PRIVATE EYE ANNUAL 2022

EDITED BY IAN HISLOP

Published in Great Britain by
Private Eye Productions Ltd
6 Carlisle Street, London W1D 3BN
www.private-eye.co.uk

© 2022 Pressdram Ltd
ISBN 978-1-901784-72-5
Designed by Bridget Tisdall
Printed and bound in Italy
by L.E.G.O. S.p.A

2 4 6 8 10 9 7 5 3 1

MIX
Paper | Supporting
responsible forestry
FSC® C023419
FSC
www.fsc.org

PRIVATE EYE ANNUAL 2022

EDITED BY IAN HISLOP

*"Not that way! That's the way they **want** you to go"*

HEIR OF SORROWS
A Short Story Special

by Dame Sylvie Krin, author of *Duchess of Hearts* & *You're Never Too Old*

THE STORY SO FAR: Charles is attending the star-studded gala performance of the new James Bond film "No Time to Live and Let Die Another Daylight to Kill"...

"**P**OP!" went the myriad flashbulbs, as Prince Charles walked jauntily along the red carpet in his black Bond Street dinner jacket, towards the Royal Albert Wolf Hall, for the glamorous premiere.

Charles was in his element as he waved and smiled and smiled and waved at his loyal subjects. At last, he thought, he had emerged into the spotlight, free of all the women in his life who had consigned him to the shadows: Her Majesty the Queen, who fortunately could not make the royal gala showing, due to an appointments clash with the racing highlights from Macau on SkyBetmore 3, and his late wife the People's Princess of Hearts who had always been the centre of attention at any event and who made him feel like a spare gooseberry in the fruitbowl of life.

At least his soul mate, Camilla, the Duchess of Consort, in her modest powder-bluebottle Bruce Oldfinger gown, was not going to steal his "thunderball" tonight. Charles smiled at his own joke, it was really rather amusing, when you came to think about it. Perhaps he should offer his services to the Bond team of writers, instead of what was her name... Phoebe Wallah-Bridget-Jones... that might pep up the script a bit! By Casino Royal Appointment perhaps? Charles' comic reverie was interrupted by his Aide-de-Memoire, Sir Alan Fitztightly, whose job tonight was to introduce him to the stars of the long-awaited film.

"Get her!" said Sir Alan, gesturing towards the immediately recognisable figure of the actor Daniel Craggy, sporting a dramatic fuchsia pink tuxedo.

"Well, the colour is certainly screaming," whispered Charles' Master of the Wardrobe, as he led his royal charge towards the renowned thespian who had reluctantly played the legendary Super-Spy since his debut in *Quantum of Physics*.

"The name is Craggy. Daniel Craggy," quipped the charismatic star of

SpectreSavers, whom Charles had seen so often saving the world from the evil machinations of cricket-loving megalomaniac Henry Stavros Blofeld and his sinister organisation, Smerk.

Now was Charles' chance to exchange banter with 007 himself, to trade quips with the laconic master of the one-liner...

"And what do you do?" said Charles, his ears turning as puce as Craggy's classic raspberry velvet jacket from the famed Mayfairlady tailors, Anderson and Clive.

"Nothing any more, Sire. I've officially

retired," said the urbane star of the Prince's favourite Bond film, *Skyplus*, set in the Scottish Highlands near the towering peak of Ben Wishaw.

"Jolly good. People should know when to retire and not just cling onto a role when they are far too old for it. Time to give way to a younger man, I say. Let the next generation take over and show that they have something to offer in a very real sense. I think a more modern approach is needed, a slimmed down eco-friendly version of the iconic brand..."

"**O**VER here!" "Over here!" "Over here!" The cries of the world's top photographers were insistent, including Sleazo Paparazzi from the Italian periodical *Snoggi*, Dick Pix from *Britain's Scum-on-Scumday* newspaper, Clic Bate from the prestigious global website the

Mailonlie, and "Flash" Bangwallop from American digital platform Buzzoff.

Charles's weary sigh could not conceal his pleasure at being the focus of attention of the world's press at the world's most glamorous premiere. He turned to Sir Alan.

"Yes, I suppose it is all part of one's royal duty however... what was the word...?"

"Appalling, Sire. Like Daniel Craggy's tux. If my partner, the Air Vice Marshal, turned up to Battle Of Britain Day wearing THAT this year, it would be ejector seats for him!"

"Over here!" "Over here!" "Over here!" continued the insistent chorus of international lensmen.

"All right... All right... I'm coming," conceded Charles, as he walked towards the battery of flashing cameras.

"Not you, sunshine," shouted Mr Pix. "Get out the way, Grandad. Let the dog see the rabbit," added Mr Bate. "Phwoarr!" exclaimed Mr Paparazzi. "Getta Loada That!"

Charles turned round to see behind him the radiant figure of Kate Middleclass, Duchess of Cambridgerton, shimmering in gold, with dazzling sequins twinkling in the bright lights.

"My God!" exhaled Sir Alan. "It's as if she were a Bond Girl herself! Only more stunning. She's like Glamourpussy Galore and Tiffany Breakfast and Ursula Undress and Vespa Matches all rolled into one!"

Sir Alan was overcome with emotion, but he wasn't the only one stunned by the Dazzling Duchess in the Albert Hall. There was no doubt who the real star of the evening was. And it wasn't Daniel Craggy. And it certainly wasn't the Heir to the Throne. It was a triumph for Katherine the Cape and, as she stood there in her diamante designer dress by Jenny Flex, she was surrounded by panting pressmen and adoring celebrity fans.

Once again, Charles melted away into the shadows from which he had only briefly escaped and thought ruefully of the name that Sir Alan had not mentioned in his roll-call of iconic beauties who swept all before them and commanded the adoration of the entire world... Diana. And his earlier Bond wordplay came back to haunt him. Di another Day, Live and let Di, Diana is Forever... Forever... Forever...

(To be continued...)

THE REASONS REMAINERS ARE THE ONES REALLY TO BLAME FOR THESE TERRIBLE SHORTAGES

1. Why did they not foresee these problems? Whining remoaners were complaining for years about all the problems Brexit would cause, but if they'd only all quit their jobs at the time and retrained as lorry drivers, none of this would have happened.

2. They want Britain to fail. It's plain to see that Remainers sabotaged a UK-US trade deal by sneaking into Afghanistan and tacitly supporting the Taliban, thus ensuring that Joe Biden's attention was distracted and that he wouldn't have time to do a simple and easy trade deal with Boris.

3. It is a known fact that Remainers spread Covid faster, due to them mingling in large urban areas and sharing coffees with each other. By artificially boosting the R number they have ensured that foreign workers have wanted to return to the UK even less than they would have done otherwise, leading to shortages.

(This is too mad even for you. You're fired. Ed.)

DEFENCE SECRETARY ADMITS LETTING DOWN AFGHAN TRANSLATORS

What's Afghan for 'sorry'?

If only there was someone in the UK who could tell you…

'I'm a Tory' reveals bisexual MP

■ A prominent bisexual woman has finally admitted to the world that she is, in fact, a Tory. "It's no big deal," she said. "My friends and family have known for some time."

But pro-Tory groups praised her bravery in helping to eradicate the stigma attached to being a self-confessed Conservative.

Said one fellow Tory, "She clearly wasn't happy with binary labels like Labour or Lib Dem, so has come out as Tory, which is a more comprehensive term for a politician who wants the best of all worlds. Good for her!"

However, some more traditional bisexuals have expressed disapproval at her revelation. "I'm not a bigot," said one, "but I just don't like what Tories get up to. It's like they want to have their cake and eat it all the time. They're just greedy."
(Rotters)

POLLY FILLER

The Eye's Top Columnist

THIS crisis has suddenly become serious. I was queuing up for petrol with toddler Charlie screaming in the back of the car when I just about heard the terrible news above his cries of "I want to watch Squid Game", because I have responsibly limited his viewing to one episode a night.

There is now officially a shortage of au pairs in Britain! OMG! What kind of Third World country have we become when we can't get girls from the Third World to come and look after our children and iron the Useless Simon's underpants?

The government had my vote up to this point, but it has finally crossed a line – and that is the the long line of willing, homesick and often stupid girls who have been graciously employed in the Filler household. The last of whom, Chi Po from Wuhan province, has unfortunately just left, after an argument about whether the hamster should be put in the dishwasher for a bath, as Charlie demanded.

So now we have no domestic help and this tyrannical and inept government is telling us all that we should pay decent wages to these workers or else they won't come here anymore!

It is a disgrace and a slap in the face to working women like myself on the front line, who are juggling career, motherhood and Peleton sessions with no assistance from the patriarchy, ie the Useless Simon, who is still on "furlough", as he calls it, or "Resident Evil Village – Level 94", as it is better known.

WHAT exactly is this government trying to do to us? Send us so stark staring mad that we vote for them again? Nice try, but I am not going to take this lying down, like Simon on the sofa, but I am going out to storm the barricades – that is, if I can find someone to look after Charlie for an hour or seven without ripping me off and without Charlie setting fire to the cockapoodle again!!!! Grrrrr!!

© *Polly Filler.*

VEGAN FOOD FAIR
TOILET
PLANT-BASED ALTERNATIVE
RSJ

FOOL SHORTAGE CRISIS

PRIVATE EYE would like to reassure its readers that there is no reason to panic about fool shortages. We have more than adequate fool supplies to fill up your magazine many times over. So do not queue outside your newsagent or supermarket, in the fear that national fool supplies are running out. We have all types of fool here to keep you entertained for hours whilst you are stuck in a three-mile tailback outside your local petrol station. Thank you.

Nursery Times

·············· Friday, Once-upon-a-time ··············

WE LIFT THE LID ON NURSERYLAND'S CULTURE OF GREED AND CRIME

by Our Investigative Staff **Peter Pandora Papers**

TODAY, *Nursery Times* can exclusively reveal how some of Nurseryland's richest inhabitants have concealed their wealth on off-shore treasure islands in order to avoid tax and to launder dirty money.

The Peter Pandora Papers paint a devastating picture of the lengths to which rich and powerful individuals will go to deceive the authorities.

Top of the list is Old Etonian Captain Hook, who has stashed his loot offshore in the former colony of Never Never Going to Pay Any Tax Land.

"I am not a pirate," protested Hook, "and I don't know the whereabouts of the Lost Money... I mean Boys."

However, Hook is not the only name in the squillions of files that make up the Peter Pandora Papers.

Also named by whistle-blowers is the so-called Crooked Man, a former oligarch who made a fortune (a crooked

sixpence) that he claims to have found on a crooked stile at the end of a crooked mile.

The Crooked Man maintains that he didn't steal the crooked sixpence and has never met Vlad the Impaler. He now lives in a crooked house (on which he has paid no stamp duty) with a crooked cat and a crooked mouse.

Meanwhile, the Owl and the Pussycat, a celebrity couple who own a pea-green super-yacht, have been exposed as deliberately taking plenty of money wrapped in a five-pound note to the distant land where the Bong Tree grows.

Said one tax expert, "It's just nonsense. They only got married by the Turkey who lives on the hill in order to reduce their tax liabilities, and the purchase of the Piggy-wig's ring for the desultory price of one shilling is clearly a scam by Sir Philip Owl and his wife, Tania Pussycat." *(That's enough Peter Pandora Papers. Ed.)*

Russian oligarch couple 'admit to owning offshore government'

Russian Oligarch couple, Lubov and Vladimir Chernukhin, have ridiculed revelations in the Pandora Papers regarding their offshore property investments, insisting they have been open and honest about their recent purchase in Britain of the Conservative Party.

"There was nothing improper about the use of a foreign shell company, set up by our good friend and adviser David Cameron, to purchase the Tory party for a very competitive price,"

said a spokesperson for the couple.

"Lubov and Vladimir have been looking at a number of foreign governments to purchase and the current Tory government was a perfect fit for them."

Lubov Chernukhin also spoke of her delight at being the successful bidder for Boris Johnson at a recent black-tie Tory fundraising ball.

"I've always wanted a Prime Minister of my own – it's so much fun stuffing Bozza into my back pocket."

'ISOLATE BRITAIN' BRINGS COUNTRY TO A STANDSTILL

by Our Economic Staff **Lorry Taylor**

A GROUP of idealists calling themselves "Isolate Britain" have yet again put their own beliefs ahead of the needs of the vast majority of the public.

Said one of the posh leaders of the group, known also as "Backbench Rebellion", "Honestly, it's for their own good, and I couldn't look our grandchildren in the face if I hadn't done something to ensure Britain was totally isolated from the rest of the world.

"I have glued myself to this

opinion, and I'm sticking to it."

Said a member of the public, "We were going along doing just fine and then these nutters appeared from nowhere and brought everything to a juddering halt. It's so selfish of them."

"Isolate Britain" is part of a larger movement – "Extinction Britain" – aiming to create shortages, keep lorries off the road and ultimately wipe out British industry, which will at least bring our national carbon emissions down to zero.

Priti Patel warns protestors

by Our Home Affairs Correspondent **Dee Lays**

HOME Secretary Priti Patel has warned M25 climate change protestors that they must ensure any future protests are totally ineffectual and go completely unnoticed by the public after securing a court order against them that could see them jailed.

"Surely these idiots blocking the roads realise that all great protest movements down the

ages – from the Suffragettes to the Civil Rights movement in the United States in the 1960s – only succeeded in the end because they were carried out quietly, politely and out of sight, without bothering any decent people going about their daily business," she said.

"People have every right to protest, provided those protests do not involve protesting because, if they do, those people will be going to jail for a long time."

NI trade groups hope for return to free movement of goods

SEVERAL trade groups have come together to voice their concerns ove r the ongoing sticking points of the Northern Ireland protocol during protracted Brexit negotiations between the UK and EU.

In an unprecedented move, the Continuity IRA, the Ulster Volunteer Force, the New IRA, the Loyalist Volunteer Force and other groups have reached

out to each other to tabulate a list of goods they want to be able to transport freely across the border with the Irish Republic, without them being subject to "spot checks'" by customs officials.

These items include: petrol, drugs, Armalite rifles, mortars, grenades, pistols, bullets, "stinger" missiles and balaclavas.

*"So, it's wild **synchronised** swimming now?"*

7

DIARY

TATE: THE AUTHORISED INTERPRETATIONS

John Singer Sargent: CARNATION, LILY, LILY, ROSE
Two unsupervised children carry paper lanterns amidst a sea of flowers. The lanterns will have been formed around an apparatus of metal made by underpaid factory workers labouring for long hours in filthy conditions. The prettiness of the picture undoubtedly obscures the horror.

When the white children walk away, the abandoned lanterns will soon become a terrifying fire hazard, scorching the earth for miles around, endangering human and animal life and causing untold damage to our fragile eco-system.

William Blake: SATAN SMITING JOB WITH SORE BOILS
Deprived of funding by successive Conservative governments, our NHS continues to struggle to provide an adequate service for millions of sick and elderly citizens. William Blake's powerful portrait of a health service driven to its knees, in the person of Job, stands as stark testament to the artist's place in society, and his responsibility to convey the message of the necessity for social change. A specially commissioned Lavender and Basil Tate Ointment for Boils, Chilblains and Blisters is on special offer at £19.89, 10 percent off for members, in the Tate shop, with a Blake-themed tube designed by Dame Tracey Emin.

Henri Matisse: THE SNAIL
Matisse casts himself as a sharp-eyed critic of society's cold-hearted treatment of snails, but he himself was undoubtedly infected by notions of White Male superiority over not only snails, clams and cuttlefish but all molluscs, as is evidenced by this, some would say, offensively triumphalist painting in which he chooses to ignore the culturo-economic contexts that prioritise the heteronormative human being over the invertebrate marine organism.

Sir John Everett Millais: OPHELIA
A woman is floating, face-up, in a murky stream or plunge-pool. She is fully clothed. In her right hand, she clutches a bunch of spring flowers. When she gets out of the water, her dress, the product of an unjust society, unwillingly maintained by underpaid workers, will be ruined and the flowers will have died.

The picture acts as a profound symbol of the degeneracy of the mercantile classes. Is the murkiness of the stream the result of chemicals pumped into it further up from a multinational biochemical company? Or is it untreated sewage, forced into the stream by privatised water companies desperate to save money so as to maximise profit margins for wealthy shareholders?

What is the painter trying to tell us? With her glassy, staring eyes, the woman is clearly a victim of the international opium trade, controlled and enforced by the British Empire, that did so much to decimate the globe in the iniquitous 19th century and beyond.

Today, women continue to fight for the freedom to bathe in clothing more suitable for water sports. Millais depicts a growing awareness that wild flowers cannot and must not be picked if we are to save our fragile environment.

David Hockney: A BIGGER SPLASH
Though no human being is depicted in this painting, the splash in the pool suggests the presence of an unknown diver. He does not resurface. Might it be suicide?

What would David Hockney have intended to say, if only he could find the word? Apparently so sybaritic and free, Los Angeles life in 1967 was in fact an historic hotbed of capitalism, misogyny, exploitation, inequality and class division, as well as a springboard for mass-murder, as evident in the specially constructed springboard to the right of the picture.

The building behind the pool in *A Bigger Splash* is empty. No one is around. There is an eerie silence. However indirectly, this painting relates to the atrocities endemic in Western overindulgence.

It seems likely that Charles Manson and his "family" have just paid a visit? Or is Hockney suggesting a more widespread holocaust, brought on by the excesses of a racist society insidiously bolstered by corrupt politicians and big business?

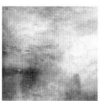

Joseph Mallord William Turner: SUN SETTING OVER A LAKE
In this heartfelt outcry against the perils of man-made global warming triggered by uncontrolled industrialisation of the landscape, Turner depicts a world consumed by sun, obliterating not just human beings but all life on earth.

Though it has often been dismissed as simply a "work of art", slavery, colonial exploitation, racism, sexual violence, transphobia, homophobia and the horrors of blood sports can all be seen in this painting by those prepared to look hard enough.

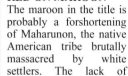

Mark Rothko: RED ON MAROON
The maroon in the title is probably a forshortening of Maharunon, the native American tribe brutally massacred by white settlers. The lack of evidence for Mark Rothko's obsessive fascination with this massacre suggests a cover-up by the patriarchal Art establishment of the time. The red in the painting stands for the river of blood. Rothko reminds us of our own association with this hideous and immoral event. No one can look at this canvas without undergoing a deep sense of guilt over their own part in the stark injustice upon which modern America was founded. Specially commissioned Remorse Tissues are available from the Tate shop at £14.95 for a packet of three, 10 percent off for members.

As told to
CRAIG BROWN

Iain Duncan Smith demands return of wartime Blitz spirit!

IN THE 1940s, Britain's workers kept going into the office even though Hitler's bombs were raining down on their heads all day, or rather only at night, which is just the same really, and they didn't sit around at home, making Zoom calls on their bakelite wifi, no, they got on their bikes, rolled up their sleeves and went into the underground to shelter from the bombers who, let's be honest, didn't lounge around and stay at home in Germany, but got up and drove to work every day in their Heinkels to deliver their vital supplies of bombs to London, ensuring that plucky Londoners could demonstrate the Blitz spirit and air-raid wardens could shout "Put that Zoom out" when people didn't observe the total blackout due to power cuts, no, that's the difference between our lazy, do-nothing, modern, stay-at-home workforce and the gallant wartime generation who didn't hide under their tables at home, as they were instructed, and certainly didn't wear any silly masks like their weak- or should I say woke-willed(!) descendants, which is why I am saying we should all stop this pathetic WFCH (Working from Country Home) that I have been doing in my wife's lovely house and shape up like the hardworking Luftwaffe did and get back to the vital job of destroying this country so that we can build back better after the war *(That's enough. Ed.)*

How to make up your £20 Universal Credit loss with just two hours' extra work

"I can't believe I'm having to explain this once again! Some people have had the temerity to suggest that I was being disingenuous! It really is quite simple – so here goes!

For those people who can work an extra 2 hours without going over their 5 hours a week DWP work allowance limit for single parents and those who are terminally ill and subject to the universal credit "63 pence in the pound" taper – if you ignore income tax and national insurance deductions, council tax reductions, the cost of child care and the fact that the national minimum wage is £8.91 per hour and not £10 – then you CAN work an extra 2 hours to replace the removal of the temporary UC £20 uplift!"

Byee!

Woman insists the Met police 'make her feel safe'

by Our Met Police Women's Correspondent **Miss Ogynist**

A WOMAN, who asked only to be identified as "Cressida", has spoken about how the Met police make her feel totally safe, especially in her job.

"I know a lot of women don't feel safe with the police, but that's not my experience," she said, her face pixelated so no one could identify her.

"From Sarah Everard's murder, to racist police taking selfies with dead bodies, to misogynist WhatsApp groups, to Daniel Morgan's murder cover-up, I'm forever in danger of being thrown on the scrapheap, but thanks to the Met police closing ranks to protect one of their own, as they did with Couzens, I feel like no one can touch me.

"When the woke mob come gunning for me, the police have my back, unlike Jean Charles de Menezes who was shot repeatedly in his."

POETRY CORNER

**In Memoriam
F.W. de Klerk, former
South African President
and joint winner of the
Nobel Peace Prize**

So. Farewell
Then F.W. de Klerk.

"Free Nelson Mandela",
Yes, that wasn't
Your catchphrase.
But you did it
In the end.

To some, you
Were a hero.
To others,
Not so much.

But these things
Are not always
Black and white.

E.J. de Thribb
(17½ years inside)

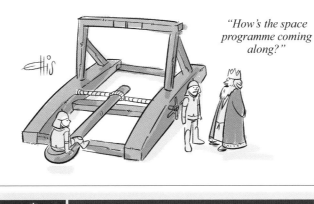

"How's the space programme coming along?"

0844 hrs Neasden officers assemble in the station for new campaign, "If you want to know the time, don't ask a policeman", reminding Neasden citizens that the Neasden Police Service (new slogan: "We're not **all** bad") is fundamentally not to be trusted with the lives or personal safety of the public. As part of the campaign, Neasden officers are dispatched across the borough with big placards saying DON'T TRUST ME, or SCUM SCUM SCUM. This will help to build trust with the community once again.

0916 hrs Officers start the morning's work of handing out pamphlets offering advice on what to do if approached by a member of the Neasden police service, reminding the public that, under new guidelines, they are legally allowed to arrest or pepper-spray an officer, or hit them with their own baton, if they suspect the officer of not being legitimate. If the officer is legitimate, the member of the public will then be arrested – properly – for assaulting an officer, but this will at least have established which officers are genuine and which are not, as presumably criminal officers won't resist arrest, or being pepper-sprayed.

0923 hrs Neasden special officers convene a meeting with the Neasden Bus Service, arranging special details for late-night patrols. As all officers in the Neasden Police Service are now considered potential suspects in a number of criminal cases, they are to be accompanied by a double-decker bus at all times, which will allow a member of the public to flag it down and get on board if they suspect a Neasden officer to be misusing their role for nefarious purposes. The logistics of ensuring that no Neasden officer is ever more than 10 feet from a double-decker bus are challenging, but in order to secure operational target of PSN (Public Safety for Neasdeners), no stone must be left unturned, apart from actually stopping criminal officers.

EYE FACT CHECK

Q: WHY has Eamonn Holmes gone to GB News?

A: It's because the QAnon Shamen, speaking through a G5 mast from his prison cell, told Holmes to leave the mainstream media's This Morning show because it is being secretly run by Bill Gates and the Democratic Party's Pizza Paedo network, and to join the only free truth-telling media left in the galaxy – Great Brillo News (surely "Great British Nutters"? Ed.), where at last he will be allowed to voice his concerns regarding something David Icke told him about how lizards are actually running the Royal Family in order to spread data harvesting microchips disguised as flu-boosters into our blood streams.

Lecturers' strike begins

by Our University Correspondent
Ed U. Catinrita

THERE were concerns today that a three-day strike by university lecturers would barely be noticed by students whose education has already been ruined by the pandemic.

"We're aware that many of the students who have had their education decimated by the coronavirus will barely notice a few days' more misery," agreed all lecturers. "But we're determined, despite this, to make things just a teensy bit worse for them.

"We've paid a terrible price for university reforms and if there's one thing students understand, it's being forced to pay a terrible price for something."

All students agreed they just want this living hell to come to an end so they can leave it all behind, graduate in peace and apply for a job in McDonalds.

Boris Johnson

Home   Create

Boris Johnson MP
● Live   385,000,000 Views

Prime Minister's Northern Rally Speech Live on Fakebook (if available)

👍 Like   💬 Comment

0 people like this

(PRIME MINISTER ENTERS TO SOUND OF BLUE CASSETTE PLAYER BELTING OUT "THINGS CAN ONLY BUILD BACK BETTER" BY D-PRESS)

Boris: Greetings from the Tory **heartlands** of **Somewhere-up-Northchester!**

(CROWD OF BORIS FANS GOES CRAZY AND GIVES HIM STANDING OVATION)

Boris: Yes, folks, I'm here. With the new three-word slogan that says **everything** about this government. Build Back **Blather**. (CHECKS AUTOCUE) Build Back **Banter**. (SQUINTS) Build Back **Booster**. Yes, **that's** the one! We've achieved so many **amazing** things, it's **hard** to know where to start, so I **won't**. Instead, I'll repeat our **brilliant** new slogan: Build Back **Better.** Hang on, **that** can't be right, we're not building **anything**, are we? We dropped the 'houses' bit after all the **nimbies** had a **whinge** about the Green Belt. Build Back **Bitter** – that's it. Wetherspoons! Oh no, we haven't got any **beer** either. Build Back **Borders**. What's **that**, Lord Frost? Oh, **don't** mention the borders, **good** point. Build Back **Bluster!** That's the one! Hats off to our **brilliant** economy, which from now on is going to be high **skill**, high **wage**, high **productivity**, high **viz**, hi-**ho silver lining**, high **sierra**, high **noon**, high as a **kite**, **Hi-di-Hi**, high **tax** – whoops!

(AUDIENCE CHEER, NOT CARING WHAT HE'S JUST SAID. THEY'LL APPLAUD ANYTHING)

Boris: And we're going to **rewild** Britain. Build Back **Beaver**! What does that **mean**? **Nothing**, who cares, but it sounds vaguely like a **double-entendre**.

(AUDIENCE BOO UNWARRANTED USE OF FRENCH PHRASE)

Boris: Whoops! I meant **innuendo**. Anyway, I'm all for **beaver** everywhere. Don't tell **Carrie**!

(AUDIENCE CHEER UNELECTED FIRST LADY AND HER GREEN, WOKE, THOROUGHLY ANTI-CONSERVATIVE VIEWS)

Boris: So Build Back **Batter**. Provided there's some **fish** to fry, which there **won't** be with President **Mackerel** and the **Barmy Barnier Beret Brigade**.

(AUDIENCE CHEER MEANINGLESS ALLITERATION AND IGNORE THE FACT THAT THEIR LEADER HAS SPENT MORE TIME WRITING THAT JOKE THAN ADDRESSING THE COUNTRY'S PROBLEMS)

Boris: You see, folks, **no** supply chain problems with the **gags**. And they're **cheap**. We've got **plenty** and they're being **brilliantly** delivered – by yours truly. No need to call in the **army** to make this speech. And hats off to my **amazing** team of colleagues. There's Liz Truss. What a support she is! And thanks to her for all those **incredible** trade deals that she's very nearly done. Priti Patel, she's **priti** scary! Particularly if you're a crusty **Swampy** type she's going to glue to a **slop** bucket in a high-security cell in D-wing.

(AUDIENCE GO MAD AT THOUGHT OF PUNITIVE JUSTICE AGAINST PERFECTLY LEGITIMATE DEMONSTRATORS)

Boris: Yes, folks, it's Jon Bon **Jokey** today, because I'm **not** going to touch on any **important** issues, like **Universal Credit**. Build Back **Beggar!**

(AUDIENCE CHEER AT SPEECH SHOWING AMUSEMENT AT THE THOUGHT OF THE HOMELESS)

Boris: I **love** Universal Credit. I'm taking the credit for **everything**. The **vaccine** roll-out, getting **Brexit** done, er, Emma **Raducando** winning whatever it was and the England **soccer** team **very** nearly **triumphing** over Europe, if it hadn't been for those **penalties** imposed by **Brussels**.

(AUDIENCE CAUGHT BETWEEN BOOING AND CHEERING AT MENTION OF WORD 'BRUSSELS'. MANY CARRIED OUT ON STRETCHERS BY ARMY PARAMEDICS STANDING IN FOR THE NHS)

Boris: Well, that's the **warm-up** done. **Now**, let me introduce the **Prime Minister** of the United Kingdom, the one and **only** Mrs Johnson!

First Lady: Thank you very much to my brilliant husband, who's done so much for the LGBT movement.

Boris: Build Back **Bugger!**

First Lady: We don't use the B-word anymore.

Boris: Quite right – 'Build'. Very poor taste. Suggests things might get **built**. Homes, hospitals, schools, infrastructure.

First Lady: I'm talking about how much you support gay rights.

Boris: Quite **so**. Don't want to **upset** the tank-topped **bum-boys**… and bum-girls! And whatever **else** they wanted to call themselves. Have I got that **right**?

First Lady: Stop. Talking.

Boris: Anyway, back to my **wife**, making a speech...

First Lady: I'm pregnant.

(AUDIENCE RISES TO FEET AND GIVES STANDING OVATION FOR NEXT EIGHT HOURS AT PRIME MINISTER'S CONTRIBUTION TO GREEN ISSUES AND GLOBAL OVERPOPULATION. FIRST COUPLE KISS AWKWARDLY THEN LEAVE AUDITORIUM TO THE SOUND OF "WALKING ON SUNLIT UPLANDS" BY KATRINA AND THE FOURTH WAVES)

GOVE'S DEPARTMENT RENAMED

It's now called the Ministry of Sound

SAUDI FOOTBALL TAKEOVER SHOCK

THE news that a Saudi-led consortium is taking over Newcastle United football club has worried players and staff.

The manager, in particular, is concerned that his position may be untenable. He told reporters, "I could be axed at any time. If I do anything that displeases the Saudis, like draw nil-nil at home, the knives will be out, and I could face the chop.

"The sack is something that every manager is aware of – the problem with the Saudis is that you'll end up in it, in bits. No offence, Prince Mohammed, just saying. Would you like to play centre forward?"

Late news

■ Reporter Iona Club has disappeared after entering the Saudi Embassy in Gateshead to ask a few questions about the new ownership. *(That's enough very bad taste. Ed.)*

"Look – I can still fit into the clothes I wore when I was 21!"

World in meltdown after Facebook outage

by Our Social Media Staff
Nick Data and **Will Selfie**

Society teetered on the brink last week when Facebook, Instagram and WhatsApp stopped working for a few hours.

There were immediately millions of complaints from parents about why the outage wasn't longer or permanent.

Said one, "Even in a couple of hours, our children's mental health had noticeably improved. And my daughter briefly talked to me, if only to say 'Dad, why is Facebook not working? I hate you!'"

However, there were those who were furious about the total failure of the platform. A number of top influencers were forced to go outdoors and run down the street showing photoshopped photos of themselves on the beach to complete strangers.

Another influencer protested, "I could have starved to death. There was no point eating a meal if I couldn't photograph it and send it to someone I've never met, hoping they'll like it. Nobody knew that my meal was better than theirs. It was a nightmare!"

Beneficiaries of the outage included TikTok, as millions of social media devotees took to the platform to post videos of themselves looking angrily in the mirror at the news that Facebook had gone down.

Mark Zuckerberg was incredibly apologetic, saying, "Nobody knows who's to blame for this disaster, but it certainly isn't me and my guess is that it is all the fault of someone called 'Al Gorithm' and Facebook will be looking very deeply into how we can avoid repeating *(cont. 2024)*

Amazon genius announces new invention

by Our Online Retail Staff
Dot Com-Boom

The billionaire boss of Amazon, Jeff Bezos, today launched a new venture that promises to revolutionise the way people shop.

"This is very exciting," he told a roomful of sycophantic reporters. "I have come up with an idea for a new experimental retail space, where people conduct transactions, spending money on items in real time. I call it a Sales Hub Of Products or a S.H.O.P."

Mr Bezos is confident that his so-called "shop" will catch on and soon there will be "shops" everywhere, possibly in a row, in a design that he has called "the high street".

"It may take a lot of getting used to for customers, as it involves walking and some possible eye-contact with strangers, rather than staring at a computer screen and clicking a mouse.

"But I truly believe this disruptive revolution in retail technology may one day replace online shopping. My only worry is that some greedy online techno-nerd will come up with a way of putting my 'shops' out of business, leaving my 'high streets' empty and boarded up."

Culture secretary to crack down on social media abuse

by **Lunchtime O'Brien**

NADINE DORRIES last night declared war on trolls who use social media to target and abuse those who disagree with them.

Said the Culture Secretary in a tweet, "These trolls are fuckwits. Anyone who sends a tweet calling other people fuckwits is a troll and a fuckwit and should be arrested at once."

When police arrived at her doorstep, she denied being an abusive troll and said she had never called anyone "a public school, posh boy fuckwit", as that would have been ungrateful to the person who had made her Culture Secretary.

facebook

ONLINE HATE GUIDE IN FULL

- ■ Zuckerberg hates being told what to do by governments
- ■ Zuckerberg hates putting any restrictions on FB users
- ■ Zuckerberg hates paying taxes
- ■ Er...
- ■ That's it

MY FAVOURITE JAMES BOND SCENE

OWEN JONES: The heart-stopping scene in *You Only Live Twice* (1967) in which Blofeld's island headquarters – centre of his ruthless multi-national industrial operation – is ultimately blown sky-high must strike anyone with an ounce of socio-economic knowledge as a perfect symbol of capitalism ultimately imploding on itself through a futile and ultimately destructive attempt to push through an outdated imperialist economic system drenched in the blood of countless millions that is, let's face it, ultimately unsustainable. My only regret is that the film's producers agreed to bend to commercial pressure and waste ultimately millions of pounds on sets, actors, cameras, technical teams, etc, when they could just as easily have conserved valuable resources and filmed a comprehensive discussion about the very same themes between leading world thinkers such as Eric Hobsbawm and/or Noam Chomsky.

JANET STREET-PORTER: Blimey! Cop a loada that! That's what I thought when I first saw so-called top hunk Daniel Craig emerge from the ocean in his sky-blue budgie-smugglers in that classic scene from *Casino Royale*.

But then I took a closer look.
Disappointing, or what?
Budgie-smugglers!
Tadpole-smugglers, more like!
Sack that camerman, someone! He must have put his lens on the wrong way round, so as to make everything look microscopic!

And whatever happened to feminism, girls?
Enough of the blokes! Let's give the women a chance!
Anyone heard of equal opportunities?

Yes, it's high time we dragged Bond kicking and screaming into the 21st century. Enough of the men! Why not have a Bond girl come out of the sea wearing nothing but a skimpy bikini? That would certainly be one-in-the-eye for those misogynist dinosaurs who still insist that women have nothing to contribute!

JULIAN FELLOWES: I'm sorry to say, many James Bond films don't quite "do it" for me. How one wishes they'd get those details right! Don't get me started! For example, that ludicrous scene in *Dr No* in which Honey Ryder emerges from the ocean soaking wet in a white bikini, while James Bond peers at her from behind a bush in jeans and wellington boots. I mean, really! Why lower the tone? After all, Bond is an Old Etonian, and Miss Ryder was probably educated somewhere half-way decent – say, Roedean or Cheltenham Ladies'. No gentleman would ever skulk behind a bush in casual dress, just as no lady would be seen in public wearing nothing but a soaking wet white bikini. Common! Common! Common! And, later in the film, she even holds her fork as one would a pen! That's why I've recently written a remake, *Dr No Thank You*, set largely in the ball-room of one of our finest stately homes. Bond wears white tie and tails and well-polished shoes while The Hon. Miss Honey Ryder looks perfectly resplendent in a gorgeous ball-gown of marine-blue silk taffeta and antique lace, which is, might I add, just as it should be.

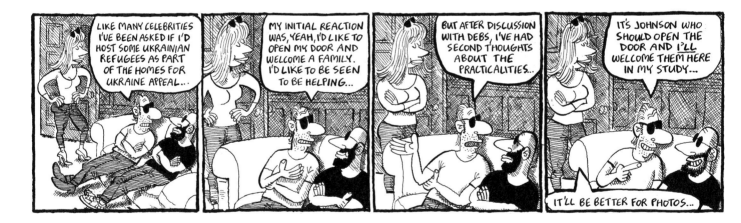

School news

St Rice Cake's, Beijing

The new, out-sourced British public school opens its doors today. There will be 3.6 million pupils per class. The Headmaster, Mr Kow-Tow, comes to us from a successful career in the Chinese Communist Party, and is committed to instilling the virtues of Xi Jinping Thought on Socialism with Chinese Characteristics for a New Era. There will be no assembly, as all assemblies are banned. Ms Wuhan is in charge of the sanatorium, which has no contact with the science labs or the biology department, and anyone who says it does will be sent to see the Head of Discipline, Mr Hit Yu. The Senior Maths Tutor, Mr Dim Sum, will be taking all lessons as there no Humanities on offer. The Bursar, Mr Hi Fee, will be directing all the money home to the charitable bank account of St Cake's, whose UK branch, run by Chair of Governors Major Scam, has recently been forced to announce an increase in fees due to Covid, inflation, Brexit and greed. The former Head of Art, Mr Ai Wei Wei, is on sabbatical indefinitely until he makes a full and frank confession of how he has let down the school, himself, his House Master and the Great Helmsman, Xi Jinping. The Long March will take place this October, just after the playing of the Great Wall Game. The school CCF will be practising the launch of the school hypersonic missile to coincide with Taiwan's Independence Day, now known as The Day of Eternal Shame. End of term and world will take place on December 11th.

WORLD OF RACING

Jockey in bullying row

THE world of racing was in shock last night after allegations emerged that a leading jockey was a habitual bully.

Said the whistleblower, Lucky Lad, winner of the 2.30 at Uttoxeter, "I know you're not going to believe me, but the jockey jumped on my back and then kept hitting me with his whip for no reason at all.

"No matter how fast I tried to get away, he just kept whacking me. And there were people in the crowd clearly egging him on. It's a disgrace. The whole sport needs looking at." *(Rotters)*

KNEEJERK RESPONSES TO TRAGEDY MUST BE MEASURED

by Our Feedback Staff **Les Riot**

PARLIAMENTARIANS on all sides of the House have agreed that the poorly thought-out kneejerk plans to ban anonymous online accounts, in the wake of Sir David Amess's tragic murder, must be hastily enacted in a carefully measured way.

"From what we know, anonymous online trolling played no part in Sir David's tragic death and that's why we must honour this man who valued freedom of expression above everything else, by savagely reducing freedom of expression online," agreed all MPs.

"It would be all too easy in the heat of the moment to bring forward draconian measures with no proper scrutiny," Home Secretary Priti Patel told MPs. "So let's do that."

The Daily Mail
AN APOLOGY

IN RECENT years we may have given the impression, through headlines such as 'CRUSH THE SABOTEURS, 'ENEMIES OF THE PEOPLE' and 'SELF-CONSUMED MALCONTENT REMOANERS', that nothing was off limits when it came to the robustness of political language and that no-holds-barred bare-knuckle debate has always been an integral part of the rough and tumble of British political life.

We now realise, in the light of the tragic murder of Sir David Amess, that nothing could be further from the truth, and that respect, courtesy and consideration should be shown towards politicians you disagree with.

We apologise for any confusion caused, and any confusion in the future when a crucial vote in the Commons doesn't go the way we want and we label the Tory rebels responsible as despicable appeasers and contemptuous Vichy elites, thwarting the will of the people, as they laugh from their ivory towers in the face of common decency and trample over...*(cont. p94)*

'We need kinder, gentler politics' agree all the worst people online

by Our Social Media Staff
Ann Nominus

All the worst people on Twitter agreed today that Britain needs kinder, gentler politics, in the wake of the horrific murder of Sir David Amess.

"We're long overdue a change in our politics, and everyone other than me needs to tone down the abuse," agreed all the people merrily dishing out abuse on Twitter.

"I am sickened by the abuse generated by hate-filled right-wing loons in support of this genocidal Naziscum government," tweeted one ghastly tweeter. "Those f***ing clowns better learn some manners or I'll unleash another Twitter mob on their sorry arses."

"What sickens me is the endless abuse dished out by hate-filled loony left Remoaners and Marxist dickwads marshalled by uber twat," tweeted another tweeter. "Those baby-faced dickheads better learn to play nice or I'll destroy them next time I'm on GB News with Farage demanding migrant boats be sunk."

All the very worst people on Twitter agreed that British politics would be a far better place if everyone agreed with them all the time.

"Ooh... double corduroy – that's brave!"

BBC UNVEILS NEW LOGO

IN RESPONSE to recent criticism, the BBC has produced a new logo to reflect a more modern BBC, in tune with the times, and responsive to government demands:

BEFORE:	B B C
AFTER:	B B C

The new Director General, Nadine Dorries *(surely Tim Davie?)*, explained: "The letters are now suitably balanced, avoid partiality, and no longer lean to the left."

POETRY CORNER

Lines on the imminent departure from earth of James Tiberius Kirk (90), Captain of the Starship Enterprise

So. Farewell
Then, William Shatner
But only for
11 minutes.

It's space, Jim,
But not as we
Know it.

You have always
Struggled with
Your weight,
But, for once,
You will be
Weightless.

Has the "Oldly Go"
Joke been done?
Oh, right,
I thought so.
How about the "Baldly Go"
For Jeff Bezos?
Oh, that too...
How about "Beardly Go"
For Richard Branson?

Hooray!
We have lift off!

It is important
For a poet to go
Where no man
Has been before.

E.J. Thribb
(Captain's Log,
Stardate 17.5)

13

Hope for global peace as UN reaches historic agreement

by Our UN Correspondent
Hugh Enn

There were sensational scenes in New York last night, as delegates from every country in the world put their differences to one side to issue a joint statement that united the globe. The statement read simply: "We don't want Matt Hancock."

From Africa to Australia, from Zanzibar to Zimbabwe, late night, behind-the-scenes negotiations were not necessary, as everyone was instantly of the same mind – that the UK's former health secretary was an entirely unsuitable person to have anything to do with the United Nations.

Said the Taiwanese and Chinese representatives in a bilateral statement, "He struggles to keep peace in his own family, let alone on the global stage."

Meanwhile, Russian and Ukrainian delegates shook hands, agreeing that "Mr Hancock's friends claimed that he is a safe pair of hands, but we've seen where those hands have been on the CCTV footage, and we have come to an alternative conclusion."

Said the Ugandan delegate, "It is true that he may be an expert on Ugandan affairs, but we still don't want him."

GILLIAN ANDERSON WINS EMMY FOR PLAYING MRS THATCHER DURING MINERS' STRIKE

I was the pits

News in brief

New evidence 'terrifying' say anti-vaxxers

■ Anti-vaccination campaigners today announced they have clinching proof that their claims are correct.

Said one protestor, outside a school in East London, "No one can deny it now. This school would normally be full of life, but it's like a ghost ship: deserted, silent. It is clear that hundreds of pupils and staff have been killed by this so-called vaccine. We are thoroughly vindicated."

A spokesman for the school, janitor Brian Mopp, said, "It's half-term, you prats."

This statement was pounced upon by anti-vaxxers as conclusive evidence of a conspiracy.

"I try to keep out of the trans debate – it's way too dangerous to take a side"

INTRODUCING

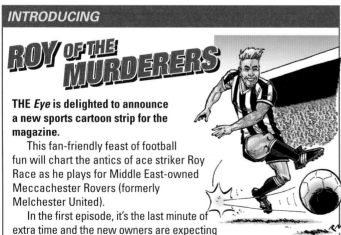

ROY OF THE MURDERERS

THE *Eye* is delighted to announce a new sports cartoon strip for the magazine.

This fan-friendly feast of football fun will chart the antics of ace striker Roy Race as he plays for Middle East-owned Meccachester Rovers (formerly Melchester United).

In the first episode, it's the last minute of extra time and the new owners are expecting a win. Or else. Can Roy get into the six-yard box, dismember the opposition goalkeeper and dispose of the remains before the final whistle blower. Will there be a penalty... of 100 lashes? Or will it go to sudden death? Yes. *(You're fired! Ed. Who commissioned this tasteless cartoon strip? They should be fired as well.)*

HEIR OF SORROWS
A Short Story Special

by Dame Sylvie Krin, author of *Duchess of Hearts* & *You're Never Too Old*

THE STORY SO FAR: Charles is continuing with his long commitment to the Green agenda as it gains momentum across the nation. Now read on...

"FILL her up, please," Charles requested politely, as he manoeuvred his prized Aston Martini GB-5 into the garage. Sir Alan Fitztightly, in his new role as Forecourt Attendant Poursuivante, unscrewed the fuel cap and prepared to replenish the supercar's tank.

"And what are we putting in her today, Sire?" he enquired, smoothing down his natty biodegradable Duchy Original overalls.

"I thought a bottle of the Pouilly Fussie '63. Nothing but the best vintage for the old girl, who has become rather thirsty of late."

"Are you talking about your wife, sir, or the car?" quipped Sir Alan cheekily, as he uncorked the bottle of classic French white wine and poured it into the petrol tank as instructed.

Charles was unamused by this display of lèse-majesté by his aide-de-edmondson. "And don't forget the cheesy whey, Sir Alan. It's the mix of the alcohol and the lactalbumin that makes the organic fuel so potent..."

"Cheesy whey?! Sounds like the Milky Way that's gone mouldy!" joked the Pumpmaster Royale, as he scooped dollops of ripened fermented curd into the power unit of the iconic 1960s' sports coupé.

"I can just hear Brian Cox off the telly talking about cheesy whey and the black holes near Uranus."

"Yes, thank you very much, Sir Alan, that's quite enough of that." Charles felt more than mild irritation at Sir Alan's irreverent tone when dealing with the very important subject of renewable energy sources. This was the future of the planet that was at stake after all and if Charles was doing his bit to save the world then it ill behoved his aide-de-campingholiday to make light of it.

"I mean, I was preaching the Green message long before anyone else and all I got as thanks was to be told I was a tree-hugging looney who talked to my aspidistra."

"You DO talk to your aspidistra though, Sire, don't you?" said Sir Alan unhelpfully.

"At least he listens! And doesn't insist on telling me louche tales of Backstairs Billy and the underfootman, dating back to the days of my dear old Nan..."

"You're full up now..." Sir Alan interjected, having decanted the last of the wine and cheese turbo-mix into the classic Bondmobile, "...which is something Billy used to say when..."

"Yes, yes, yes." Charles had had enough of his equerry-as-folk's bawdy badinage and gunned the Aston into life before it spluttered and hiccoughed down the drive of High-Di-Highgrove House, weaving drunkenly under the heady influence of its rich alcohol/dairy energy supply...

AS Charles drove through the bucolic landscape of the Couttswolds, he ruminated on the success of his lifelong campaign to bring the Green agenda to the fore.

Perhaps, at last, his role would be recognised and his achievements applauded. Organic Socks, Yoghurt Aftershave, Nettle Trousers... all his ideas and all ahead of their time.

He turned on the radio to Classic FU where Alexander Armstrong-Jones was mellifluously enthusing about a relaxing new recording of Vivaldi's Four Seasons Pizza by the London PhilHammond Orchestra.

"But first, the news..." soothed the pleasing baritone.

Charles was not pleased by this interruption and put his foot down involuntarily on the accelerator to power his wine 'n' cheese chariot up to an impressive 27mph.

"...and here are the headlines. Kate and Wills have taken the Green world by storm and made it their own. At last the Royals have gone Eco and their appearance at the EarthShock Awards has set the agenda for the future of mankind. Karbon-Neutral Kate was wearing a stunning recycled gown by Zara Boomdeeay whilst Woke Wills sported a dashing velvet green Vaping Jacket by catalogue king, Johnny Bobrummel."

Charles turned the knob on the radio angrily and channel-hopped through the broadcasting ether... "Honestly," he thought to himself, "it is so unfair. All those decades campaigning for red squirrel sanctuaries, writing letters to the Under-Secretary of State for Shrubs, planting hedgerows in one's own ha-ha... and now, one has been supplanted by one's very own offspring..." Charles did his best to try and feel pleased that the baton of ecological responsibility had been passed on to the next generation, but he could not contain his feelings of injustice. "I mean, it really is..." he told himself...

"Appalling! It's the only world to describe the state of the planet. And guess which Royal has now weighed into the debate?"

The radio had tuned into the Radio Two show of veteran broadcaster, Jeremy Wine.

Charles cheered up as he drove slowly through the sleepy village of Clarkson-on-Prime. Perhaps, at last, he would receive the credit he deserved.

"It's only the Queen!" exclaimed the excitable Wine. "Yes, Her Maj has been caught on camera attacking the powers that be for being all talk and no trousers regarding global warming and climate change. Well, now the climate has changed completely and we have all warmed to the sustainable, recyclable monarchy. Long live Her Majesty the Green!"

Charles groaned as Jeremy segued effortlessly into the melancholy sound of the Carpenters singing *Rainy Days and Other Extreme Weather Events*, while thinking to himself "my cup of misery runneth overfull".

But then came an ominous knocking sound, as the Aston Martini began to slowly grind to a juddering halt in a thick cloud of vinous fondue-scented smoke…

(To be continued...)

"I'm guessing this is your first attempt at chicken stock"

@Vilmissimo

BUNG TO RIGHTS

It's a *question* of integrity

Ok, I'll ask it – for £100,000!

GARRICK CLUB SINNER

Poor old Owen has paid a heavy price

Not as much as Randox

WHIPPING UP RULE BOOK

We've got to save the sleazeball

But what about Paterson?

Keir Starmer WRITES

HELLO! Well, we've had amazing news! A single poll (conducted last week) showed that Labour are now finally ahead of the Tories!

By the way, in completely unrelated news, last week I tested positive for Covid, so lots of other people were doing the job of Leader of the Opposition instead of me. I'm sure this has nothing to do with this amazing poll result, which I'm sure has been down to my longterm planning and diligence thus far!

I do have to thank Ed Miliband and Angela Rayner for standing in for me in PMQs and the LOTO budget response. I do worry though that they were a bit too vigorous in attacking the government and calling them to account!

I did try to tell them that by being nasty to the government they are in serious danger of offending those people in the country who are hard-core Conservative voters. Incredibly, they both seemed to think that wooing people who will never vote for us under any circumstance is a waste of our time!

It is worrying, I know, watching Ed and Angela "oppose" the Conservatives in such a way that borders on the rude. Why can't they be like my other front benchers, Anne Onymous MP and Ian Cognito MP, who spend their time productively retweeting articles from the Independent on their Twitter feeds?

Well, I'm back now, so we can all get back to normal. I'm planning to have the Labour party implode in a fresh spasm of in-fighting next week, so everybody can get back into a reassuringly familiar routine!

Sincerely, Keir.

That Garrick Club Telegraph Dinner

To start

Chicken-liver Paté-son

Plotted shrimps

Scot-free egg

100,000 squid risotto

Main course

Lynn's Owen-brand Country Foods porky sausages

Toady in a hole

Grouse fresh from the Moore

Wild Bore (Garrick speciality)

Well and truly cooked goose

Unjust desserts

Plummy duffer

Spotted dickhead

Eton Mess with three-line whipped cream

To follow

A selection of sleezes, with homemade in-a-pickle

To drink

Beaujeau Nouveau

RIVER SEWAGE CONCERN

by Our Environmental Staff
Sue Widge, Hugh Jeturd and Lou Paper

SOME of Britain's most prominent rivers have expressed concern about the disgusting state of Westminster.

"It's like an open sewer in there," said the River Avon. "They really need to clean up their act. The place is full of turds. You walk though Westminster and suddenly there's another shit right in front of you. It's revolting."

The River Severn agreed, saying, "Wherever you go, you have to hold your nose. The stink is totally unbearable."

The Thames added, "I'm starting to worry that the effluence from parliament will wash over and pollute my already filthy waters."

The government has promised to act on the state of Westminster. Said one leading Tory wet wipe, "We're appealing to the floater voter, so we're going to look into this disgraceful issue and do nothing at all. One thing's for sure, you won't find us doing a poo-turn."

News in brief

Assisted Dying Bill's future 'in the balance'

■ Supporters of the Assisted Dying Bill said last night they would do whatever it takes to keep the bill alive.

Meanwhile, those against assisted dying are doing all they can to kill the bill off as soon as possible.

With the Assisted Dying Bill facing a long, painful future, many are suggesting that rather than suffer a slow demise in the UK, it might be preferable to be debated in Switzerland.

Westminster Round Up

Tory MPs last night decided that they will wear masks after all. "It's for Health and Safety reasons," said one prominent Conservative. "If we don't wear masks, people will recognise us as the Tories who let **Owen Paterson** get off scot free, and will probably hurl abuse at us." Said another, "I'm wearing a mask so no one can see my red face."

Parliamentary Standards Commissioner, **Kathryn Stone**, was last night accused of being biased against Brexiteers when it came to dealing with complaints about the conduct of Members of the House. Said one Leaver, "She is clearly a Remainer who is targeting those of us who wanted to take back control of our own greed... And regain our ancient freedom to lobby the government in exchange for large amounts of cash." Said the Commissioner, "It's done. Get over it. If you don't like the result, suck it up, Loser!"

A new **Standards Committee** has been announced, which will have a toughened remit to make sure that there are no standards in Parliament ever again. Under the proposals, any MP who displays any sign of probity, honesty or integrity will be hauled before the committee and then suspended for 30 days. Or possibly forever. Said Iain Duncan Donuts, "There are a few rotten apples in the barrel and we should be put in charge of everything."

The **Chair** of the new Standards Committee, replacing the old Standards Committee which had too many standards, has been announced as John Whittingdale MP. Mr Whippingdale is an expert in scandal, having been at the centre of a number of a lurid episodes with a sex worker, for which he was investigated by the former Standards Committee. "I was severely punished, which I thoroughly enjoyed, and then I faced the Standards Committee," said Mr Whiffytale. "They gave me a good spanking, which I can't recommend highly enough."

The **Prime Minister** has NOW decided not to have a new standards committee and not to appoint John Whittingdale, and not to support Owen Paterson. He said, "This is not a U-turn and my previous decisions were nothing to do with the investigation by the Standards Committee into my own standards regarding my free holiday in Mustique." He added, "That is a ridiculous suggestion – as though I would indulge in petty revenge, when I've got free holidays courtesy of my chums to worry about."

(That's enough sleaze. Ed.)
(No, it isn't. PM.)

"When I finish here I have to go to my second job in the nursing home and this evening I've got my waitressing shift"

"BOO! Sleaze!"

Those renamed Oxford institutions after accepting Mosley donations

Oxford University............ The British University of Fascists
St Peter's .... St Spanker's
Lady Margaret Hall .... Lady in German Uniform Hall

(That's enough bad taste. Ed.)

Lines on some further developments in Scottish politics

'Twas in the year of twenty twenty-one
That the Scottish First Minister surprised everyone
Not by a new scandal or going politically rogue
But by appearing on the cover of the magazine *Vogue*.
Now, with no disrespect to the wee lookalike Krankie,
The *Vogue* cover girls are usually long and lanky,
But her supporters all said that Nicola was "a model leader"
And now she had proved it to the fashionable reader!
Her critics, however, said it was an act of egotistical vanity
When she should focus on the climate and the threat to humanity.
For this all coincided with the COP26 summit in Glasgow
And the dilemma over the new oilfield known as Cambio,
How could Ms Sturgeon claim that her party was Green
When no greater supporter of drilling had Scotland ever seen?
Jobs versus the enviroment – what an unhappy choice
For the leader who claims to speak with Caledonia's voice.
Fossil fuels? Is it "Och Aye" or is it "No Nay Never"?
Any answer from the SNP leader has to be fiendishly clever.
How to solve this dilemma and not lose the populist vote?
Maybe a photo in "cream roll-neck jumper and stylish beige coat"?

© *William McGonagall 1867*

Who should be the next Parliamentary Commissioner for Standards?
You choose who should replace Kathryn Stone in the hot seat to regulate MPs' behaviour

Sepp Blatter

Lex Greensill

Neil Hamilton

Jeffrey Archer

the late Bernard Madoff

Del Boy

Owen Paterson

Kathryn Stone again

Boris Johnson MP
● Live   385,000,000 Views

Prime Minister's Live COP26–Stream

👍 Like   💬 Comment

0 people like this

Boris: I'd like to **welcome** the world to this stream and, like **all** British streams, it's **totally** transparent and clear and **devoid** of any **faecal** content whatsoever. So, **on** with the **big** speech. Tonight, fellow **worldsters**, we stand on the **brink** of history. And my message to you **is**: Come on, let's **pollute** the world, sod the future generations, let the snowflakes **fry**, let's **stink** up the planet! **Whoops**, no sorry, that's the **other** speech I wrote. I **always** write two, clears the mind, helps the **Bozzter** decide what he thinks. Then I run them past the **boss** and Carrie says "The **green** one, you idiot."

(NO REACTION FROM EMPTY HALL, AS ALL DELEGATES OUT BUYING GLENFIDDICH WHISKY AND TINS OF LUXURY SHORTBREAD FROM GLASGOW COSTCO)

Boris: So, it's **one** minute to **midnight** – which is when I wrote this speech – and **time** is running out. The Sword of **Damocles** is hanging over James **Bond** as he tries to **defuse** the ticking **bomb** that's going to **blow up** the world. Should he cut the red wire or the **green** wire or should he just get his **wires** crossed and come up with **another** metaphor? So, **football**! It's 5-1, Humanity United are **trailing** Climate Change Rovers in extra time in the **final** of the **World Cop**. They think the planet's all over, it **isn't** now – if we can pull **one** goal back or maybe **two**.

(AIDE HANDS HIM PIECE OF PAPER)

Boris: What's this? **Cripes**! That's good! We seem to have got an agreement to **reduce** metaphors to net **zero** by 2030. Well, that's a result! It's **5-2** now! Well done to the boys in **green**!

(AIDE WHISPERS IN HIS EAR)

Boris: Ah, sorry, **methane**! Not **metaphors** at all. Because one of them's a **flatulent** outpouring of **toxic** gas that does no one any good and the **other's** methane. You may ask, **why** are we suddenly talking about **methane** when **I** thought we were all worried about **carbon dioxide**...?

(AIDE WHISPERS IN HIS EAR)

Boris: Ah! It's because the President of the United States **says** so. Quite right, the **Donald**!

(AIDE WHISPERS IN HIS EAR)

Boris: I knew **that**! It's the **Joe**. And without **further** ado, let me introduce...

(AIDE WHISPERS IN HIS EAR)

Boris: Well, wake him **up**, then! Lady and gentleman, I give you President Biden to announce this **historic** agreement.

President Biden: We're all agreed that China and Russia should have turned up, but they couldn't be bothered. They didn't even sign the methane agreement. What does that say? Is it time to go home now? Where's my jet?

Boris: **Great** speech, Joe! Let's get **off** our phones and give him a big **COP** round of **applause**!

(DELEGATES STILL BUSY ON PHONES, REALISE THEY COULD HAVE BOUGHT WHISKY MUCH CHEAPER ONLINE AND HAD IT FLOWN TO THEIR OWN COUNTRIES. THEY ORDER MORE ANYWAY)

(FROM OUTSIDE, WE HEAR GRETA THUNBERG SAYING: BLAH BLAH BLAH)

Boris: Quite **wrong**, Greta, my young **crusty** friend! In here, it's all **blah-ther, blah-ther, blah-ther,** which is **completely** different. Cue my other slightly **older** friend, Prime Minister Modi, our very own **Star** of India, who's got some **madrastic**, **fantastic** ideas about stopping the world heating up into a **Vindaloo**!

(AIDE HOPES NO ONE IS LISTENING, WHICH THANKFULLY NOBODY IS)

Prime Minister Modi: I'm fully committed to reducing our carbon emissions to net zero...

Boris: Hurrah, **India** on board! Planet **saved**! **Bozza** takes credit!

Prime Minister Modi: ...by 2070.

Boris: Yikes! **2070**? You'll be **dead** by then!

Prime Minister Modi: And so will everyone else.

Boris: Well, it's **progress** of sorts! **Phew**, is it **hot** in here or is it just me? So, what's **next** on the agenda? Ah, time to introduce the most **important** person in the world...

(ENTER CARRIE SYMONDS WITH AGREEMENT TO END DEFORESTATION)

Boris: **Blimey!** 5-4! **Another** one! Back of the **net** zero! These agreements are coming **faster** than new managers at Newcastle United! (LOOKS AT PIECE OF PAPER) And **this** agreement's particularly brilliant because we'd already agreed it in 2014. **Ace** recycling, guys! Hats and **masks** off to my old chum, President Bolsonaro, who **couldn't** be with us for the very understandable reason that he couldn't be **bothered**. Brazil, where the **nuts** come from! No offence, **Bolso**! (AIDE WHISPERS IN EAR, THEN RUNS OUT OF THE DOOR)

Boris: You've **resigned**? You **can't** resign! I'm about to do the **big** closing speech. Well, **Bozza** stands alone to save the planet. (FROM OUTSIDE, THE SOUND OF GRETA THUNBERG AND SUPPORTERS SINGING: "YOU CAN SHOVE YOUR CLIMATE CRISIS UP YOUR ARSENAL!")

Boris: It's **Emission Impossible**! This planet will **self-destruct** in five seconds! Your **mission**, Bozza, should you choose to accept it is...

(DELEGATES STREAM INTO HALL, HAVING HEARD THAT PRIME MINISTER OF UK HAS FINALLY FINISHED, AND DEBATE THE PROBLEM OF RAPIDLY MELTING ICE IN THEIR WHISKY GLASSES)

ECO CHAMBER

Makes you wonder, doesn't it? Are we humans all alone in the universe?

Apparently if people were to die out, within five years the earth would begin to recover

Don't worry, we're bound to invent some device for removing CO_2 from the atmosphere

GLOBAL CLIMATE CRISIS: LEADERS UNITE

Putin: "We've agreed to save a lot of energy"

Xi: "By not going to COP26"

COP26 recycling initiative praised

by Our Climate Change Correspondent **Cat Astrophe**

There was widespread praise today for the ongoing commitment to recycling at COP26, with the amount of recycled empty promises from previous climate change conferences reaching record levels.

"First, we had the recycling of the deforestation pledge, which was promptly ignored both by Brazil's government and illegal Amazon rainforest loggers a decade ago, then we had the recycling of the big banks' commitment to no longer invest in fossil fuels, a commitment they first made back at the Paris Conference and then quietly shelved," said a leading environmentalist.

"This level of recycling is unprecedented and will probably only be matched by COP27 when these announcements are recycled yet again.

"COP26 is shaping up to be the most environmentally friendly climate change summit yet, with the tonnes of recycled empty promises easily offsetting the carbon generated by the hundreds of private jets flying the rich and powerful to and from Glasgow."

EXCLUSIVE TO ALL ADVERTISERS BUYING SPACE DURING COP26

Hello.

We just want you to know that we've learned the word 'sustainable'.

Yes, we know our business consists of trawler fishing/ making furniture out of the rainforests of Borneo/flying thousands of planes a day, but we want you to know that we are really trying to do this sustainably.

We've done a lot; there is a lot more to go. We know we have to do better at telling people how great we are at being sustainable.

And that's why we have

committed to our plan: by 2030, we will have doubled the number of adverts we run telling people we are doing whatever it is we do sustainably.

By 2050, when you are fighting over the last cup of water in Europe, we will be running nothing but adverts telling you that this whole situation is nothing to do with us.

That's our promise to you. For our children.

[Insert meaningless corporate squiggle here]

POETRY CORNER

In Memoriam Mo Drake, advertising genius

So. Farewell
Then Mo Drake.

"Beanz Meanz Heinz",
Yes, that was your
Catchphrase.

They even changed
The spelling on
The can of "Beans"
To "Beanz" –
That is quite
A legacy.

Now, no one
Can call you
One of the
Haz Beanz.

E.J. Thribbz
(17½ varieties)

Revolutionary new source of decarbonisation finance proposed

A THINK tank has proposed a brilliant new source of carbon-cutting finance which could change the entire global situation at a stroke.

A spokesman for the think tank said, "The idea is very simple. Every time someone at the Telegraph, Mail, Spectator, Express or GB News says 'Yes, but what about China, they're not doing anything at all, so it's pointless us doing anything?', whoever says that has to pay for someone to get a heat pump installed.

"Our preliminary statistics have suggested that the government's target of 600,000 heat pumps to be installed each year could be met in about four days, which would free up enormous amounts of time and energy."

"Oh dear! Looks like we've just missed them"

DIARY

ADRIAN CHILES

There's nothing in the world I love more than beans on toast. In a word: truly scrumptious. Don't listen to the so-called gastro snobs with their fancy sauces, "kiwi fruits" and French-style "mayonnaise" (what's that when it's at home?)

Tucking into my beans on toast this morning got me wondering just how many beans are there in your average small tin? Fascinating question, to my mind – and one that, frankly, I've never seen satisfactorily answered.

So I got to counting. And the answer gave me a bit of a jolt. On the many occasions I'd given the matter serious thought, I'd guessed at a figure around the 200 mark. But the actual figure turned out to be a whopping 212, though obviously it must vary a bit from can to can.

Not bad value, to my mind, when all is said and done, and with a nice slice of buttered toast to form a sort of "bed" beneath the beans, it's positively delicious.

Which is more than can be said for the kiwi fruits of this world!

Yeah, whatever. That's what I thought when I read in our local paper that there's going to be a new mini-supermarket situated just off the ring road, left at the roundabout. I didn't mind one way or the other.

Sorry, but you don't have to have an opinion on everything. I can take a new mini-supermarket just off the ring road, left at the roundabout. Or I can leave it. Some things just don't particularly interest me, and that's one of them.

So for now I'm reserving judgement, if it's all the same to you.

Don't get me wrong. I can see the point of lifts. All things being equal, they save you the effort of going up and down stairs. And that must be quite a few stairs if you're talking the Empire State Building in New York or the Shard in London or any other building of similar height elsewhere in the world, for that matter.

But I've never liked being inside them – lifts, that is. I don't know why. Perhaps it's something to do with being stuck inside a confined space. Nevertheless, I always take consolation that I won't be in them for long, as they travel very swiftly these days.

So, all in all, the lift is a good thing. Just don't ask me to be in one for a minute longer than I need!

Funny how sometimes it's the obvious things that you don't really notice, or at least not until you do.

Let me explain. Talking with some mates in my local boozer the other day, I got to wondering why zebra crossings are called zebra crossings and not antelope crossings or dolphin crossings or some such. Fascinating question.

At that moment, one of my mates pointed out that it was because the crossings have black and white stripes – just like the aforementioned zebras, if you will.

Now it seems obvious, but it had never struck me before. As I said just now, sometimes it's the obvious things that you don't really notice – until you do.

As told to
CRAIG BROWN

DEVIL IN REBRAND SHOCK

by Our Social Media Staff
Old Nick Clegg

The Chief Executive of the Infernal Regions, Mark Beelzeberg, confirmed today that he is changing his name to reflect his new priorities and developing moral responsibility in a changing underworld.

"I think people had the perception that I was in some way evil, encouraging hate and sin, which could not be further from the truth," he lied.

"What I'm trying to do with this rebranding is to reposition Hades as a sort of user-friendly space, a nice warm environment, where people from all backgrounds can be tortured with pitchforks, have their innards roasted, and burn for eternity should they so wish."

He continued, "That is why from now on I would like to be known as Metaphistopheles rather than my old name, Beelzeberg, which is now rather dated."

When asked to define what the Metaphistopheles universe is like, he said, "Well, the best idea is to go and have a look at Facebook, where our algorithms will lead you to the darkest regions of hell. If you want someone to vouch for me, I could refer you to one of the tormented souls who work for me, otherwise known as Sheryl and Nick."

Facebook 'changes name'

by Our Technology Correspondent
Meta Thunberg

IN AN attempt to put months of controversy and criticism behind it, Mark Zuckerberg today confirmed that Facebook was changing its name to something he believes will allow the social media company to make a fresh new start and no longer be hated and despised: "The Liberal Democrats".

"This incredible new name was the idea of our Head of Human Shield Resources, Nick Clegg, or 'you there', as I call him affectionately. He says The Liberal Democrats is a name associated in his country with decency, honesty and success."

"I'm certain this is another great call by Nick Clegg and not something he'll have to be saying sorry for at some point in the future."

Yorkshire County Cricket Positions in Full

- Bully Mid off
- Bully Mid on
- Backward Square Leg
- Deep Cover-up
- Extra Cover-up
- Whistlebowler
- Sticky Wicket-keeper
- First Slip
- Second Slip
- Third Slip
  (OK, we admit there were a few slips by the complainant as well)

BOYCOTT SHOCK

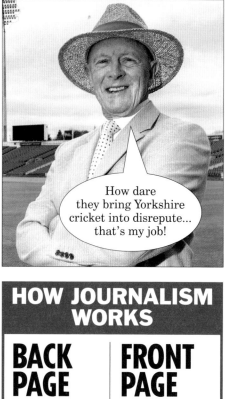

How dare they bring Yorkshire cricket into disrepute... that's my job!

HOW JOURNALISM WORKS

BACK PAGE
■ WHY oh why does cricket have such a terrible problem with racism?

FRONT PAGE
■ WHY oh why do we allow floods of migrants into the UK?

Welcome to the Metaverse! A digital realm of endless possibilities awaits you!

I saw you looking at this on Google. Do you want to buy it?

Pandemic? Pandemic!

Look at my dick

New study: Jeff Bezos may have been to space

by Our Fulfilment Centre Correspondent **Ima X. Hausted**

UNCONFIRMED reports suggest that Jeff Bezos may have been to space recently, based on the fact that he mentions it every single time he goes anywhere or does anything and makes a huge brouhaha about the fact he's been to space, is basically Neil Armstrong and that this has completely changed the way he looks at life.

"From the footage, the reports cannot be verified, as he appears to have only filmed his entire journey from about 94 angles, taken several other people to space with him, and made a massive deal of it," said one space expert, pushing open his door to reveal a hundred envelopes from Jeff Bezos announcing that he's been to space and it was amazing.

"But the preliminary evidence certainly suggests that he may have been to space or, at least, very, very high in a special plane, which is nearly the same thing."

Industry experts have announced that, if Bezos has been to space, it doesn't really make a difference to the rest of us, but it's very nice for him and there's definitely no reason for us all to ignore Bezos when he talks about it and pretend not to have heard when he mentions it for the billionth time.

"Can I call you back? I'm just having a drink with my best friend"

CHINESE WHISPERS

A VARIATION on the classic parlour game of misunderstandings

In this case, the first player makes a statement such as: "I was sexually assaulted by a senior member of the Communist Party."

The next player whispers in her ear: "You didn't mean to say that or you'll never play tennis again."

The next player repeats this whisper whilst changing it slightly: "You didn't mean to say that or you'll never see your family again." The next player in the chain does the same thing: "You didn't mean to say that or you'll never see daylight again."

Finally, it comes back to the first player (Peng Shuai) who whispers sheepishly: "I never meant to say that, it's all an enormous misunderstanding, and I am very happy to support President Xi and his Thought on Socialism with Chinese Characteristics for a New Era."

It's a marvellous party game, for all members of the Party, ie everyone. Compulsory fun for all the family.

....

NEXT WEEK: "Charades" – how the West responds.

YORKSHIRE CRICKET CLUB BOARD CONVENES EMERGENCY MEETING OVER RACIST BANTER CRISIS

Good to see they're all in their whites

Time wasters calling 999

by Our Ambulance Staff **Si Ren**

THE ambulance service has revealed some of the most ludicrous requests from members of the public calling 999.

Said a spokesperson, "We had one caller today who said that they'd fallen down the stairs and could we send an ambulance. Really?! We haven't got any ambulances available – they're all far too busy helping people with genuine complaints."

She continued, "We've had calls from time wasters giving birth, having heart attacks, with axes stuck in their heads – you name it!

"Honestly, these people really need to keep the emergency lines free for those who want to know how to get to sleep, how to resuscitate their goldfish, or what to do if they've swallowed their filling when eating a Greggs' pastie".

From The Message Boards

Members of the online community respond to the major issues of the day...

Art historian offends students

Guys, I see TV art critic Andrew Graham-Dixon has upset students during a Cambridge Union debate about 'good taste' with his highly critical impersonation of Hitler. The Union's Equalities Officer found it 'absolutely unacceptable' and 'utterly horrifying' and one undergraduate felt 'physically sick'. Other officials called on the President, Keir Bradwell, to resign, while the Union's LBGTQ+ Officer added that it was 'unprofessional' of him to have had two glasses of wine at the dinner before the debate and admitting to being drunk. Bradwell apologised for not intervening and promised to create a blacklist of speakers including Graham-Dixon. Under pressure he then changed his mind and announced that, 'There is no policy to ban anyone – it's a free speech institution.' A career in politics beckons methinks! – *Bogbrush*

Two measly glasses at dinner? Slippery little shit should be sacked for that alone. – *Anglia Potatrix*

Graham-Dixon's performance was indeed horrifying and unacceptable, and his sickening impersonation made my flesh crawl. Stooped and cowed, whining and bleating, he bore no relation to Der Führer. I have added him to my own schwarze Liste and there will be no U-turns! – *Legion of the Damned*

I saw Graham-Dixon's documentary '100% English', which examined the DNA of people who believed themselves to be of pure stock (including one lady who claimed a thousand years of Anglo-Saxon heritage). All were proved to be imposters with foreign blood. Keep up the good work Sir! – *Odal*

Spot on Odal, we must remain vigilant. White singers are rightly condemned for adopting corn rows and Bantu knots. The Rolling Stones have even stopped performing 'Brown Sugar' (whose miscegenistic lyrics understandably cause outrage) and we can at last enjoy 'Midnight Rambler' and 'Stray Cat' without the nagging fear they might spoil it all with that sordid song. – *367485*

Do you mean misogynistic? – *Bogbrush*

This comment has been removed by the moderators – *367485*

As a plain man with a thousand years of Angelfolc blood coursing through my veins, I ignore chatter about Anglo-Saxons, Adolf Hitler, Andrew Graham-Dixon, and other alien entities. I simply toil to build a secure homestead for my wife (when I meet a woman suitably fair and fecund) and our future sons, Raedwald, Aethelweard and Edmund. – *Athelstan*

I suffer from alopecia barbae and can only grow hair directly under my nose. I'm doing Movember with my usual 'Adolf' tache but this year I'm calling it Andrew! – *Phil Trum*

Time to end the disastrous educational experiment. – *Sword of Truth*

BIBLICAL TIMES

Friday 26 November 2021

Children of Israel tell Moses 'Commandments must be reformed'

BY OUR BREXODUS STAFF
ARCHIE COVENANT AND BERNIE BUSH

The Commissioner for Standards of the Chosen People, a Mr Moses, has come under fire and brimstone over his controversial 10-point code of conduct.

Angry members of the Children of Israel said it was unfair to expect them to obey these strict rules, which prevent them from doing whatever they want.

Said one, "Ok, some of us have been dancing around a graven idol and worshipping false gods. And, let's face it, our neighbours' oxen are pretty damn covetable, but these practices have been going on for years and have been perfectly acceptable up to now. Why make a fuss?"

Said another, speaking from his secretary's bed, "Oh, come on, what's adultery got to do with my wife? I mean, God!

Why can't I take his name in vain?"

Said a third, "Where does it say 'Thou shalt not steal'? Ok, it's on the tablet, but it's not as if it's set in stone. Oh, it is? Here's a solution, why don't we kill Moses?"

The Children of Israel have now agreed to hold a vote and set up a new standards committee that doesn't include Moses or God.

The new chairman, Mr Mammon, said, "Under the new rules, it will be perfectly permissible to worship both God and Mammon, providing the God bit is kept to under two hours a week and doesn't interfere with your primary job, which is the adulation and celebration of the Deity of Dosh, who is everywhere by the way."

Our thanks to the authors of the Book of Second Job for additional reporting.

Jennifer Arcuri breaks her silence for the 19,735th time

by Our Technology Correspondent
Lee Gover

BORIS JOHNSON's former lover, Jennifer Arcuri, sensationally broke her silence for the 19,735th time over her affair with the Prime Minister, as never-before-published diary extracts sensationally revealed Boris Johnson to be Boris Johnson.

"Boris said he wanted to be the throttle to propel my business to success," Arcuri revealed in the diary extract, "but the truth was that he just wanted to camshaft me."

Everyone agreed that this revelation is definitely the one which will finally see Boris Johnson brought to account for his links to the American businesswoman, though possibly that might have to wait until the 19,736th time Arcuri breaks her silence in another Sunday paper in two weeks'...
(cont. p94)

Parliamentary Regulation

Senior Backbench Tory MP, Sir Bufton Tufton, writes:

THE Prime Minister's disastrous proposals to prohibit members of parliament from taking jobs as consultants may look attractive in theory, but in practice it will discourage a whole class of persons from entering the House of Commons. That class consists of people who are not just career politicians, obsessed with the minutiae of government, but includes those who have wider interests – such as making money, making more money and, most importantly, making more money still. Parliament would be a much duller place if it were to be deprived of the input of colourful characters who are not merely politicians – in fact, some may have no interest in politics at all. Instead, they have a deeper hinterland which involves a life-time interest in matters such as filling their boots, feathering their own nests, and sticking their snouts in the trough. It is essential that there is a wide breadth of such experience in parliament and this commercial expertise makes for a more rounded politician, particularly if the job involves a large lunch. This ill-considered and badly thought-out piece of regulatory folly will result in a lacklustre lower chamber, which will find itself desperately short of spivs, chancers and crooks, who all contribute to the rich, in fact very rich, tapestry of Westminster Life. Am I getting paid for this? Right. Three thousand quid paid into my British Virgin Islands account. No questions asked. Questions cost extra.

© *Sir Buff-Envelope Tufton of Cash 2021*

"I know where you're coming from, Maestro, but I suggest you omit the 'Have a banana' from the chorus"

World's smallest violin manufacturer cancels all leave

THE world's smallest violin manufacturer today cancelled all leave and announced plans to ramp up production after Tory backbenchers expressed incredulity that a ban on second jobs would mean they would have to live on just £80,000 a year.

"This is great news for our company, we've never known such a sudden demand for our products," said a spokesman.

GOVE DEFENDS £164M PPE CONTRACT FOR CLOSE BACKER

I know a good supplier when I see one

Paul Dacre 'bewildered'

by Our Media Correspondent
Noah Clue

ANNOUNCING the withdrawal of his bid to be Ofcom chairman, the former *Daily Mail* editor, Paul Dacre, has lashed out at lefty civil servants who, he claims, were determined from the word go to stop him getting the job.

"How on earth did we get to the point in this country where we are so polarised as a society that we can't see the attributes and talents of someone from the opposite side of the political spectrum?" a clearly wounded Paul Dacre said to reporters.

"When did it become the norm that just because someone holds views you dislike, they are to be demonised and destroyed at all costs?

"I am totally at a loss to understand how this wretched and awful turn of events came to pass, but I'll now be returning as Editor in Chief of the Mail Group to try and work out this mystery."

COP 26
THAT FINAL AGREEMENT IN FULL

We the undersigned nations agree:

- We will agree to sign an agreement
- The terms of that agreement will be agreed
- The timing of that agreement will also be agreed
- The agreement will be so agreeable that nobody will be able to disagree
- This agreeable agreement will last as long as we agree agreeably
- By 2030 we will all achieve net zero disagreement on agreements
- No nation signing this agreement will be judged to have been disagreeable
- Er...
- That's it...
- For the planet

COP

Watered-down COP

STANLEY IN SEX SCANDAL

Like father, like son

Don't like either of them

THE SPECTATOR

— *EXCLUSIVE* —

'WHY I FEEL SORRY FOR RACHEL JOHNSON'

by Ghislaine Maxwell

WE shouldn't be judged by our family. And yet it's plain to see that sexual misconduct runs absolutely rife in that family. That awful father!

Well, it's no wonder the kids ended up so messed up, you know – I met her at Oxford and it was clear then that the dad was a terrible fraud and it's plain to see that the rest of them are *(cont. for 94-year jail term)*

GEORDIE GREIG'S SUDDEN DEPARTURE FROM THE Daily Mail

Those possible reasons in full...

- The triumph of Evil.
- Not getting Lady Rothermere into smart party.
- Refusing to run "Hitler not so bad after all" piece.
- Purchase of all Geordies by Saudi Arabia.
- Plans to turn focus on online operation and restructure as seven-day print operation to reduce costs.

(This is too boring. Ed.)

French demand right to go on Mortimer and Whitehouse 'Gone Fishing'

IN AN unexpected twist to the post-Brexit fishing crisis, President Macron himself has insisted that he appear in the current series of the popular BBC2 reality doc.

A spokesman for the French Premier has demanded that the President has the right to don waders, cast his line and catch at least one British trout by the end of the programme.

He further demands that Bob Mortimer cook him lunch and that he be allowed to engage in light-hearted but strangely affecting banter with Paul Whitehouse about their health issues, as clearly set out in the terms of the Brexit agreement.

Failure to agree to President Mackerel's terms will lead to a blockade of all British ports, Jersey's electricity supplies being cut off, the Channel Tunnel closed, and the Christmas Special "Bob 'n' Paul Go Ice-hole Fishing at the North Pole" (with special guest, Santa, discussing his elf issues) be removed from the French schedules in perpetuity.

LATE NEWS: *Captain Birdseye arrested in Le Havre for breaking Crispy Cod Fritter protocol and exceeding breadcrumb finger quota.*

UK aims for net zero

NO FISHING

WARNER.

SAY 'AHH'

AAAAARGH!!

GP ONLINE CONSULTATION

BUFFERING

Troops called in to help army cope

THERE is increasing disquiet that the military has yet again been called in to help bail out another British public service that's woefully short of manpower.

Said one General, "It's a sorry state of affairs when our lads, who have been trained to inject vaccines and drive heavy goods vehicles and ambulances, are asked to don battle fatigues and take up arms to defend the border of an ally against military incursion."

He continued, "Fighting is not what our fighting forces signed up for. They're just not prepared for this – it will take months for them to readjust to the unfamiliar business of warfare."

When asked for an alternative to sending British troops to help the British troops, the General suggested maybe some Eastern European HGV drivers and nurses could be given special temporary visas to come to Britain, in order for them to be sent to the Ukraine.

(Rotters)

Q Boris Johnson   Home   Create

Boris Johnson MP
● Live   385,000,000 Views

Prime Minister's Live Stream on Fakebook

👍 Like   ○ Comment

0 people **like this**

(PRIME MINISTERS PRESS CONFERENCE)

Boris: So, **fire** away, let's start with the **Mirror**, which, as you know, I'm too busy to look in! **Still** got it! Not Covid, **obvs**.

Ivor Scoop: What's this about you having Christmas piss-ups in Downing Street when we were all supposed to be in lockdown last year?

Boris: Well, Ivor, not much of a scoop, is it, a year **late**? But I can assure you no rules were broken. We **strictly** adhered to the rules of Twister, Sardines and Blind Man's Buff – you know, the one where you put the **blindfold** on and **grab** the nearest person and guess who

they are. **Top** party game! Matt Hancock was **brilliant** at it. The main thing is, **everyone** was wearing masks, even if they **were** over their eyes. And **I know**, because **I** wasn't there!

Simon Briefcase: Careful, sir. We don't want to prejudice any public inquiry.

Boris: Bloody inquiries – led by bloody **judges**! We've had enough of them, laying down the law as if they were... well, judges! Time for a **new** legal system where **ministers** decide what the law is that they're **not** breaking! And **then** they should be allowed to appeal to the **supreme** authority – the Prime Minister. **Bozza**! **Myself**! Master of the **Sausage Rolls**! Right, that's **sorted** – time for one **last** question. Kay Burley, Sky-eyed News?

Kay Burley: Don't you think it's really hypocritical of you to be having a boozy party with colleagues when the rest of the country is obeying lockdown regulations?

Boris: Wow, Kay, you're **totally** and utterly **shameless**! You should be working for **us**!

Conservative Party announces name change

That shortlist in full

■ The Conservative Perfectly Legal Gathering

■ The Conservative Drinks Reception In Accordance With All The Rules That Were In Place At The Time

■ The Conservative Tiny Soirée With Almost Nobody In Attendance Really

■ The Conservative Small Essential Workplace Get-Together *(That's enough stupid names. Ed.)*

"What party?"

FRUSTRATION FOR THOSE STILL STUCK WITHOUT POWER

by Our Meteorological Staff
Gail Force

THERE was anger throughout the North (of London) at the continued absence of any power in a number of homes belonging to members of the Labour party.

One furious resident, a Mr K. Starmer, complained, "We've been out in the cold for so long – it feels like years, because it is years. I feel so isolated up here in the wilds of Islington. I can't remember the last time I was able to turn on the television and see a Labour party in power."

He continued, "I blame Storm Arsol, which caused a very damaging landslide in the last election, and left us completely cut off – communication lines are

down. We're trying to reconnect, but it may take another 17 years for the damage to be repaired."

Another powerless victim of the recent Storm Arsol, a Ms Angela Rayner, said, "I've no idea what's going on. Did Keir really say that? He didn't tell me. But something really needs to be done. Just look at the House – it's full of scum!"

LATE NEWS
■ "You're not helping, Angela!" says Labour leader.

LATE LATE NEWS
■ "Leave it, Keir, she's not worth it!" says Yvette Cooper.

LATE LATE LATE NEWS
■ Storm Arsol sweeps across nation again for another landslide.

CHINA SHOCKED TO BE NAMED BY MI6 CHIEF

What's bugging him?

You, of course

MI6 Chief reveals China is biggest international threat

IN OTHER NEWS

■ Secret intelligence sources suggest Pope is agent of Catholicism

■ Covert surveillance of woods indicates bears may be source of faeces

Clerihew Corner

Sheikh Mohammed bin Rashid Al Maktoum
Got a nasty shock in an English courtroom.
Because of the ghastly things that he did,
He must pay his ex-wife half a billion quid.

Sarah Vain

Putting the 'Me' into Meghan (although the piece is supposedly about William)

TAKE two brothers, who've had the same sad history, but who have turned out very differently. One is a caring, empathetic and responsible role model, who has selflessly devoted his life to Royal duty and saving his injured subjects as an Air Ambulance pilot. The other one has devoted his life to suing the *Mail*.

One has a beautiful, intelligent, well-dressed wife. The other has a wife who sues the *Mail*.

One speaks movingly and openly about his mental health issues on a pod cast. The other one tries to do the same, but is too busy suing the *Mail* for his podcast to be anything other than embarrassing loopy rubbish.

One has genuine desire to save the planet. The other is selfishly wasting paper to make writs to sue the *Mail*.

One has three lovely children whose pictures he generously shares with the world. The other has three unlovely lawyers, who ungenerously try to prevent any pictures of his children appearing anywhere in the world, ever. I could go on... *(Please do. Ed.)* But isn't it now crystal clear that Wills and Kate are great, and Harry and Megs are the dregs?

***

HAVE you noticed, as I have, how Harry's beard is incredibly stupid? One thinks of other men, of similar age and background, who have resisted the temptation to grow a stupid, selfish, litigious beard – I'm thinking of, say, Prince William, whose delightful, clean-shaven, diligent and responsible visage stares out at us every day from the pages of the *Daily Mail*! Prince Hairy(!), on the other hand, is beginning to look as stupid as his stupid beard! I'm sorry to be so harsh, but it's true.

***

MEGHAN MARKLE and her silly writ-happy beret – have you ever seen anything sillier? Apart from her husband's beard? Honestly, if I were the judge in, say, a high-profile copyright and privacy action, I would consider the beard and beret as conclusive proof that the ridiculous couple's litigation should be thrown out of court! Case dismissed!

by the Rev Wilbert Tawdry

THE NEW ADVENTURES OF THOMAS THE TANK ENGINE

"**WHY** are you looking so down in the dumps ?" said Thomas to his new friend, Henry the High Speed Train.

"I'm steaming!" said Henry unhappily, although he wasn't, of course, because he was electric. "It's the Fat Conservative," he explained. "He promised that I would be going all the way to Leeds, but now he's done a U-turn."

Thomas laughed. "He does a lot of those! So where are you going now?" he asked.

Henry blew his whistle furiously, "I'm going nowhere!"

"Well," said Thomas merrily, "at least you're going there fast!"

All the other trains and replacement buses laughed at poor old Henry who had believed what the Fat Conservative had promised, as Henry was shunted towards the sidings… *(to be discontinued)*

A Doctor Writes

AS A doctor, I am often asked, "Doctor, will you treat me for Covid, which I have contracted because I have refused to be vaccinated?"

The simple answer is "Yes, because I have to", although the more complex answer I would like to give is "Stuff you, matey, you deserve it. I would prefer to carry on treating the backlog of cancer patients!"

What happens is the anti-vaxxer, or *idioticus onlinus conspiritalis Qanonsensicalis*, as they are technically known, is admitted to Intensive Care suffering from extreme breathing difficulties.

The doctor is then obliged to consider their Hippocratic Oath rather than the other form of Oath – namely "Fuck off!"

If you are worried about doctors being cross with you, there is an easy and simple remedy. Get yourself jabbed.
© *A Doctor 2021*

DAILY⚔BREXPRESS

HURRAH FOR SEWAGE!

by Our Environment Staff
Lou Flush

YES, it's jobbies for everyone! Now we have severed ourselves from the yoke of the hated EU, we can finally exert our sovereignty and release genuine British sewage into our rivers!

Yes, we can now cover ourselves in glory, bathing in what has been flushed from the throne of kings, this septic tank, this toilet seat of Mars, this demi-john!

And now, the best part of all! The whole nation can join with us at the Daily Brexpress and take part in that fine British pastime – turd polishing!

Simply reach into your local stream or stretch of coastline, grab hold of a British turd, take it home, polish it, varnish it and wear it in your lapel on British Jobbie day, when we remember our brave soldiers who fought and died in trenches full of excrement, so that we can do exactly the same all these decades later!

··

■ **DISCOVER how far we are up shit creek on pages:**
2, 3, 4, 5, 6-94

"It's a very effluent area"

Film highlights
Trainstopping

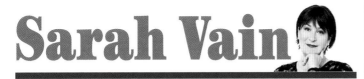

Black comedy about a group of low-lifes addicted to the rush of getting high-speed rail programmes cancelled.

Bozbie, Shapps, Spad and Posh-Boy (an off-form Jacob Rees-Mogg) get their thrills from the destructive habit of "trainstopping" – involving not injecting cash into the system.

Set in the economically depressed North, they'll do anything to satisfy their compulsion – over-promising, lying and cheating – as they maintain a front of respectability while inhabiting the sleazy world of dregs.

Don't miss the scene where Bozbie rants, "Choose money, choose a freebie, choose a holiday in Mustique, choose an old Etonian, choose another Old Etonian, choose a friend of Carrie's, choose me, choose a car, choose a bus, but don't choose a choo-choo to Leeds because there isn't one."

EYE RATING:
Money down the train

What are the new Covid rules?

- ■ Work from home if you can...
- ■ But you don't have to
- ■ Masks must be worn everywhere...
- ■ But they aren't being, are they?
- ■ Umm...
- ■ Er...
- ■ That's it | HM Government

COMMONS COCAINE SHOCK

It's a three-line whip

Are knighthoods too easy?

Asks A. Level-Student

I know everyone says this, but isn't it time we admitted that knighthoods have really become a bit of a joke? I mean, it used to be something you really had to work for, but nowadays they just give them to anyone. It's unfair to single out individuals, but let's take Gavin Williamson as an example. He completely messed up the lives of school kids and students, but nobody seems to care about his poor performance, and they're going to give him a knighthood anyway. It just proves that you can be useless and get one, regardless of talent, work, application or anything else. It's just done on the single assessment that if you're given one, you'll shut up and go away. If this sort of low-grade inflation continues, knighthoods are going to become meaningless. At the very most, Gavin Williamson should get a CBE, but it'll probably be upgraded to a knighthood (A*A*A*).

Lines on the Great Scottish Invasion of 2021

'Twas the eve of the year two thousand and twenty two
When Scotland was under attack from the Covid flu.
Nicola Sturgeon told folk, with a serious frown,
That she was shutting all the nightclubs down.
She then also told them that they could not travel,
But her well-laid plans would soon unravel.
For no true Scot quietly at home will stay
When it's time to celebrate Hogmanay.
The clans all descended across the border
In search of a dram or two or ten to order.
To the land of the Sassenachs did they all debunk
And ended up in Newcastle, gloriously drunk
For there was, they joked, "grog on the Tyne"
To help them sing rousingly *Auld Lang Syne*.
"Same again, barman," the merry Caledonians clamoured,
As their English friends helped the Scots get "hammered"!
I hope this cheeky historical quip doesnae make readers cranky,
And get me in trouble with the First Minister of Scotland.

© *William McGonagall 1867*

The Eye's Controversial New Columnist

This week, like most sensible commentators, I am angry about Big Bird from *Sesame Street*. In case you haven't heard, the feathered person in question has been caught promoting the woke leftist agenda of having a Covid vaccine. Mr Bird has been outed by Republican State Senator Wendy Rogers as a communist. I agree, but I will go further! I have had my eye on *Sesame Street* for some time (purely in my capacity as a columnist and not because, as a baby, I like to watch such things) and I believe it is nothing more than a training ground for Russian spies. Think about it: they spend all their days learning English words, working out how to "count" things (very important when spying on western defences) and training how to hide in dustbins. I do not find it a coincidence that popular characters "Bert" and "Ernie" bear a striking resemblance to Putin spies "Boshirov" and "Petrov" – agents who were sent to this country to "count" Salisbury cathedral. And I find it telling that Big Bird is yellow and Elmo is red. It is obvious they represent the alliance between communist China and Putin's Russia. I cannot believe that we are wasting time talking about Climate Change and potential famine in Afghanistan when we should all be focusing on this shocking fact that we have the fluffy red menace in our *(cont. p94)*

"Mummy, why doesn't Action Man have a willy?"

"He was ahead of his time"

HELLO! Well, I had a painful reshuffle last week! Actually, I had two!

The first reshuffle was the one I conducted of my shadow cabinet while Angela Rayner was making a speech. The second one was when Angela grabbed me in the corridor, slammed me against the wall and reshuffled my testicles with her knee! Thank heavens none of my "shadow secretaries of state" got "ejected out of my cabinet", if you catch my meaning!

I know Angela was upset that I derailed her speech about Tory sleaze, but she should think of it like this: we are making real inroads against the Tories with Angela's line of attack; so if I HADN'T derailed it with a pointless bit of party management, the British public would have just got confused! Branding is very important in politics, and the Labour brand under me is snatching defeat from the jaws of victory!

But that aside, I think my proper reshuffle was a huge success! You can't have missed that I put Yvette Cooper back on the front bench. If you're not familiar with her work, Yvette was a minister in Gordon Brown's cabinet, a shadow minister under Ed Miliband AND the wife of Ed Balls. If that doesn't have the smell of electoral success, I don't know what does!

In other news, I said the word "Bullshit" last week to describe the PM. I know it shocked and offended a lot of people, but that's the kind of politician I am. Fearless, tough-talking and not afraid to use "B" words! "Bastard", "Bollocks" and "Batshit" have all been loaded on my autocue and we're ready to roll!

Obviously, my fearlessness does not extend at the moment to using the words "Brexit" and "Blair", but perhaps when I grow a pair to replace the ones Angela has squished, I might whisper them quietly when no one is listening!

Sincerely, Keir.

DUMB BRITAIN

Real contestants, real quiz shows, real answers, real dumb!

Radio 1 Breakfast Show

Arielle Free: Who was the first man to walk on the moon?
Caller: Louis Armstrong.

Pointless, BBC1

Alexander Armstrong: Which American sprinter won four gold medals at the 1936 Berlin Olympics?
Contestant: Jesse Jackson

Armstrong: We're looking for a country that took part in the 2014 Commonwealth Games.
Contestant: North Korea.

The Chase, ITV

Bradley Walsh: In the state of Israel, belonging to which religion makes you a citizen?
Contestant: Muslim.

Walsh: Which American rapper's name is an anagram of Kenya?
Contestant: Jay-Z.

Walsh: Croci is the plural of what small spring flower?
Contestant: Daffodil.

Walsh: The Fischer-Sozin attack is an opening in which board game?
Contestant: Cluedo.

Walsh: Which British prime minister's wife gave birth in 2010?
Contestant: Winston Churchill.

Walsh: Jellied moose nose is a delicacy in Alaska and which Commonwealth country?
Contestant: Italy.

Lightning, BBC2

Zoe Lyons: Helen of Troy was known as "the face that launched a thousand…" what?
Contestant: Bullets.

Tipping Point, ITV

Ben Shephard: The first televised Presidential Address from the Oval Office in 1947 was given by which American president?
Contestant: George Washington.

Shephard: Joe Biden served twice as vice-president under which leader?
Contestant: Jeremy Corbyn.

Shephard: In his epic poems, Homer often refers to nectar as the drink of the gods, and which other substance as their food?
Contestant: I know he likes doughnuts. I think I'll go with doughnuts please, Ben.

Shephard: The Volga, Europe's longest river, flows into which inland body of water?
Contestant: The River Nile.

Shephard: Famously used by Sir Francis Drake, the Golden Hind was what mode of transport?
Contestant: A car.

Shephard: Which brothers, pioneers in aviation, are honoured in the USA every year on December 17th?
Contestant: Is it the Marx brothers?

Shephard: Which Conservative party politician was known by the initials "IDS"?
Contestant: Margaret Thatcher.

Shephard: In 1855, which nurse established the British Hotel for sick and convalescent troops during the Crimean War?
Contestant: Marie Antoinette.

Shephard: Fletcher Christian led a mutiny aboard which ship in 1789?
Contestant: The *Titanic*.

Shephard: Who was on the throne when Tony Blair became prime minister?
Contestant: Queen Victoria

Shephard: What word comes after brook, brown or rainbow to give a type of freshwater fish?
Contestant: Dolphin.

Shephard: Ciabatta bread originated in which European country?
Contestant: India.

Shephard: What kind of animal is a Bavarian mountain hound?
Contestant: A cat.

Shephard: Solar wind is a term for a stream of particles emanating from which large celestial object in our solar system?
Contestant: The moon.

Shephard: "Madchester" is a term to describe the music scene in which north-western city?
Contestant: Newcastle.

Shephard: Which large striped member of the cat family features in Henri Rousseau's 1891 painting *Surprised*?
Contestant: Zebra.

Shephard: In which European capital city can you cross the River Liffey by using the pedestrian walkway called the Ha'penny Bridge?
Contestant: Is it Germany?

Shephard: Richard the Lionheart was king of England in which century?
Contestant: The twentieth.

Shephard: In 1952 Prince Charles became the Duke of which English county?
Contestant: Wales?

The Tournament, BBC1

Alex Scott: The name of which day of the week is an anagram of "dynamo"?
Contestant: Tuesday.

Impossible, BBC1

Rick Edwards: Which major government report is often referred to as the blueprint for the welfare state: Beeching, Beveridge or Brandreth?
Contestant: Well, I don't think it's Beveridge because that's a drink.

Michael McIntyre's The Wheel, BBC1

McIntyre: The category is food. I am looking for any green fruit or vegetable.
Big Narstie: Orange.

On the Ball, Radio 2

Michael Ball: Which world championships are currently taking place at the Crucible Theatre in Sheffield?
Caller: Rugby.

Celebrity Weakest Link, BBC1

Romesh Ranganathan: "Friends, Romans, countrymen, lend me your…" what?
Gemma Cairney: Heads.

Ranganathan: What is 7 times 7?
Dick (of Dick and Dom): 14.

Ranganathan: How many beds in a twin hotel room?
Gemma Collins: One.
Ranganathan: Was there any part of you that thought "twin" might have something to do with it?
Collins: I only stay in suites and penthouses.

Ranganathan: The film genre known as "romcom" is an abbreviation of the phrase "romantic…" what?
Esme Young: Peanut?

Ranganathan: Which "J" is a geological era in which the dinosaurs roamed the Earth?
Anton du Beke: Germanic.

Ranganathan: What "B" is the nickname for the Yeoman Warders who guard the Tower of London?
Chunkz: Border Control.

Christmas University Challenge, BBC2

Jeremy Paxman: Name the composer of this piece. [piano music plays]
Jackie Clune: Bobby Crush.
Peter White: Winifred Atwell.
Paxman: No, it was Robert Schumann.

Ant & Dec's Limitless Win, ITV

Ant (or was it Dec?): In which year did man first step on the moon?
Contestant: 1912.

Mastermind, BBC2

Clive Myrie: Which knighted Scottish singer and music hall entertainer was known for such songs as "Roamin' in the Gloamin'" and "I Love a Lassie"?
Contestant: Sean Connery.

Myrie: What part of a house is known in Cockney rhyming slang as the "apple and pears"?
Contestant: The toilet.

Myrie: Which controversial British music impresario, who died in 2010, was the manager of the Sex Pistols?
Contestant: Robert Maxwell.

Myrie: Which 19th century UK prime minister had the nickname "Dizzy"?
Contestant: Dizzy Gillespie.

Tenable, ITV

Warwick Davies: Name an EU country of seven letters.
Contestant: Ecuador.

Popmaster, Radio 2

Ken Bruce: Who had a number one in 1990 with "Nothing Compares 2 You"?
Caller: Des O'Connor.

Breakfast Show, Magic FM

Harriet Scott: What "V" spews lava?
Caller: Vulva.

Boris Johnson MP
● Live   385,000,000 Views

Prime Minister's important message streaming on Fakebook, Instagroan, Twatter and all other platforms except DIKPIKTM

👍 Like   💬 Comment

0 people **like this**

Boris: Yes folks, everything is going up! **Electricity** bills, **gas** bills, **water** bills, **national insurance**, **taxes**, **inflation**, **cost** of living, **all** are being levelled **up**, **up**, **up**!! They're calling it the Year of the **Squeeze**, which sounds pretty **good** to yours truly. I'm **all** for a good **squeeze**.

First Lady: Watch it, Fat Boy, or you're going to the spare bedroom, as soon as we've sellotaped the gold wallpaper back up again.

Boris: Yes, but my point **is**: **everything's** on the rise – including Keir Starmer's **popularity**. Which is an **amazing** achievement and all down to **me**. Because, to be honest, there's **nobody** around of my stature, with

the political **bottom** to fill my trousers. The **swivel-eyed** brigades in the shires are all going **doolally** for **Liz Truss**. And, no offence, Liz, **who** in their right mind would **trusst** you? **Geddit**? See, I haven't **lost** it. Not the Prime Ministership, but my **gift** for **boffo Bozza bantz**, which is another crowd-pleasing skill **lacked** by the Trusster, who's only able to riff on **cheese** and **pork** markets. And to be **honest**, no one's going to give the top job to someone who **flip-flopped** on Brexit, was a **useless** Foreign Secretary and spent **all** their time arranging **photo** opportunities, while **plotting** disloyally behind the Prime Minister's back.

First Lady: Hahahahahaha! At last you've said something funny.

Boris: Where's Simon BriefCase – or is it Simon PackedCase? I thought he was **still** Cabinet Secretary. If he's having a **leaving** party, I want to be the **last** to know about it.

Simon BasketCase: I'm still here, helping Sue GraySuit with her inquiries, over a bottle of business wine and a plate of fact-finding cheese.

Boris: Excellent. Now time to concentrate on the **new**, exciting

opportunities ahead – such as the **opportunity** to **renegotiate** the **entire** Brexit agreement.

Simon CaseClosed: I thought you said that you had "Got Brexit Done"?

Boris: Yes, but I want to move **further** and **faster**!

Simon CaseReopened: Prime Minister, that rather does sound like finding yourself in a hole, and pledging to keep digging.

Boris: Nonsense! Piffle and **dePfeffel**! It's just a case of **undotting** the 'I's, and **uncrossing** the 'T's... and then **completely** crossing out all the **other** letters in the words in the Brexit Agreement that we don't quite **like**. Such as "Brexit" and "Agreement".

Simon CaseClosedAgain: So who will be in charge of this impossible and gargantuan task?

Boris: Lizard Truss! **That's** who! That should shut her **up** for a few years, and keep her **so** busy she won't have time to take pictures of **herself** trying to look like a **leader**. Clever, eh? Chummy **Machiavelli** had nothing on Nicolo di Bernardo dei **Bozziavelli**!

Simon CaseDismissed: Oh dear.

MAXWELL TRIAL LATEST
EXCLUSIVE TO ALL PAPERS

SHOCKING, UNPLEASANT PAEDO BEHAVIOUR THAT YOU DON'T WANT TO READ ABOUT
Bumper court supplement pages 1,2,3,4,5-94

FEARS OVER GHISLAINE MAXWELL'S HEALTH
by Our Court Staff **P.D. O'Phile**

THERE was growing concern over the well-being of Ghislaine Maxwell, as images emerged from court showing the socialite looking "badly drawn".

A spokesman for the family said, "She's not herself, she looks more like Sophia Loren or Carol Vorderman... she isn't the Ghislaine we know."

Her Defence Attorneys agreed, "Our client has been painted in a very bad light, and she's clearly been smeared. And, to be honest, I don't like how I've come out either."

Court officials defended the depiction of the accused, saying, "She's not that badly drawn, not compared to other defendants. OJ looked like Martin Luther King, and Johnny Depp looked like Rasputin on a bad day."

Maxwell's accusers were delighted by their depictions, explaining that they were keen to remain anonymous and now there was no risk of anybody recognising them.

The trial still has weeks to run, and the jury will have to decide whether or not Ghislaine Maxwell has been framed.

THAT HEARTFELT PRINCE ANDREW APOLOGY THAT HE DIDN'T MAKE IN FULL

In the light of the Ghislaine Maxwell verdict, I can no longer remain silent as regards the suffering that has gone on.

One must always remember the victims, those innocent princes who have, through no fault of their own, seen their lives and indeed lies ruined as a result of the events of 20 years ago.

I am sorry, from the bottom of my heart, for myself and I offer my sympathies and condolences to me for the horrific ordeal that I have endured. I can only hope that I will now be left alone to rebuild my life as best as I can, and return to public life by attending nightclubs, performing duties such as skiing in Verbier and assisting the travel industry by flying everywhere for free.

Yours insincerely,
His Royal Highness
the Duke of Porkies

Genuinely smart motorway

EXHIBITION

WHY THIS ARTIST IS A COLONIALIST BASTARD AND YOU ARE STUPID FOR LIKING HIS STUFF

R&J

That Foreign Secretary £1400 'Biz With Liz' Luncheon with Those Very Important US Government Officials In Full

To start
Foreign Offal
Yankee Noodles in Peanuts sauce

Fishy course
Dover Soled Out
Expenses Claim Chowder

Lack of entrees
Arm and a leg of lamb with minted sauce and gravy train
Spring greeds
Trade Veal (off)

To follow
Bananas Frittered
Waffles with syrup
Assorted British Cheeseys (Red Leicester Wall, Shropshire Ex-Blue, Hard Brexit Cheddar)

To drink
Bubbly Blonde 1985
Free Port 2027

(Bill to be sent to J. Public. No border cheques, please)

THE ALTERNATIVE VOICE

DAVE SPART (Co-Chair Of The Dalston Pro-Hamas Puppet Theatre And Organic Baking Collective)

The awarding of a knighthood to the neo-Con War Criminal and Genocidal US Stooge Tony 'Bliar' is a totally and utterly disgraceful disgrace, which completely devalues the honours system which has already been completely devalued as an anti-meritocratic proto-zionist sop to the elite cabal of military industrial complex capitalists who control every aspect of the oppression of the working classes and er… er… I therefore join with my comrades at the *Daily Mail* in condemning this honour of Phoney Blah Blah which rewards the wrong sort of imperialist warmongering ie not the kind perpetrated by the progressive anti-Western Russian regime of Vladimir Putin, and instead whitewashes the blood on the hands of the tyrannical Weapon of Mass Destruction Tony Blairstrike who should be on trial at the Hague rather than feted at Buckingham Palace by the outdated anti-democratic symbol of tyranny ie Her Majesty the Fascist… er… in fact so utterly and totally and totally and utterly appalled am I that I am sorely tempted to give back my own award for services to counter-counter-revolutionary creative arts co-operatives in Neasden, but if a damehood is good enough for our sister in the socialist struggle Vanessa Redflag, then it would be churlish of me to deny that Dave Spart OBE has a convincing ring to it and… *(continued p94)*

Nursery Times
········· Friday, Once-upon-a-time ·········

SOMETHING STINKS IN NURSERYLAND

by Our Sewage Correspondent **Wee Wee Willie Winkie**

THE Nurseryland Water Company today accepted it may be partly to blame for the outpouring of effluent into the waterways and seas of Nurseryland from its own sewage pipes.

The problem first came to the attention of a female sea-shell seller, who sells sea shells by the sea shore, but more recently it is claimed by the sea-shell seller that "she smells faeces by the WC shore".

Said a spokesperson for the Nurseryland Water Company, "If she smells faeces on the WC shore, then I'm sure she smells sea shore wee smells."

Said the sea-shell seller, "The faeces smells shall seriously shatter my sea-shore shell sales."

Elsewhere a sea-faring owl and a pussycat complained that their formerly beautiful pea green boat was now pee yellow.

Said an irate owl, "Thanks to the sewage, we are now going to the Land Where the Pong Tree Grows."

As anger grew around the coastline, a sailor who went to sea sea sea, to see what he could see see see, said that all he could see see see was not the bottom of the sea sea sea, but what had come out of bottoms in the sea sea sea.

But a spokesman for the Nurseryland Water Company was unapologetic, saying, "We're making giant golden-egg profits. If you think we're going to fix this, you're living in Neverneverland."

On other pages

● Rapunzel in tower nightmare: "I'm trapped by an evil developer, I can't sell my home till the government helps pay my cladding bill" **3** ● After huffing and puffing, Big Bad Wolf "delighted" to be given triple-pig heart transplant **17** ● Sleeping Beauty's isolation period cut down from 100 years to 5 days **94**

How to keep your house warm as energy bills double

1. Find as many stories you can about the Cost of Living Crisis and then fashion them into a suit, with at least 17 layers, which will keep you and your family warm all year.

2. Wait until your elderly neighbours have both frozen to death, then break into their house, boil their kettle and use that water to fill your own bath back at home.

3. Break into Conservative Party headquarters, take a thousand copies of their manifesto from the 2019 general election and burn them, particularly the bit which says that they will be introducing "new measures to lower bills" because energy costs are "a major source of financial pressure" for lots of families.

News in brief

Antarctica 'Beset by Invasive Species'

■ The natural environment of Antarctica is being ruined by an invasive species that has "hitched a lift" on ships to the pristine marine ecosystem, a new scientific study has revealed.

The invasive bacteria – known as "humans" – are believed to have travelled into the area on ships from over 1,500 areas they have previously ruined around the world.

"These non-native organisms endanger every ecosystem they inhabit, changing the local environment to fit their own nefarious ends and making it difficult for any indigenous species to co-exist with them," the report concluded.

"You must lose your attachments"

CONSPIRACY UPDATE
GHISLAINE MAXWELL SPECIAL

Well Ghislaine Maxwell has been well and truly convicted for sex-trafficking minors, but we know beyond a shadow of a doubt that's what they WANT us to believe! So what's the truth?

QANON fan MAGA435 thinks he has the answer, and he supplies it via his gun-festooned website:

"It is reelly convenent that no-one is talking about Hillary CLINTON and her pizzagate now! I think we can see what is hapening here! It is such an old scam to destract us from a ficktional sex trEfficking ring by puting a REAL one in the news! Do not be fooled! These PIZZA PEEDO ELITES are trying to make you FORGET all the things they didn't do!"

TRUTH-IS-OUT-THERE4356 has a scoop, delivered via his Facebook page accompanied by a picture of a fish:

"I believe this is an actual photo of Ghislaine without wearing her human skin. I took this several years ago but no-one took any notice. Perhaps now you will believe me! Notice that the real Ghislaine is an aquatic fish monster – I warn the authorities now that if she is left alone for a second she will attempt to escape into the ocean like her father – you have been warned!"

On a final note DeltaMale@Incel.org.uk has sent this very interesting blog he's just written:

"I think the fact Ghislaine was convicted by a jury, many of whom were women, and none of whom were paedophiles, just shows how much of a kangaroo court this trial was! Perhaps for the next trial we might have some sex offenders on the jury so we might finally get some sort of balance..?"

Food for thought, DeltaMale! The mystery continues!

Levelling up scheme begins to pay dividends

by Our Levelling Up Correspondent **Phil Hole**

At last the government can point to genuine evidence that its investment in levelling up is working.

In East Sussex, £330,000 from the government's "Levelling Up" fund has been used to repair potholes on the driveway of former Tory peer Nicholas Gage.

Said one local, "It's amazing how successful this levelling up has been. Beforehand the road looked like the surface of the moon, now it has been completely levelled, and all the potholes have been filled up with crisp £50 notes. It's a triumph for government policy, and it's certainly improved the access to my caravan."

Critics, however, queried whether the 87-year-old so-called "Virile Viscount" was a suitable recipient of public money for his drive, commenting, "With a wife who is 38 years his junior, the old boy is going to need a hole in the ground sooner rather than later."

"Bad news, darling. Looks like we'll have to cancel dinner with your parents"

NAY

South China Morning Post Truth

HONG KONG LATEST

THERE was no raid by hundreds of security police at pro-democracy media outlet Stand News, and there were no arrests for "conspiracy to publish seditious publications".

The arrests never happened early on Wednesday and searches of the journalists' homes were not also carried out.

Said a police spokesman, "If these things had happened, people might imagine that China was in some way a repressive tyranny, but as they didn't, we can continue to rest easy, believing China is the champion of international press freedom. Now, please excuse me, I have a statue not to remove."

American tanks fail in attempt to invade Hong Kong in 2021

INFORMATION   DISINFORMATION

wilbur

OMICRON VARIANT WILL 'DEVASTATE THE UK AND NOT DO ANY SIGNIFICANT HARM' AGREE COLUMNISTS

by Our Omicron Expert **Dr A.R.M. Chair**

UK COLUMNISTS today all agreed that the Covid Omicron variant will wreak devastation on the UK/be such a mild variant it'll prove no more deadly than the common cold, and that the unprecedented surge in case numbers will overwhelm the NHS/barely even fill half the beds in ICU, as it is now clear we have entered the deadliest stage of the pandemic/the end point of the pandemic where a weakened strain fizzles out harmlessly.

The public breathed a huge sigh of relief/gasped in terror that the end was in sight/we're all doomed.

POETRY CORNER

Lines on CEO Jack Dorsey leaving Twitter

So. Farewell
Then Jack Dorsey.
You've announced
You're leaving Twitter,
But we all say that before
We end up going
Back to find out what
Laurence Fox said about
What Owen Jones said
About what Piers Morgan
Said about what
Andrew Neil said
About Laurence Fox.

Still, you can look
Back with pride at what
Twitter has contributed
To global debate:
"You are a fascist Nazi!"
Yes, that was one
Catchphrase.

"You are cancelled!"
That was another.

"I hope you die of cancer",
That was possibly the
Most popular, if not
The finest.

E.J. Thribb
(17½ followers)

The Alternative Rocky Horror Service Book

**Number 94
Baptism of convert
to Christian faith**

Reverend Flannel: Hello, everyone, it's great that there's so many of you here.

(Congregation of two sponsors and one refugee sit down)

Reverend Flannel: Peace be with you.

Christian Convert: Allahu Akbar.

Reverend Flannel: Yes, God is indeed great in a very real sense, and this is the point in the service where I have to ask you whether you genuinely turn to Christ and renounce the devil and all of his works.

Christian Convert: Yeah, whatever.

Reverend Flannel: Now, I have to ask you, as would-be convert *(and here the Reverend may give one of a number of plausible names)*, whether you do indeed come from Syria or Iraq or Jordan, or possibly Dubai?

Christian Convert: Yes, indeedy.

Reverend Flannel: Super. Are there any questions you'd like to ask, as we welcome you into our community?

Christian Convert: Where's the nearest B&Q? I need to buy some fertiliser.

Reverend Flannel: Gardening – how lovely. A really English hobby. And maybe your sponsors would like to say something at this point.

Sponsor 1: He's a nice lad and keeps himself to himself,

Sponsor 2: He's always in his bedroom listening to a lot of enthusiastic preachers online.

Reverend Flannel: Marvellous. Now I think we've just got time to baptise you with this holy water.

Christian Convert: Careful, bro. Don't wet my batteries.

Reverend Flannel: And isn't that a marvellous metaphor for the recharging of faith in all its mysterious ways. Let us pray.

THE PRAYERS

(Congregation kneel, one rolls out prayer mat and faces Mecca)

Reverend Flannel: Dear Lord, or Lady, or however thou identifiest thyself. Let us pray that we, in your wisdom, haven't had the wool pulled over our eyes and we beseech thee that just because we're trying to be nice to people, let them not take advantage of us in a right royal way.

Sponsors: Amen.

Christian Convert: Inshallah.

Reverend Flannel: Now let us all sing together that great hymn of faith: "Holy, Holy, Holy… war".

© The Church of England 2021.

DIARY

HOLLY WILLOUGHBY'S LIFE LESSONS

1. At one time or another, we all feel anxious, which is another word for anxiety. OK, your team of lovely, lovely professionals may keep telling you how great you look, but you don't always believe it, owing to childhood insecurities. So always keep a mirror close by, just to be sure.

2. It's good to breathe. My own special technique is to breathe in, then breathe out, then breathe in again, then breathe out again, then in, then out. Build this into a routine, and before you know it you'll be doing it without thinking. Now you can count yourself a true breathing expert, just like some of the iconic icons I've interviewed on *This Morning* over the years, including Dawn French, Ed Sheeran and Nelson Mandela.

3. Candles are so versatile. You can put them in drawers, or take them out and light them. The best way to light them is by taking a match or lighter to the stringy bit. Placed in the centre of a table, they can really light up a room, though if you want extra light it's probably best to switch on the main electric lights too. It's up to you.

4. Whether you are working behind the counter in your local McDonald's, or presenting the top-rated award-winning TV show *Dancing on Ice*, just remember: you're special.

5. Choose manageable goalposts. If you set the goalposts too high and too wide then you'll never be able to score that goal. Or you will, because the goalposts will be so high and so wide that it's easy to kick a ball in. But if the goalposts are too low and too narrow – say, six inches by six inches – then no football could get through them.

6. It's great to be natural. But once you've done that, it's best to put some basic cosmetics in your handbag, including dark black waterproof mascara, eyelash curler, lip scrub, lip balm, a good concealer, a pinky lipstick, eyeliner, moisturiser, eyelashes, blusher, body make-up, concealer, tissue, compact with fine milled powder and a small brush. Just to give you that natural look.

7. Some people might fear stepping out of a luxury limousine and onto a red carpet to be photographed looking drop-dead gorgeous in a brilliant designer ballgown before entering a glamorous prestige TV awards ceremony where they've been shortlisted for no fewer than five awards. But we human beings have a great capacity to face up to every difficulty that life throws in our direction.

8. It's negative not to think positive, and the best way to be positive is not to think negative.

9. So think positive!

10. Be kind to yourself. Why not buy a pair of Moonstone Drop Earrings with Moon and Starburst Studs, £460 from the Holly Willoughby Collection?

As told to
CRAIG BROWN

HS2 ARCHAEOLOGISTS MAKE ASTONISHING FIND

by Our History Correspondent
Roman Rhodes

Archaeologists working for the HS2 project have reported an extraordinary find, discovering traces of what experts are calling "the largest white elephant ever to have existed".

"The size and scale of the white elephant is mindboggling," said one excited trowel-wielder. "It stretched from London to the North, but not quite to Leeds for some reason, and cost upwards of £90 billion.

"We've never seen such a perfectly preserved white elephant as this one."

A HS2 spokesman said the plan was to put the enormous white elephant on display to the public by the mid-2030s, but admitted this could be delayed by a second discovery of what's being described as the biggest black hole of money they have ever seen.

The Mike Nesmith I never met
by **Philippa Website**

MIKE NESMITH was in the group "The Monkees". "The Monkees" were very important because they started a craze for pop groups to name themselves after animals that were spelled incorrectly, such as "The Beatles", "The Byrds" and "Lionel Ritchie".

Mr Nesmith was also heir to the company that invented liquid paper. Liquid paper is an early form of correction, where you could obliterate mistakes using a little brush to paint out the errors. Nowadays, of course, you can correct obvious mistakes easily on a computer, by speed-reading stuff on the internet like I do and *(You're fired. Ed.)*

ONLY IN

Read the incredible revelations in our sensational 94-part exposé of Hugh Hefner

◼ The man who created Playboy wasn't a committed feminist.

◼ The man who stuck bunny tails on women's backsides did not always treat women with respect.

◼ The man who had a harem of women a third his age was, to be honest, a bit of a chauvinist.

◼ The Pope who wore a big white hat and lived in the Vatican was a bit of a Catholic.

◼ The bears who lived in the woods also used the area for a bit of a shit.

◼ Hugh Hefner was also a bit of a shit.

On other pages

◼ The truth about the old man who made a lot of money out of pictures of naked women
(You're fired! Rupert Murdoch, 94)

Laurence Fox engagement announced

THIS week, Mr Laurence Fox was delighted to announce that he has become engaged.

The engagement in question is to perform at the birthday party of Simon (2). As news of the surprise engagement hit social media, his former agent tweeted, "We are thrilled – if surprised – that Laurence has finally got some acting work."

Mr Fox will be showing off his mastery of balloon animals, as well as his repertoire of entertaining one-liners, including: "Why did the chicken cross the road? To avoid getting vaccinated", "Knock! Knock! Who's there? An Eastern European. Go back to where you came from," and – most hilariously – "I'm running for Mayor. Vote for me!"

....

Late News
◼ **Children's party ends in tears** There was a tantrum when Laurence Fox stormed out of the party, throwing Simon's toys out of his pram, after a three-year-old insisted he wear a mask and pointed out the anomalies in his anti-vax thinking.

POETRY CORNER

**In Memoriam
Mike Nesmith, actor and musician, second to last surviving member of the popular musical group The Monkees**

So. Farewell
Then Mike Nesmith.

"Hey, Hey, we're
The Monkees",
That was your
Catchphrase.

Now you have taken
The Last Train
To Clarksville,
So let's hope
You were
A Believer.

E.J. Thribb
(17½ minutes of fame)

DAVE ROCK

WRITES FOR THE GNOME

MAN, it so breaks my heart that my old buddies Neil Young and Joni Mitchell are leaving Spotify. They bring shame on the great name of Rock Music by not standing with me, Eric Clapton, Kid Rock, Kanye and Meat Loaf, and being against the evil vaccine.

I'm sure you've heard that we're all forming a super group to protest against the Man. We're the Anti Vaxxxers (that's three 'x's) and if you buy our song on Spotify, over eight cents from the first three billion sales will go to a militia in New Jersey who make their own placards.

None of us have taken the Vax so far, and we're all okay, apart from Meat Loaf, obviously, but as anyone in rock will tell you, what's the point of being in a group if one of them isn't dead?

I speak for Rock itself, man, when I tell you, if Rock stands for anything, it's standing against getting suspicious shit being injected into your arm without exhaustive trials and further tests. I'm sure if my old buddies, Lou Reed and Janis Joplin were here now, they'd be saying the same
(cont. p94)

GLOBAL TOURISTS LEFT CONFUSED BY TRAVEL REGULATIONS

Am I allowed to go to Mustique?

Am I allowed to go to Ukraine?

Am I allowed to go to Taiwan?

Am I allowed to go to sleep?

FOY, WHAT A SCORCHER!

by Our **Entire Staff**

IT WAS the scandal that rocked High Society and set Fleet Street on fire!

And the intriguing central mystery at the heart of it all was "Why was Claire Foy on every page of the *Telegraph* for weeks?"

Was it because she was playing the fruity Duchess in a TV drama about a sex scandal? Yes.

But there was still one question remaining: "Who was the so-called Headless Man?"

Was it the editor of the *Daily Telegraph*, who completely lost his head and put in pictures of Claire Fwor to make up for the lack of real news? Yes.

And would it lead to a messy divorce between the editor and the readers? No, of course not, because he knows that's what the Tellygraph readers really want!

ON OTHER PAGES

■ Foy oh Foy! says Simon Huffer **p2**

■ Moore Foy, please! says TV's Charles Phwoore **p3**

■ A breath of Fresh Claire, says Tom Uttleyobsessed **p4**

■ Ashes disaster – Duchess of Argyll not involved, by Sir Geoffrey Foycott **p94**

Daily Telegraph Friday 7 January 2022

Letters to the Editor

Historical Inaccuracies in BBC Bonkbuster

SIR – Is there no one at the BBC who can be bothered to check any of the details in their so-called period dramas?

I refer of course to the outrageous travesty that was broadcast under the title *A Very British Scandal*. And scandal it most certainly was!

For those of us unfortunate enough to sit through all three episodes, with a notebook and pen at hand, the litany of inaccuracies was overwhelming. Where to begin? From the very first shot featuring the 1963 Austin Mitchell Traveller to the final scene depicting the post-coital smoking of the Rothschild Kingsize no-filter cigarette, almost every detail was historically illiterate.

The Traveller in question should not have come with Dunlop tyres, as these were unavailable, due to a well-reported strike at the rubber plantation in Kuala Lumpur in 1962.

The Rothschild Kingsize was a brand only available to children and no responsible newsagent would have sold them to a member of the aristocracy over the age of 21.

I do not want to bore your readers by listing every single shocking aberration, but may I further point out that the so-called headless man was not in fact naked in the infamous polaroid at the centre of the scandal, but was in fact wearing socks and sock suspenders, as was appropriate in the presence of a Duchess wearing only pearls. I know this because the so-called "headless man" was a very good friend of mine, and I had only purchased – I mean, he had only purchased – the classic Argyll socks from Messrs Gieves and Wooster that very morning after a fitting the previous week.

For the BBC to get this essential detail wrong, calls into question the veracity of the entire enterprise. If the so-called sock scenes are not to be trusted, then how can we believe any of it? And indeed whether the Duchess of Argyll ever existed outside the tawdry imagination of the BBC, with its slipshod communist screenwriters?

I'm so furious I will have to watch all three episodes again, whilst my good lady wife is out volunteering at the booster centre car park in the coastal village of Givegood Head.

Sir Herbert Fairbanks Junior Gussett
Dunblowin', Duncan Sands, Cesspoole, Dorset

We're Married!!!!
TV comedian Sid Twatt and his wife Nora take the listener through their absolutely crazy life together, answer audience questions and stage an amusing not-quite-argument which they definitely haven't tightly scripted. This podcast is #1 in 37 countries, and has sold out the O2 Arena for the last six weeks.

Messpod This podcast – previously *It's Alright To Be A Complete Mess* – hosts a new celebrity each week, explaining how they're not actually incredibly thin and wealthy and successful, but are in fact a disastrous mess, just like you, you pathetic bastard. Guests have included Sting, Twiggy and His Holiness the Dalai Lama.

The Crime A former investigative journalist from the BBC, Derek Serious, spends 37 hours interrogating a horrible murder before concluding the police probably did get the right man, all things considered. Episode 25, *Acid Bath*, won a Grammy.

The Entrepen-Hour This brilliant business podcast is so good that it fits an hour of content into just 33 minutes of human time. Listen up to learn all the business hacks to hack your way to a more efficient life of business hackery. Guests have included Jeff Bezos, Lex Greensill and Bernie Madoff.

Cage against the Machine The John Cage podcast features two celebrities listening to a recording of John Cage's *4'33"* each week, and then not discussing it. Then, the next week, two other celebrities listen to the previous week's recording, and don't discuss that one, and so on. A riveting listen. Guests have included Pope Francis, Leigh Francis, Francis Rossi, and Ross Kemp.

Daily Middleton

BRILLIANT KATE PLAYS PIANO FOR CHARITY WHILE LAZY, TALENTLESS MEGHAN SELFISHLY STAYS AT HOME DOING NOTHING

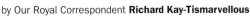

by Our Royal Correspondent **Richard Kay-Tismarvellous**

BEAUTIFUL Kate Middleton, Duchess of Cambridge, today wowed the entire nation with her virtuoso piano performance, which had music critics gasping in admiration.

Kate, looking beautiful in red, tinkled the ivories with her elegant fingers, giving a flawless rendition of the complicated and technically demanding *Chopsticks in C* by the composer Franz 'Civil' Liszt.

Meanwhile, across the Atlantic, Meghan Markle, who can barely play a single note on a recorder with those fat fingers of hers, managed to contribute no musical gifts to the world whatsoever, although she is very good at blowing her own trumpet and banging the drum for her money-grabbing schemes.

The assembled listeners were in no doubt about Meghan's failings, with one saying "Even when she wasn't playing a musical instrument, the useless Meghan made a number of mistakes, one of which was to sue the Mail on Sunday, another being to win the case. We would all much rather hear the beautiful, wonderful, fabulous, beatific, unlitigious Duchess of Mozart *(cont. p2-94)*

IT'S A STATUS CYMBAL

BORIS PARTY SHAME

Government's New Plan to Save Prime Minister

MILITARY TO BE BROUGHT IN TO CLOSE DOWN BBC, LEVEL UP IMMIGRANTS, END DRINKING CULTURE IN THE NHS AND SCRAP COVID REGULATION FOR ENERGY BILLS

by Our Political Staff
Des Pratt and **Di Straction**

IN A SERIES of well-thought out knee-jerk policies published today on the back of an envelope, the government laid out its strategy for appealing to someone, or anyone really, with a list of words designed to be thrown together in no particular order on the front of a newspaper.

The policies include levelling the BBC, ending immigration into the military and scrapping culture in energy drinks on sale in the NHS.

"This is what the public really want," slurred a Downing Street spokesman, opening his third bottle of Sauvignon whilst sitting on a broken swing in the garden.

"If this doesn't work, we will have no option but to send in the military to Downing Street and arrest Sue Gray."

"Are you the stripper?"

SUE GRAY INVESTIGATES

The most brilliant investigator since Sherlock Holmes tries to solve the greatest mysteries of the age:

■ **Whether the gathering of staff at Number Ten broke Covid rules.**

■ **Whether the gathering of bears in the woods was responsible for smelly mess.**

■ **Whether the gathering of Papal enclave at Vatican involved Catholicism.**

⊙ WORDLE ✿

It's the game everyone is playing

Now *Private Eye* joins in the fun (and steals the idea from the bloke who thought it up!!). You have six guesses to find the word that the public is looking for!!

B	O	R	I	S
B	O	O	Z	E
P	A	R	T	Y
L	Y	I	N	G
S	H	A	M	E
S	O	R	R	Y

More tomorrow, with the Eye's new puzzle sensation – Turdle!

MASKEMATICS

Some current secondary school problems

1 38% of the teaching staff are self-isolating. Draw a graph showing the Head's blood pressure rising exponentially.

2 Outside it is 0°C-4°C. Inside, below 15°C is a health risk. How many windows can you safely have open in class?

3 The government promised CO2 monitors six months ago. Calculate the probability that they will ever arrive.

4 All six catering staff have Omicron. Draw a pie chart showing what pies will now not be available at lunchtime.

Boris Johnson MP
● Live   385,000,000 Views

Prime Minister's No Question Time Live on Facebooze

👍 Like   💬 Comment

0 people **like this**

(THE ACCUSED ENTERS WITH HAIR CUT, TIE STRAIGHT AND SHIRT IRONED. THE PRIME MINISTER, FOR IT IS HE, READS OUT THE CASE FOR HIS DEFENCE, TRYING TO LOOK CONTRITE)

Boris: People of Britain, this is a **historic** moment. I have said **sorry** to **someone** for **something**. It has **never** happened before. You will no doubt all have seen my **heartfelt**, **sincere** and extremely **carefully worded** and **convincing** apology to the House of Commons. You will have heard me talking about sharing your **pain** at loved ones dying alone and all that sort of **stuff** that I trotted out so **movingly**. And I'm **sure** now no one can be in **any** doubt about how very, **very** sorry I am that **you** the public have formed the opinion, however **misguided** and technically **inaccurate**, that I have done something **wrong**, even though I **haven't**.

(THE PRIME MINISTER TURNS PAGE SOLEMNLY AND LOOKS GENUINELY DISTRESSED... AT HOW MUCH MORE OF THIS HE'S GOT TO READ OUT)

Boris: What would be **wrong** would be for **me** to comment further on the public's regrettable **misinterpretation** of the events which are under investigation by the **official** enquiry conducted by the **independent** civil servant working **directly** for Number Ten. This is Sue Graysuit, who was brought in after Simon Case, or rather, Simon SuitCaseFullofBottles, had to step down, due to an unfortunate **misapprehension** of his independence, having potentially attended a work-related wine and cheese **crisis** meeting in Downing Street. So, while I await the **conclusions** of the enquiry, it would be entirely **unethical** for **me** to answer **any** questions about **anything** I have done for the past few

years, apart from the **successful** rollout of the **vaccine** and the **fantastic** job **my** government has been doing **fighting** the virus. This **triumph** was achieved under extremely **difficult** circumstances, such as being **unjustly** investigated over work-related gatherings with **incredibly** diligent staff who, let's face it **deserve** a drink, especially when the weather is so **lovely** and all the **bars** are closed and you can't even go to the **park** without the police arresting you for **breaking** government Covid regulations. So, **apologies**, I **won't** be saying anything further about this disappointing **failure** in public perception **other** than to say I am as **furious** as you are at the way things were handled that evening (note passive tense) and absolutely **livid** at the way things turned out (note passive tense again, ie none of it my fault).

(PRIME MINISTER TAKES DEEP BREATH AND LOOKS GENUINELY ANGRY... AT BEING MADE TO EXPLAIN HIMSELF FOR ANYTHING TO ANYONE)

Boris: Notwithstanding my commitment not to say anything further, I **am** just going to make the following points to **clarify** any **confusion** in the public's mind regarding the so-called "party":

1. It was **definitely** a work-related event, because **Carrie** was there. Why on **earth** would she be there if the business of running the country was **not** being conducted in the garden extension to the office?

2. I **had** to be at the meeting because the invitation read "**BYOB**", which everyone knows stands for "Bring Your Own **Bozza**", ie **my** presence was required by my Principal Private Secretary Marty 'Party' Reynolds.

3. **BYOB** also stands for "Bring Your Own **Booster**", which proves **all** the Covid protocols were being followed at **all** times, even though **technically** at the time it could be argued that we didn't have a **vaccine**, let alone a **booster**.

4. It was **clearly** a very **important** decision-making work meeting, because **everyone** involved was under the influence of alcohol, which is the **best** way to create **effective** national policy on pandemic control, as **any** scientist would testify, if **drunk**.

5. **Ignore** 5. It's **not** very convincing, now I read it again.

6. There are **no** photographs of this meeting, so **technically** we don't **know** whether it took place or **not**, even though it did. But if Dominic Cummings **doesn't** have any pictures, and Rishi Sunak **wasn't** in Number 11 disloyally taking **snaps** of the garden from the balcony, there is **no** concrete proof that the regrettable alleged event **ever** occurred.

7. It **wasn't** a party, as there is **no** video record of Michael Gove **disco-dancing** and throwing dad-shapes to the sound of the Westminster Village People hit "**BYOBMCA**".

8. It couldn't **possibly** have been a party, as there are **no** CCTV images of former Health Secretary Matt Hancock handling some **very** complicated **briefs** with his special advisor and old university friend in a socially distanced office garden shed.

9. **Finally**, the party that **never** took place cannot possibly have **been** a party, because if it **had** been, **I** would have resigned in **shame** at the grotesque **hypocrisy** involved in leading a government which told the public they could **only** meet **one** other person outdoors, whilst inviting a **hundred** people to have a **piss-up** in the garden. The fact that, as a man of **integrity**, I have **NOT** resigned, is **absolute** proof that Ms Graysuit should conclude her **independent** enquiry by letting me off completely on **all** charges.

(THE PRIME MINISTER LOOKS RELIEVED THAT ORDEAL IS OVER)

Boris: **Phew**, think I got away with it! With one **bound** the Bozzter is **free**! It's time for a **party**! Get Marty Party on the case! Or have I thrown him under the **bus** yet? BYOB – Bring Your Own **Bus**! See what I did there? Bozza is **back** and the **bants** are flowing like the **champagne** we keep nicely chilled in the party **fridge** – which doubles up as somewhere to **hide** for yours truly! See you all at the garden office extension coronavirus **policy** meeting! Remember **BYOB**, Believe Your Own **Bollocks**!

(SOUND OF POPPING CORKS)

CABINET DISMAY OVER BORIS PARTYGATE SCANDAL

DOWNING STREET

HOW DID THIS NUTTER GET INTO WINDSOR?

by Our Royal Correspondent **Elizabeth Cross Bowes-Lyons**

QUESTIONS were being asked at the highest level after last week's discovery of a dangerous criminal inside the grounds of Windsor Castle.

The intruder was caught on CCTV cameras driving around the park and walking freely between buildings. He was identified as His Royal Highness Prince Andrew, who is known to the police on both sides of the Atlantic and considered "a potential threat to women".

Prince Andrew's relatives were said to be devastated at his latest actions and a spokesman told reporters: "Something has gone badly wrong with Andrew. He used to be an ordinary, fun-loving member of the family, but he became isolated and demotivated during lockdown. He began associating with the wrong sort of people, ie paedophiles, and it went downhill from there. Now, tragically, we have no option but to disown him."

When finally confronted by police and asked what he was doing, wearing wellingtons and carrying a loaded gun, the Duke of York claimed he was there for "an ordinary shooting weekend" and it was not his intention to "kill off" the monarchy for good.

THOSE PLATINUM JUBILEE PUDDINGS

Your suggestions in full

- Plummy Duffer
- Dick Spotted
- Sponger Cake
- Inbred and Butler Pudding
- Inability to Suet Pudding ✦ Sweaty Toff Pudding *(above)*
- Andy Snaps with Clot Cream ✦ Gooseberry Fool
- Jelly with Cowardy Custard ✦ Monarchy crumble

Radio Highlights

Barry Gardiner's Question Time

Friday, 3pm (Radio 4)

Recorded live from Brent North, tune in as a specially invited audience of MI5 agents and police officers quiz Labour MP Barry Gardiner about the problem of moles, Chinese plants and how his garden is full of Magicmoney Trees.

Questions will include: "What's the best way of spending half a million quid that a nice Chinese lady gives you with no strings attached?", "What do you think about the oppression of Hong Kong and the Uighur Muslims?" and "How stupid can you actually be?"

EYE RATING: *Nearly as good as David Attenborough's new TV series "Little Red Planet".*

Couch potato

You tuber

Han-z-z-zard

Prime Minister's Questions, continued from page 94

Gary Angry (Oop North, Lab): The Prime Minister has still not apologised for breaking the rules and breaking the law at a time when thousands were unable to see their dying loved ones while he was sipping Chardonnay with his cronies in Downing Street. Does he not agree that he should resign immediately in disgrace?

The Prime Minister: I thank the Right Honourable gentleman for his question and I refer him to the answer I didn't give earlier.

Norman Toady (Lymeswold, Con): Would the Prime Minister like to join me in congratulating himself for his continued support for cheese-making in my constituency, which has boosted output by an astonishing 0.03 percent in the last year?

The Prime Minister: I thank my Right Honourable friend for drawing the House's attention to the amazing success of the Lymeswold cheese industry and I do not have to point out that the Opposition's own cheese policy is, for want of a better word, crackers.

Tory Members: Ha! Ha! Ha!

Labour Member: You're past your sell-by date! You're smellier than any cheese! Get back in the wine 'n' cheese fridge!

Mr Speaker: Order! Order! I won't have anyone calling the Prime Minister a liar, even if he is one!

Irma Suckup (Stoogeminster, Con): Would the Prime Minister like to join me in congratulating myself for asking a very long question about trouser-press wiring regulations, thereby running down the clock to enable him to avoid answering the more serious charges against him regarding hypocrisy and the supposedly shameful flouting of rules he himself has made and blah, blah, blah?

The Prime Minister: I'd like to refer my Right Honourable friend to the job I offered her earlier.

Tory Members: Ha! Ha! Ha!

Labour Members: It's brown-trouser-press time for you, Boris! Your pants are on fire!

Mr Speaker: May I repeat that I will not have the Prime Liar called a Minister!

Ed Whohe (Nowheresville, LibDem): Can I just say something, Mr Speaker?

Mr Speaker: No, that's all we have time for...

(House empties to go to bar to discuss "worrying culture of booze" in Westminster)

POLICE BURGLARY SHOCK

THERE was widespread amazment today amongst police forces after an experiment by Greater Manchester police revealed that investigating burglaries and crimes actually works.

"The pilot scheme involved the police not simply hanging up the phone and saying 'sounds likes an insurance job to us' when people phone in to report a burglary," said a Greater Manchester police spokesman.

"Instead, we send officers to the property, who then investigate the burglary, examine the clues and hunt down and arrest the criminals responsible. Incredibly, doing our job actually works, who could have ever guessed?"

The Met Police in London say that, while the experiment was fascinating, they currently have no plans to start investigating crimes that have already happened. *(Rozzers)*

NEVER TOO OLD

A new love story by Dame Sylvie Krin, author of
Heir of Sorrows and *Duchess of Hearts*

THE STORY SO FAR: The Nonagenarian Media Moghul is ruing the day that he invested in the health innovation technology firm Theranonsense run by Elizabeth Holmesick...

"**S**TREWTH!" exclaimed the billionaire tycoon, as he pedalled furiously on the Peloton Ride of Death, a Christmas present from his young bride, the 65-year-old former supermodel Leggy Hall. "How could I have been so bloody stupid? Even a blind dingo in a blacked-out billabong could have seen that shifty Sheila coming!"

"Why now, don't you go frettin' yerself, Rupert!" soothed the 7-foot tall southern belle from the land of Texan Guns and Roses, removing the newspaper that he was attempting to read as he cycled nowhere doggedly on his exercise machine.

"It's an easy mistake for an old fella to make. There she was, a sassy blonde bombshell, batting her eyelashes and wiggling her start-up. And there you were with 125 million crisp greenbacks ready to slip into her cute li'l investors' account!"

Leggy smiled knowingly, as the similarity in the two women's story arc was not lost on her.

"I feel like a bonza bozo!" continued the most powerful man in the world, dismounting from the static bicycling device and slumping into a chair in front of his 94-inch plasma Panasonic Hedgehog TV screen. "The bastards in the newspapers are calling me 'Dupert Murdope'!"

Leggy loyally stifled a snigger while her furious antipodean beau ranted at his humiliation in the *Washington Last Post* under the cruel headline "There's no fool like an incredibly old fool."

"Remind me to buy the buggers up and close them all down!"

Leggy massaged his tense and hunched shoulders, as Rupert's pulse race to a dangerous 30 beats a minute.

"Let's jus' chillax, honey bun, in front of some relaxin' escapist telly fare – somethin' to take your mind off your worries and woes."

Leggy selected the Sky Atlastresort Channel, knowing that the TV Titan liked to watch his own channel. But what was this?

There on the screen was an elderly, foul-mouthed media mogul with useless sons and a scheming daughter... and there was a much younger woman bringing him a bogus health elixir to prolong his life.

"Who is this Logan bloke meant to be? What a fucking drongo! Why doesn't he sort out his shit-for-brains family? And why is he falling for the half-baked hussy with the snake oil who is clearly after his wonga? He's as much use as a toothless croc taking on a one-legged wombat in Goolagong Gulch."

Leggy smiled indulgently again, as the uncanny parallels between reality and streaming fiction played out in front of the still twinkling limpid pools of loveliness that were her eyes. But Rupert had watched enough of the multi-award winning factertainment drama, *Fuccsession*, and switched over to the headlines on Foxed News.

"British Prime Minister Boris Johnson is under pressure after further revelations of illegal lockdown partying in his Downing Street backyard. Will the Boris party be pooped? Or will the Comeback Kid live to party on Dude! Coming up next... 'Why Trump is still great'."

Rupert turned off the television in disgust and reached for his Swansung Smart phone.

"Is that the Times of London? Get me the editor... whatshisname... Ditherow?"

A nervous voice came across the Atlantic from the Newscorpse offices at London Bridgerton, all the way to the 94th-floor Spenthouse apartment in New York's Old Manhattan district.

"Yes, sir. It's me, sir."

"Ditherow! Listen up, yer toffee-nosed Pommy whinger! From now on, we put the boot into Boris. You hear me?!!"

"Yes, sir! I am just writing that down. Put boot into Boris... Any reason, sir?"

"Jeezuz, Ditherow! Do I have to do everything myself? The Brit Buffoon has lost the plot. His judgement has gone to Kerbluey! He's gotta go! He's a loser! And nobody loves a loser."

"Very good, sir. And what shall I write about the conviction of Ms Holmes and the discrediting of Theranonsense, sir?"

Rupert threw the phone down in fury.

Leggy secretly wished that the miracle blood-testing technology from Theranonsense had really worked, so that she could now check to see whether Rupert's blood was actually boiling....

(To be continued...)

WHY AREN'T WOMEN HAVING CHILDREN BEFORE THE AGE OF 30?

It's a mystery.

ON OTHER PAGES

- Houses more unaffordable than ever before
- Dating apps make romance miserable
- Constant warnings that it's the apocalypse *(more bad news until page 94)*

PRIME MINISTER REDACTS SUE GRAY REPORT

Boris ~~Johnson~~ ~~clearly~~ did ~~break the regulations and then lied about it and did~~ nothing ~~to stop drunken parties which were quite plainly both legally and morally~~ wrong

Nursery Times

·········· Friday, Once-upon-a-time ··········

NEW ALLEGATIONS SURFACE ABOUT GRAND OLD DUKE OF YORK

by Our Royal Correspondent **Nicholas Wicked-Witchell**

THE beleaguered Grand Old Duke of York has been hit by new claims that he slept with a large number of teddy bears.

Said one Royal Watcher, "It doesn't matter how old the teddy bears are, it's totally inappropriate for a grown man to share his bed with one, let alone 72 of them." One bear added, "Let me tell you, it was no picnic. When these allegations come out in the newspaper he will be totally stuffed."

Lawyers for the Grand Old Duke of York denied he ever met the bears, or ordered his staff to arrange them in precise order, and any photos of him taken with any teddy bears are totally fake.

Meanwhile, the Queen of Hearts has removed the title "Grand", so he is now just known as the Old Duke of York, and has been heard marching around the gardens shouting, "Off with his HRH"!

"Don't disturb the bears – Prince Andrew's practising being in front of a jury"

FRIDAY, FEBRUARY 4, 2022

HAVE THESE TRAITORS LOST ALL SENSE OF PROPORTION?

And should they all be hanged, drawn, quartered and shot at dawn for deliberately undermining the Prime Minister's heroic battle to win World War Three against Russia?

by **Ted Verysilly** and **Paul Facre**

THE ridiculous focusing on the so-called "partygate" scandal is just another example of how the enemies of the people, ie the Labour Party, the red wall Tories, the BBC, the civil service blob, the police, the teaching profession, the nurses, the judiciary, all other newspapers, social media, the BBC again and, above all, the hated Geordie Greig, have lost all perspective on reality and have gone literally stark staring bonkers!

For God's sake, there is a war on and if these fifth columnists don't stop asking silly questions about trivial events from long ago then the Prime Minister is going to lose the war and we will have President Putin in Number Ten with snow on his boots before the week is out.

There is only one way to deal with these quislings and that is to put their heads on spikes outside Traitors' Gate and have their eyes pecked out by ravens.

Only then will reason and sanity prevail in modern Britain.

Johnson believed implicitly that it was a 'Smirk Event'

by Our Political Staff **Smiles Jupp**

THE prime minister has infuriated the entire nation by insisting that his shameful appearance at Prime Minister's Question Time was not in any way inappropriate.

Video footage clearly shows the prime minister sitting on the front bench having a laugh with colleagues at the nation's expense as he is accused of breaking lockdown regulations.

While he is grilled by opposition leader David Davis he is seen shaking his head, rolling his eyes, yawning and grinning inanely.

"He is clearly having a party and enjoying himself," said one exasperated critic, but the official Number Ten spokesman denied the accusation.

"The prime minister is smirking as he has done throughout the pandemic. This PMQ appearance was, he believed, a smirk event and he just popped in for 25 minutes to do some smirking with his smirk colleagues and then he left to go to a birthday party."

Said a supportive Tory MP, Sir George Useless, "Nowhere in the rules does it say that you are not allowed to smirk in the House of Commons. The public understand that the prime minister is smirking very hard on their behalf and it is time we stopped banging on about parties and let him get on with his important smirk."

"Great! Could you speak again, but this time say the opposite?"

1936 BERLIN	2022 BEIJING
Olympic organisers allow Games to take place *before* genocide	**Olympic organisers allow Games to take place *during* genocide**

What You Missed

Winter Olympics

That Freefall Four-man Skeleton Snowboard Cross Luge Halfpipe commentary in full

Phil Airtime: Thanks, Clare, and wow that's a quadruple knee-grab double rodeo with a 17/190 switchback pancake followed by what looks like a corkscrew armadillo with a 450 out/in triple double in pike position which is super tasty for the third round oh my God she's only gone and done an elbow jerk topper which takes her right up to possible medalling which would be the first time since the Chernobyl nuclear winter games in '83 that's a double wow from the judges as the young Yemeni physics undergraduate grabs fat air for a record back-scratcher and would you believe it…

(Continued for 94 hours on all little red button channels)

THOSE BEIJING WINTER OLYMPICS EVENTS IN FULL

- The Spyathlon
- The Dieathlon
- The Bobslay *(surely "Mobslay")*
- Very Cross-Country Skiing
- Not Nice Hockey
- Not-at-all-free Style Skiing
- Reputation Downhill
- Dissidents Pursuit Skating
- Covid Figures Skating
- Men and Women Skeleton
- Ski Jinping *(surely "Xi Jumping")*

WINTER OLYMPICS HIGHLIGHT

CROSS-COUNTRY SKIER IN FROZEN PENIS DRAMA

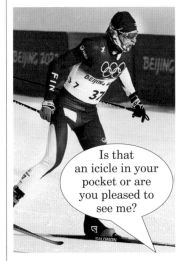

Is that an icicle in your pocket or are you pleased to see me?

POETRY CORNER

Lines on the plan by the government to save the planet by legislating against single-use plastic sauce sachets in takeaway food establishments

So. Farewell
Then sauce sachets.

Ketchup, mayonnaise,
Mustard, HP, salad cream,
BBQ, vinegar.

Yes, you have all
Had your chips.

It is Tartare for now.
May you
Rest in peas.

E.J. Thribb
(17½ milligrams of
sauce per sachet)

DIARY

AN AUDIENCE WITH ADELE

Celebrities, including Gordon Ramsay, Mary Beard, Peter Andre, Angela Rayner, Piers Morgan, Michael McIntyre, Jeffrey Archer, Ed Balls, Ben Okri, Joe Pasquale, Tim Rice and Major James Hewitt, hover around the entrance to the London Palladium.

ALAN "CHATTY MAN" CARR: OMIGOD! The atmosphere is TOTALLY ELECTRIC! Everyone is GAGGING for a bit of Adele! She is LITERALLY the greatest singer in the world! And we're all about to be SEEING HER! You know what? I'm almost doing a WHOOPSY in my pants, I'm that EXCITED!

GRAHAM NORTON: We're going to be AMONGST the first people in the world to hear these songs, and that's LITERALLY one of the greatest privileges known to mankind.

Inside the Palladium, the celebrities begin asking questions...

DAWN FRENCH: Adele, my love! One thing's for certain – the Vicar of Dibley would have gone totally nuts over you!!!!

Audience laughs, cries, roars its approval

ADELE: You crack me up, you do, Dawn! You know wha? I feel like I'm gonna piss my pants!

Audience screams with delight

DAWN FRENCH: But my question is this, my love. Your music is so relatable, and so many millions of fans adore you, do you have tons and tons of people coming up to you to tell you all about their break-ups and their relationship issues?

ADELE: To be honest not much though now you mention it like to be honest yeah a bit though not much if I'm honest but like sometimes a fan will come up and stuff like that and like now you mention it they'll say I got them through this terrible break up or stuff like that, like now you mention it.

Audience rise to their feet and applaud. Close-ups of Nadiya Hussain, Gregg Wallace, Amol Rajan, Ian McKellen and Nadine Dorries, all in tears.

ADELE (*sings*): Wecda aveetwarwarwar!!!!
Rarlinin de dee-eee-eee!!!!
Yewad myart insaarrd yraan!!!!
Anjew playdit to the be-ee-ea!!!!

ANDREW LLOYD WEBBER: Adele, to me your performances rise to the level of pure artistry. In so many ways your extraordinary voice reminds me of the time I was writing Phantom, which, I suppose one might say, was not so very long after the phenomenal international success of Superstar and Cats, which, I can modestly say became Broadway legends, so what I wanted to ask you, frankly, is, where do you get your ideas from?

ADELE: I'm just like to be honest I get them from like real life like if I'm in the shower I like see all this water coming down and I think to myself like this is like a shower of tears and heartbreak and that because frankly life's not always easy know what I mean and I say to m'self let's see shower rhymes with tower and power and heartbreak like rhymes with I don't know bake and lake and so if I'm honest yeah that's basically it.

ANDREW LLOYD WEBBER: Genius!

Standing ovation. Close-ups of the Countess of Wessex, Peppa Pig and Gareth Southgate in tears.

ADELE: Who's next? Emma Thompson! You're like so like brilliant!

EMMA THOMPSON: You are rightly idolised for your huge talent by literally everyone around the world, and not only that but you're probably the greatest superstar who's ever lived. But what I'd like to know, Adele, is – how do you manage to stay so normal?

ADELE: Aww, thanks Emma so I have so many great people rooting for me like people who keep my feet like firmly on the ground there's my aerobics instructor and my personal coach and like my household operational manager and my dietician and my interior decorators and my in-house mindfulness guru and the lovely lovely girl who does my nails and all my fabulous drivers and my stylists and the swimming pool guys and my fashion co-ordinator and my publicity people

and they all make sure I keep me darn twerf did I mention I left my marriage it was so painfaw.

EMMA THOMPSON: Amazing! That's the most brilliant and honest answer ever!

Audience stands and applauds. Close-ups of Eamonn Holmes, Stormzy, Edwina Currie and Idris Elba in tears.

EMMA THOMPSON: Just one more quessie, if I may. Was there one person in particular who inspired you when you were growing up?

ADELE: Well, there was this like teacher she left in year eight but she got me really into literature I've always been obsessed with English and now I write lyrics and that.

EMMA THOMPSON: Well, she's here today!

Ordinary person is given one minute twenty seconds to come up on stage and thank Adele for all she has achieved.

ORDINARY TEACHER: Hello I'm so proud of you goodbye.

ADELE: Brill! Now you got me so moshinaw I'm literally crying or I would be if I was. Last questions?

GRAHAM NORTON: Sound of Music or Mary Poppins?

DAME JUDI DENCH: Sean Connery or Daniel Craig?

LORD SUMPTION: Kit-Kat or Mars?

RISHI SUNAK: Pfizer or Astra-Zeneca?

ADELE (*sings*):
Goweeee-eee-ee-ee-eas yonme bebeh
Ah wuzsteala charld
Din ged da chyanz to
Feee-eee-eee yawhirl around
Had no tam dechoose
What ah chose todo
So go wheeeeeeeaz yonme.

Audience cheer and dance and applaud and weep. Close-ups of Jimmy Carr, Dame A.S. Byatt, Rebecca Long-Bailey, Chris Packham and Naomi Campbell sobbing.

ADELE: Thangs guys you were a right larf so glad you could make it I awmost peed in my wotsits.

As told to
CRAIG BROWN

LEVELLING UP 'UNDERWAY'

Everyone in the South will soon be as poor as everyone in the North

KATE BUSH DOES A BIG SHOP

"You're running up that bill"

Turds to sell entire back catalogue

by Our Music Staff and Turdologist **Al Bum**

THE music world was rocked to its core by the news that the popular music group The Turds had joined the long list of stars selling their entire life's work to the highest bidder.

First it was David Bowie, then Bruce Springsteen, then, unbelievably, Bob Dylan. But now, in a huge shock to their fans, the last surviving Turd, Spiggy Topes, has announced that he is to sell the rights to classics such as *Yesturday* to the Cashin Music Group (based in the Virgin Records Islands) for an undisclosed sum (£5).

Diehard fans, Sid and Doris Rocker, were disappointed. "We never thought the Turds would sell out – there were always plenty of seats at their gigs – but now Spiggy has let us all down."

In his defence, Topes said, "Now my fans will be able to stream Turds morning, noon and night. This Turd-streaming idea has been floated before, and I have to think of my future before my career goes down the toilet.

"This sum will assure me of a can of own-brand cider and a packet of cheese and onion crisps I can call my own."

A book of Spiggy's lyrics called *In My Own Turds* is available in all good charity shops for the price of 99p (reduced from £780).

ASHCROFT'S NEW CARRIE BOOK

It's the tragic story of a sad old man obsessed with a younger woman

Don't be so hard on yourself

HOW WE CAN SEE INSIDE THE MIND OF VLADIMIR PUTIN, BY REMEMBERING THAT HE IS A CHESS MASTER/JUDO BLACK BELT/ICE HOCKEY CHAMPION/ TOPLESS HORSE-RIDING ICON

by Our Metaphor Staff **Ann Alogy**

As the world holds its breath and Ukraine teeters on the brink of war, what will be Putin's next move/throw/shot/giddy-up?

What will be the end game/ ippon/net buster/camp pose with which Putin will confuse the West?

Only by thinking of him in terms of knight to bishop 4/ morote seoi-nage/puck off/is this butch enough for you? can

NATO frame its military response to what is the most serious threat to global peace since the Second World War.

Will it be a case of tipping over the board/pulling the foamy mat from under his feet/ramming him into the side wall/or putting a jumper on because it's a bit cold? *(That's enough of this peace. Ed.)*

© *All newspapers.*

Defence Secretary announces holiday cancellation

IN a historic moment in British politics, Defence Secretary Ben Wallace today revealed he will do his job for the duration of the Ukraine crisis, rather than, as is normal for a government minister, going body-boarding or sunning himself on the beach in Crete.

Mr Wallace's remarkable display of diligence has stunned Westminster, but a spokesman has confirmed that his astonishing self-sacrifice doesn't stop there.

"The Defence Secretary is working so hard, dealing with

the next world war, that he also missed the final of the *Masked Singer*, but don't tell him what happened because he's hoping to watch it on catch-up."

The spokesman added, "If the situation on the Ukrainian border escalates, there is a very real possibility that he will have to pull out of dinner with Simon and Angela, that new couple who've moved in at Number 54, though he has no plans to cancel his highly important bid to solve tomorrow's Wordle puzzle."

(Rotters)

THE ALTERNATIVE VOICE

DAVE SPART
on the Ukraine crisis

AND SO yet again we see the disgusting spectacle of warmongering Western powers uniting to bully a free and democratic country, namely Russia, a country in which President Putin has a personal mandate of an extraordinary 194 percent of his own population, despite which the repellent alliance of quasi-fascistic neo-lib hegemo-orthodoxical slave states, ie Britain, France and the USA, are pouring arms into Ukraine in a manifest attempt to distract from their failures at home and ramp up invasion fears to cover up the truth – ie that the real villains are NATO who have fabricated this entire situation to threaten Germany's energy infrastructure by threatening the Nord Stream pipeline which will keep Germany dependent on the Russian teat for oil which is the only thing preventing the Germans from invading Ukraine from the other direction as they did in 1941... er... er...

"He's a rescue"

Let's Parlez Franglais!

Numéro 94

Le diplomatic mission avec le monde sur le brink de guerre

Macron: It's good to parler.

Putin: Quoi?

Macron: Pardon?

Putin: Qu'est ce que you said?

Macron: Eh? Je can't hear you.

Putin: The West n'est pas listening.

Macron: Russia n'est pas listening.

Putin: Ma table est plus big que yours.

Macron: Vous êtes closer à Kiev than vous êtes to moi.

Putin: Ce meeting est pointless. Mais pas aussi pointless as un meeting avec Liz Truss. J'ai une plus grande table pour her. Ha ha ha.

(Monde ends)

© Kilomètres Kington 2022

Keir Starmer WRITES

HELLO!

I don't think you would have failed to notice that an angry mob descended on me last week. Don't worry about me; I've tussled with nutters before!

I was once beset by an angry mob that called themselves "the Labour Party". I don't know if you've heard of them? They are a raucous mob, fuelled by an irrational hatred of well-groomed lawyers and conspiracy theories about mysterious people in suits who are plotting to sell them down the river!

They seem to have decided to latch onto me for some reason, I can't think why! For a long time they followed me around, to conferences, to press junkets, to, well, everywhere really! In a way, they're the complete opposite to the other mob – they seem to be cross that I AM going after a peculiar crusty old white-haired man! Well, there's no pleasing some people!

But, unpleasantness aside, I am indebted to the PM for uttering his baseless conspiracy nonsense about me and Mr Savile. If that hadn't happened, the story of Johnson's utter depravity might have become old news and everybody might have lost interest. And now this story about me being assailed in the street really puts me in a very good position on the moral high ground.

You might say that Boris "Fixed it for Me!" Well, you might say it, but I couldn't possibly, as that would be in very poor taste indeed!

Yours carefully,
Keir

Gove issues ultimatum to builders

MICHAEL GOVE has issued an ultimatum to the house-building industry, saying he will force through a £4bn towerblock safety strategy unless executives give him an alternative plan by the end of the month.

A spokesman for the builders said they would definitely be getting Gove that estimate by the end of the month... well, actually the end of the month could be a bit tricky, as they have this big job out in Brentford and the site manager is an absolute slave driver... but they'd definitely have one to him by mid-May at latest, well, June 1st, tops... and they could always knock off half a billion for cash in hand – why make the VAT man rich, hey?

"...is there anything in the Police Bill about passive-aggressive irony?"

love

Exclusive to all papers
AN APOLOGY

IN COMMON with all other newspapers, we may recently inadvertently have given the impression that we thought the Duchess of Cambridge was in some way great.

Headlines such as: "You're Great Kate", "Catherine the Great" and "Isn't Great Kate Great?", may have reinforced the impression that we considered the wife of our future monarch to be great.

We now realise this could not be further from the truth and that, in fact, Kate, the Duchess of Cambridge, is totally wonderful, and amazingly fantastic in everything she does. We would like to apologise to our glorious future Majesty for any offence we may have caused by what we accept is an appalling and baseless slur on her brilliantly splendiferous name.

Our hope is that our front-page headline today goes some way towards correcting any inaccuracies in our previous reporting, viz: "Totally wonderful and perfect in every way, Saint Kate brilliantly picks up rugby ball and dazzles fans with her amazing skills, then tells children's story better than anyone ever, whilst wearing a fantastically amazing jumper which all proves that spoilt, greedy Meghan is utterly finished and washed up".

ON OTHER PAGES: Camilla is great but not nearly as great as Kate who is beyond great (*see above*).

Who should replace Cressida Dick as Met Police Commissioner? You decide...

Coleen Rooney aka Wagatha Christie

Hercule Poirot

Sue Gray

Ted Hastings

Judge Dredd

Inspector Clouseau

Peppa Pig's PC Panda

Boris Johnson

BORN TO BE QUEEN CONSORT

A new short story from the pen of DAME SYLVIE KRIN,
author of *Heir of Sorrows* and *Never Too Old*

THE STORY SO FAR: It is the eve of the 70th Anniversary of Her Majesty the Queen's accession to the throne and Charles is isolating in his bubble, having caught Coronanationvirus, once again. Now read on...

CHARLES lay back and contemplated the smooth waters lapping at the edges of the cast-iron McPartlin & Donnelly Victorian bathtub.

Yes, he thought to himself, as he launched the miniature RMS Sir David Attenborough scientific research vessel on an exploratory mission to the overflow, there had been some choppy waters, but now, at last, it looked like plain sailing for the ship of state.

Charles smiled at his own metaphor as Sir Alan Fitztightly, his Companion of the Bubble and Loofah Bearer Royale, gently massaged his noble shoulders. The unguent organic Duchy Originals Hay and Dung bath balm swirled peacefully around the replica Boaty McBoatface submersible which Charles had now sent to the depths of the bath to find the soap.

"You know, Sir Alan, I really thought we were in a spot of bother there, what with Andrew on the run from the FBI, Harry going lala with Mystic Meghan, and poor old Fawcett getting caught up with the shifty sheikh and losing his titles of Keeper of the Colgate, Aquafresh Adjutant, Marshal of the Macleans and..."

"You were indeed in trouble, Sire," coughed Sir Alan. "I feared I could hear the tumbrils rolling and Madame Guillotine sharpening her blade..."

Charles shivered at this revolutionary riposte from his aristocratic aide, the last of the Humphshire Fitztightlys.

"Don't be so dramatic, Sir Alan, we are not at one of the Air Vice Marshal's fancy dress parties where he goes as Marie Antoinette."

"Please yourself," said Sir Alan, tartly, "as Backstairs Billy used to say when one of the underfootmen declined his invitation to show him around the linen cupboard in the days of your dear old Nan..."

"Yes, yes, thank you, Sir Alan... my point is that I've managed to navigate the stormy seas and get the royal barge back on an even keel. As the commemorative plate from China with the misprint has so appositely put it... this jubilee thingy is royal lovely jubbly!"

Sir Alan smiled at Charles' reference to the popular situation comedy of yesteryear *Only Fools and Horseguards* and, at that very moment, Charles' new smart/casualphone rang with its distinctive *Tiktok the Priest* anthem ringtone.

Sir Alan shimmied over to the mobile device in its Rory Stewart tartan case.

"It's the palace, Sire. To mark her Seventieth Year, Her Majesty has made an announcement which she thinks you will be very pleased to hear."

CHARLES made no move to leap out of the bath and run naked towards Yesminster Abbey, as he had been in such a situation too many times before. Instead, he breathed deeply, as he had been instructed on the Archewellnness Foundation Mental Wealth App by none other than Life coach Harry, the Duke of Suxxess himself.

Think of clouds on a beach, perhaps on the moon... Empty your mind and your wallet as you drift away on a sea of tranquility... but it was no good. Sir Alan continued excitedly, "Her Majesty acknowledges that you have waited a very long time for this moment and has graciously decreed that this is the moment for your dearest wish to be granted and for the highest royal title to be bestowed on..."

And before the aide-de-very-camp could stop him, Charles arose from the soapy depths like Britannia herself rising from the azure main to command the waves in the great patriotic aria.

He then jumped from the baignoire onto the marble floor, sending foamy Covid-infected tides cascading down the stairs as he dashed along the corridor shouting, in what Sir Alan could not help noticing was an accent not dissimilar to that of Russell Crowe in the cinematic entertainment *Gladiator*... "My name is Carolius Tertius Maximus, Commander of the British Legions, General of the Imperial Armies, Loyal Servant to the True Empire, Father to Noble Sons and Husband to..."

"Yes, the announcement is about Camilla. She's to be Queen Consort. As we all expected. It's no big deal."

But it was too late. Charles had disappeared in his birthday suit in the direction of the Mall and the last that could be heard was the sound of the Monarch-in-Waiting's cry, "I will have my inheritance in this life... or the next."

(To be continued...)

British wading birds

UKRAINE WAR: IS PUTIN LOSING IT?

UKRAINE LATEST

PUTIN SENDS IN TANKS, BIDEN SENDS IN THOUGHTS AND PRAYERS

IN a dramatic escalation of the Ukrainian conflict, US president Joe Biden last night authorised the deployment of large numbers of thoughts and prayers to the warzone.

The president promised to send in further thoughts and prayers if the initial barrage of prayers and thoughts fails to achieve a Russian withdrawal.

Biden said, "This country is committed to deploying as many thoughts and prayers as are needed. There will be no shortage of either thoughts or prayers as long as I am Commander-in-Chief of the most powerful military force on the planet."

The British prime minister echoed his ally's strong commitment by saying, "Our thoughts and prayers are with the Ukrainians as well, although we don't have as many as the Americans. Our thoughts/prayers contribution is world-beating, even if some of it doesn't work very well in the field."

A Ukrainian government spokesman said he was delighted by the level of support in both thoughts and prayers coming from the West, although Ukrainians had been thinking and praying for something more substantial – possibly rifles, tanks, missiles and even some troops.

President Biden concluded his dramatic intervention, however, by declaring, "There won't be boots on the ground, but there will be knees on the ground, as we pray," before closing his eyes in what looked like a prayer but turned out to be a nap.

(Rotters)

WAR COVERAGE IN FULL

DAILY EXPRESS
UKRAINE – EU TO BLAME

DAILY Mirror
UKRAINE – BREXIT TO BLAME

THE TIMES
Not sure if EU or Brexit to Blame as Mr Murdoch Hasn't Told Us Yet

theguardian
Ukraine – United States to Blame

The Daily Telegraph
Ukraine – BBC to Blame

The Sun
IT'S WORLD PHWOAR THREE – UKRAINE'S FRUITIEST FREEDOM FIGHTERS!

FINANCIAL TIMES
Ukraine – Will your share portfolio be affected by Armageddon?

Daily Mail
UK MUST WELCOME REFUGEES
(Is this a mistake? Ed.)

What You Missed

Exclusive to all news channels

Patsy Flakjacket: I'm reporting live from an underground carpark in Dblvhk and the latest news is that it's not clear what's going on… I'm hearing reports of heavy fighting to the north, or possibly the south, or maybe the west, and I've been told that there have been explosions in the city… from where I'm standing, I can see literally tens of other news reporters desperately trying to find out what's going on as the news blackout continues into yet another day… Joining me now from over there by the kiosk is our Defence Correspondent, Chris Hardhat… Chris, just how difficult is it to find out what's going on?

Chris Hardhat: Well, Patsy, the news I'm getting from my sources is that we can't say for sure what the military situation is as of now. There are rumours that there is nothing on social media, but I can't confirm that. What I can say is that, like you, I've seen TV reports of other journalists saying that they've heard explosions and reports of heavy fighting.

Mike Anchor *(in Studio):* Thanks, Chris. Thanks, Patsy. Take care now, and we'll be back for another live update in a minute when we've asked some experts from the Centre for Strategic Warology Studies if they can speculate as to what might be going on, but first over to Sally Sunshine for the weather in Kyiv.

Sally: We can't say for sure what the weather is like, but unconfirmed reports suggest…

(Continued for 94 hours)

"Look, Pestilence is exhausted… War, why don't you pop down there and have a go?"

PUTIN'S UKRAINE PLAN

"You are a peacekeeping force"

"Which piece would you like us to keep?"

"All of it!"

GLENDA SLAGG

She's the gal they call 'Storm Glenda' – Fleet Street's top blowhard who's full of wind and a bit wet! Geddit????

■ ANT AND DEC – what a disgrace!!?! Who do you think you are, using "womanface" and dressin' up as ladies in drag???!! And don't tell us it was for the kiddies – the only thing you're doing to littl'uns is scaring the life out of them with your fake boobies and manly bits tucked up where the sun doesn't shine!!!!???? As for your drag names – **Lady Antoine Du Bec and Miss Donna Kebab** – give us a break!!!?! Laddy Carcrash and Hideous Miss Take more like!!??! Geddittt!!!!??? I'll tell you whose act IS a drag – and that's YOURS, Ant and Dec!

■ COME on, snooty sister columnists, leave poor old Ant and Dec alone!!?! Forget "womanface"!!!? What about "po-face"?!?! There they were, trying their darndest to raise a giggle and a few bob for the poor kiddies – and suddenly there's a pile-on of ferocious feminists and terrifying transistors *(Is this right? Ed.)*. Has the whole world suddenly lost its sense of humour, for Gawd's sake??!!? What a drag!!!!! Geddit!???

■ FOR gawd's sake, Madonna, act your age!!?! That's 63, by the way – not 16, as you might think from recently released pix from the senior citizen siren!!!?! Sorry, Madge, no offence, but go easy on the Photoshopping *(see pic)*!!?! Whatever you might want us to believe, you're no longer a spring chicken – you're not even an autumn chicken, you're a Christmas turkey!!??!! Just sayin'. No offence, love your work!!!?!

■ ALL hail her Madge-sty!!!?? That's Lady Madonna I'm talking about – the Gorgeous Glam Granny *(subs, please check)* who's still got it at 63!!??!! Go, girl!!?! Who cares if you've used the odd app or ten to turn the clock back – you may be no spring chicken, but you're a game old bird!!??! No wonder everyone's just "Crazy for You". Geddit???!!? (It's a Madonna song title, btw, millennial subs who haven't heard of anyone pre-2021!!?!)

■ PSSSST!!!?! Glenda's gonna let you into a li'l secret, but don't tell anyone!!?! Wordle!!!?! Sounds nerdy, but it's an addictive game of wits that pits you against yourself and your own vocab!!??! Remember – you read it here…

■■■■■

…(that's FIRST!!??!! Glenda got it in 7/6)!!??!!

Byeee!!

Madonna releases new photos

Nursery Times

STORM DOROTHY CAUSES CHAOS

by Our Meteorological Correspondent **Windy Miller**

A TRAIL of destruction has been left by the latest extreme weather event to hit Nurseryland, as Storm Dorothy wreaked havoc, lifting a farmhouse from Kansas and depositing it on an unsuspecting Wicked Witch, believed to be from the East.

Said one lion onlooker, "I was absolutely terrified, but then I always am."

"On reflection, it was the wrong day to try skipping down the Yellow Brick Road (B2086)," said a scarecrow. "It was a pretty brainless thing to do, but that's me all over."

A small dog added, "It was crazy, I went full Toto."

Munchkins, meanwhile, were glued to their screens, watching flying monkeys on Big Vet TV attempting to make a smooth landing at Emerald City Airport, with commentary such as "Easy, easy, easy, go on, son, he's crabbing, look at him crabbing, man, go on get it down, woahhhh, he's down, he's up, he's down, he's going round again, he didn't like it, too much turbulence, woaahhh!!"

Also having difficulty in the conditions was Peter Pan, who was never never going to land and a Dumbo jet whose enormous ears could be seen flailing around in all directions, as it tried to avoid being hit by the flying circus tent.

On other pages

● Storm Jack brings down beanstalk **3** ● Storm Wolf blows down two out of three pig homes **12** ● Storm Daniels blows President *(hang on, this is a children's newspaper. You're fired. Ed.)*

● **Exclusive picture of clean-up operation after recent storms**

THE BBC'S AMOL RAJAN AND NOVAX DJOKOVID

Do you have a favourite spoon?

Yes, it's the one that you are using to spoon feed me all these easy questions.

So you are not anti-spoon?

Oh no. I am definitely not an anti-spooner. I just feel that everyone should have the right to choose whether or not they have a spoon.

Fair enough, Novax...

I don't think you should force people to have spoons if they don't want to.

Do you want to have spoons?

I don't think there's enough scientific evidence to prove that spoons are the right item of cutlery for transferring soup into your body. You must listen to your body and respect what it says. If it says "No to Soup" then I would have to consider very carefully whether I should accept a spoon solution to a wider holistic problem.

So what you are saying is that you would give up the chance to win more titles rather than agree to a compulsory or mandatory spoon?

Yes, for me it is that important. It's not about spoons, it's about liberty, about freedom and about landing you in the soup.

Has anything amusing ever happened to you in connection with a spoon?

Yes. This interview. It has made everyone laugh except your colleagues on the *Spoon Today* programme.

Thank you very much, Mr Freud... I mean, Mr Djokovid *(starts coughing ominously)*

NEXT WEEK: *Tom Cruise, "Me and My Cruise" (sponsored feature by Viking Saga Rhine Tours Ltd)*

Boris woos Saudis

by Our Ethical Staff **Phil Petroltank**

THE Prime Minister, Boris Johnson, has defended his decision to visit Saudi Arabia and discuss increased oil exports, saying, "Prince Mohammed bin Salman has only killed 80 people this week, which is hardly any compared to Putin. It is important we judge regimes ethically, and Salman also hasn't killed any prominent journalists for ages – unlike Putin.

"So you can see," he added, "why I have to build bridges with Saudi Arabia – which is something I am very good at. In fact," he concluded, "I might build a bridge from Northern Ireland via Westminster across the channel all the way to Riyadh, with a garden on top, which will bloom in the desert and strengthen links between our two great countries."

Prince Mohammed bin Salman said, "With oil prices going up and Russia out of the picture, I am going to make a killing. And I'm also going to make some money."

Hollywood Rumours

With **Baz Bamigbyebye**

FOLLOWING the successful adaptation of hit Playstation computer game "Uncharted" into a mainstream blockbuster, other studios are desperate to snap up similar ideas.

Rumours are circulating that casting is already underway for *Wordle – The Movie*, with Tom Holland contracted to play the cheeky but down-on-his-luck vowel hero, A.

Also slated are Aisling Bea, to play feisty consonant and love interest B; Jack Dee has been possibly miscast as good-natured, happy-go-lucky F, whereas Ben Whishaw is a safe choice for Q, as is Judy Dench for M.

Killing Eve star Sandra Oh is expected to make a guest appearance, though no one knows what role she may be given.

Hopes are also high for rap star Jay-Z to play the twin roles of J and Z, in a career first. Will our hero solve the six-step five-letter puzzle in under two hours 47 minutes? Or will there have to be a sequel?

The biggest mystery about this film is Y. *(That's enough five-letter-based humor. American Ed.)*

WAR UPDATE

1. No-fly zone to be established after all

The UK government has confirmed that there is to be a no-fly zone over the skies of Britain, but only for Ukrainian immigrants.

Said Priti Patel, "Rest assured, no one's flyin' in. They're not comin' while I'm runnin' the Home Office."

The RAF is on standby to escort any Ryan Air flights containing Ukrainians back to Poland (at a charge of £47, toilet not included).

2. Facebook ban in Russia

The Metaverse has been taken offline in Russia.

Said spokesman Nick Clegg, "This is outrageous, where are Russians going to get their inaccurate information from now? What are those poor Russian bots going to do with themselves all day if they can't bombard the West with stories about how the Ukraine invented Covid and needed to be invaded to stop Bill 'Hitler' Gates?"

3. Huge left-wing anti-American demonstrations held

In response to the war in Ukraine, left-wingers throughout the world have joined together to blame America for failing to act as global policeman.

Said one long-term activist, Dave Spart, "Er… basically, it is sickening to see the US failing once again in its responsibility to police the world and er… failing to employ the military industrial complex against the neo-fascist, imperialist, war-mongering er… Russian non-communists er… so what we are demanding is American covert CIA-led interference, er… destabilising foreign governments, engineering regime change, and er… basically AMERICA IN!"

4. Brexit bonus real after all

"There can be no doubt we are nimbler, more flexible, and can respond more quickly, thanks to Brexit," said an EU spokesman last night.

"I was sceptical at first, but there's no denying it. Without Britain dragging its heels, we can move much more speedily and let thousands of desperate refugees in, without unnecessary red tape and classic British non-Brussels bureaucracy."

UKRAINE APPEAL

LITTLE OLLY GARK is only 59, but has tragically lost everything, due to the horrific war in Ukraine. Through no fault of his own, Olly has had to flee from his home in Belgravia and is now forced to find refuge wherever he can. We are asking you to open your hearts and give generously to little Olly and his fellow victims of conflict.

£1m will pay his children's school fees at St Cakes School.

£2m will pay for his wife to feed and clothe herself. For a month.

£5m will buy him a standard peerage.

£10m will buy him a British law firm to prosecute journalists.

£35m will buy him a small mansion in Holland Park.

£150m will buy him a premiership football club.

£500m will buy him a basic superyacht with helicopter pad.

£1 will buy him the Independent and Independent on Sunday newspapers.

Please give now to our emergency crisis charity campaign. Make your generous donation to the "In the Red And Cross Appeal", c/o Bank of Zurich, Cayman Islands.

Pravda

FRIDAY, MARCH 18, 2022

RUSSIAN INVASION TRIUMPH

by Our Wartime Staff
Lunchtime O'Dessa

IN A heroic victory for Mother Russia, the forces of western capitalism have been repelled. The evil businesses that have been desperately trying to take over our brave nation have retreated in disarray and have been forced to return to where they came from.

The hated armies of McDonald's and Coca Cola have surrendered. Starbucks and Ikea and Apple have also waved the white flag and have given up their campaign to annex Russia and call it part of the West. With the West in total disarray, even energy giants Shell and BP have abandoned the struggle and conceded defeat.

Said our glorious leader, Vlad the Insaner, standing outside the deserted ruins of a McDonald's which had advanced as far as Red Square, "The War is over. The enemy could not cope with our resistance to their attempts to conquer our country with fizzy drinks, Chicken McNuggets and milky coffee. From now on, our gallant comrades will be able to enjoy our own patriotic fast food Happy Meals. These include a delicious Potato in Potato Bun with a free toy (a potato). All children and their parents who buy the Happy Meal will be happy or they will die."

Elsewhere, a spokesman for President Vlad told Pravda, "Our stategy against the West is working. The United States, Europe and the UK will soon have no foothold in Russia at all and will then collapse. The entire capitalist system will grind to a halt and, denied our money, they will sue for peace and invite the triumphant forces of the Russian economic miracle to run the entire world. *(Is this right? Ed. I don't want to get shot.)*

Outrage as Russia bombs military base

by Our War Correspondent
Phil Graves

THERE was shock around the world as Russia stepped up their assault on Ukraine by deliberately targeting a military base five miles from the Polish border.

Said a horrified UN observer, "This is a stunning escalation by Putin's army. No one was expecting them to attack a facility filled with soldiers and weapons when there was a perfectly good hospital nearby.

"Why they did not strike the undefended kindergarten up the road or even the apartment block full of civilians next door is inexplicable."

A Russian spokesman was quick to deny responsibility. "This is a ludicrous claim designed to discredit the reputation of the precision bombing of innocent targets. It is fake news.

"All those supposed soldiers killed were actually pregnant women and old-aged pensioners. The alleged military base which actually carried out the attack on itself was in fact an orphanage."

MPs: 'GIVE ZELENSKY A KNIGHTHOOD'

Wow! You really think I'm as great as Gavin Williamson?

"Aw, look! His first taking offence!"

47

Boris Johnson MP
● Live   385,000,000 Views

Prime Minister's State of The Nation Address, from The War Room, Previously 'The Party Room aka Disco Central'

👍 Like   💬 Comment

0 people **like this**

(ENTER PRIME MINISTER, SHOOING OUT A DANCING MICHAEL GOVE, THE LAST REMNANT OF ANOTHER, MORE CAREFREE ERA. THE PM IS DRAPED IN A UKRAINIAN FLAG, AS THE RUSSIAN SOUND SYSTEM PLAYS THE RED NOSE ARMY CHOIR SINGING "TIE A BLUE AND YELLOW RIBBON ROUND WHAT'S LEFT OF THE OLD OAK TREE")

Boris (serious face): As **Supreme** Commander of the wartime coalition, I know that the world is looking to **me** for leadership and I shall **not** fail, unlike Putin. **Putin must fail**. That is our d**ecisive** new slogan which we've launched this very day. It's got **three** words, you see, and that **always** works. **Three Words Work**. See. Remember "**Build Back Better**" and how I cleverly turned it into "Build Back **Butter**"? Well, I say to you now, Putin Must **Wail**. Putin Must Sail. Home. OK, that's got **four**. Putin Must **Fall**. You see. We're on track again. **On Track Again**. **On Frack Again**. Which we will be, when the **gas** runs out.

Guto Harri-Kiri: You're rambling! This is worse than Putin. Get on with the Six-Point Plan.

Boris: Yes. **Six-Point Plan**. I have in my **hand** a piece of paper, with six points on it – oh no, perhaps best not to reference pieces of paper, **Munich**, Neville Chamberlain, **appeasement**, Prime Minister **replaced**...

Guto Harri-Enfield: You don't want to do that!

Boris: Right. Listen **up**, Putin! Here's some **bullet** points. Not **bullets**, obviously, don't want to **over-react** to the World War that's developing. Best not to poke Comrade **Bear** with a **stick** and get him all **grumpy**...

Point 1 **Mobilise**. We started with thoughts and prayers and now we're going **full-on** with **speeches** and **applause**. We may not have boots on the ground, but we've got shoes on the ground, as we give the Zelenskmeister a standing **ovation**. Take **that**, Ruskies! We may escalate this response, to a **clap** a week on our doorsteps, possibly even banging **saucepans**.

Point 2 **Support**. Everyone to support **me**. Including useless smartarse lawyer Keir **Harmless** and Scottish fatboy Ian **Blackpudding** (good work on the **nicknames**, Mark Spencer! Who says this government's doing **nothing**?). I want a **total** ceasefire and no more **cheap** shots to be fired about oligarchs, parties, donations or **feeble** Six-Point Plans.

Point 3 **Increase**. Boost the number of points to at **least** half a dozen. Anything **less** than six looks a bit half-arsed.

Point 4 **Halt**. Stop **any** refugees from getting **into** Britain. **That** should keep the backbenchers on board, which is **vital** for the war effort. **And** the ceasefire (see Point 2).

Point 5 **Renew**. Guto Harri-Krishna's contract for this **brilliant** Six-Point Plan. **Hang on**!

Guto Harri-Harri-While-Spad-Lasts: Sorry, boss. I didn't think you'd actually read the plan, as you don't read anything else. And you do tend to throw your chief advisors under the bus when things go wrong.

Carrie (voice from upstairs): No, he doesn't. I'm still here.

Boris: Where **was** I? Oh yes...

Point 6 **Strengthen**. Strengthen my position so they can't get rid of **me**, even when they slap me with a **big** police fine that proves I lied to Parliament all along, etc, etc, **boring**, snooze, who **cares**, there's a **war** on, don't you know?

(PUTS ON CHURCHILL-STYLE BOILER SUIT AND STARTS PAINTING WATERCOLOURS)

Boris: Of course, that **weasel** Putin prefers to call the war a "**military operation**", but that's just elusive semantics. Come on, Vlad, why not cut to the chase and call it a "work gathering"?

(PHONE RINGS)

Boris: Someone's on the other line. It could be **Putin**, capitulating in the face of my **devastating** Six-Point Plan.

Guto Harri-Potter: It's more important than that. It's Lord Lebedev of Moscow. They're onto you about ignoring the spooks' advice and pushing his peerage through.

Boris: Gadzooks! A **real** security crisis! Lord **Luvvaduck**, how are you?

Lebedev: They're saying it's dangerous that the son of a KGB officer should have a voice in the House of Lords.

Boris: That's **balderdash**! You can't be arsed to turn up. So **what's** the problem? Too busy having your **picture** taken with Sir Ian McKellen and singing **songs** from the shows with all your **luvvie** thesp mates.

Lebedev (sings): How do you solve a problem like Mariupol?

Boris: Yes, that's **terrific**, Evgenners! And **don't** worry, everyone knows that the only reason you got a peerage is that you backed **me** for Mayor when you were running the Standard. Nothing **dodgy** about that. Absolutely **transparent**. Free press at its **best**.

Lebedev: I tried making it free, but I can't even give it away. Anyway must go. I've got a beard-trim in five. Not had one for ten. Ciao! Mwah, mwah.

'LORD LEBEDEV PASSED SECURITY TEST' SAYS PM

Have you got the right papers?

Yes, I've got the Evening Standard and the Independent

Boris: Regards to your **dad** – but he's probably listening in **anyway**.

Lebedev Snr: Hello, Boris!

Boris: Cripes, you don't know **who** you can trust nowadays.

Carrie: Not you, that's for sure. Now just sign these visas – we've got to get the poor things out of Kyiv.

Boris: OK, my sweet, **who** are they for?

Carrie: Fido, Rex, Tiddles, Hammy and Goldie.

Boris: If **anyone** asks, I had **nothing** to do with it.

Guto Harri-Kane: Is that Point Seven?

Boris: Double **cripeski**!

(PRIME MINISTER EXITS TO NEW CHELSEA FOOTBALL SONG, SUNG BY MASSED UKRAINIAN ARMY CHOIR, "BLUE AND YELLOW IS THE COLOUR, POLITICAL FOOTBALL IS THE GAME, WE'RE ALMOST ALL TOGETHER, AND NOT GETTING INVOLVED IS OUR AIM")

New Black Dr Who

School news

St Cakes

Sanctions Term resumes today. There are 3 boys in the school (down from 397) following the permanent exeats taken by many pupils after the half-term break.

FSS Novichok (Oligarchs) is no longer Head of School. KGB Polonium (McMafias) is no longer Senior Praefectum. Ivor Thermobaric-Missile (Vlads) is no longer Captain of Wargames.

The Master in Charge of Computer studies, Mr Botski, is on sabbatical until further notice. He has been replaced by supply teacher Mr Hugh Awei who comes to us from the highly respected Beijing Academy For Xi Jinping Thought on Socialism with Chinese Characteristics for a New Era.

The CCF trip to the Isle of Wight has been cancelled due to the bulk of the cadets being conscripted by the Russian Army.

The Sailing Club has been suspended until further notice due to the School Superyachts being impounded in Monaco, Gibraltar and Bodrum.

The Headmaster, Mr R.G.J. Kipling, is the subject of an Unexplained Wealth Order and will be unavoidably busy helping the authorities with their enquiries. His tutorials on Moral Philosophy for the Shell, Bomb and Removal classes will now be taken by Ms Cherry Fancy, the Senior Mistress of our sister school, St Crumpets, which has unfortunately closed due to an unexpected absence of girls.

The School Production of Dostoyevksy's *Crimea and Punishment* is cancelled due to a boycott by the remaining parents (Mr and Mrs Double-Barrell-Bombe). The school concert, Tchaikovsky's *2022 Overture*, has been replaced by a selection of patriotic Elgar classics, including *The Enigma Machine Variations*, *Nimrodliddle*, and *Land of Hype and Tory* (from the *Pomp and Circumstancesbeyondourcontrol Suite*).

The end of term, and indeed the end of the world, will be on July 7th.

"...and finally, for £50,000, what is a woman?"

Keir Starmer WRITES

HELLO!

Well I'm sure you've noticed there's been a bit of a kerfuffle about J.K. Rowling!

J.K. says I've misrepresented the law by saying "trans women are women", but, if may say, Jo, love, I think you'll find you're incorrect. I know it's a bit difficult for a woman to grasp the finer points of legalese, but it's actually a bit of a grey area!

Allow me to gently mansplain the situation to the poor dear: if we just define a man as "a person with testicles" and a woman as "a person without testicles", then we open ourselves to all sorts of confusion, don't we? As that would make me a woman and Angela Rayner a man!

The Labour party has a proud history of fighting for women's rights to participate in politics, so I feel I am giving J.K. Rowling that right, to participate fully in Labour politics, by implying she needs to shut up and agree with the party line as I see fit to define it!

It's a very difficult situation. J.K. is a very strong-minded person, with unbending principles, who is not afraid to speak her mind. Which is probably why, tragically, she has no place in the modern Labour party! I will be sad to see her go.

Back to work now! I'm working on how to make my poll lead magically disappear!
Sincerely,
Keir.

THIS WEEK

MARR VS GOVE

Me and My Spoon – the new LBC show that everyone is talking about. Now with top inquisitor Andrew Marr. At last, Marr is free of the shackles of the BBC – so watch out, world, as he no longer has to pull his punches, but can at last be his own controversial, opinionated, no-holds-barred interrogator of the powerful! He's wild, he's fearless, he's a maverick.

This week, Andrew puts a leading member of the government under the spotlight and talks all things spoon to Michael Gove.

So, Mr Gove…
Yes, Andrew?

Do you have…
Yes?

…a favourite spoon?
No.

NEXT WEEK: *Andrew Marr Grills Bear Grylls.*

LATE NEWS

A statement from the actors playing the charactors of Harriet Potter, Hismione Granger and Ron Weasley-Words to explain why the author was not included in the Hogwarts reunion.

"We're excluding her for being exclusionary".

BERCOW GUILTY OF BULLYING

Out of orrderrrr! Out of orrderrrr!

News in brief

Bercow conduct branded shameful

■ The Conservative Party has roundly condemned the former Speaker, John Bercow, after an inquiry found him guilty of "bullying".

Said Home Secretary Priti Patel, "His bullying falls way below the standards of bullying that we expect in parliament. Compared to me, he was a pathetic pussycat. He should have been sacked. Unlike me."

The former chief whip, Mark Spencer, agreed, "Bercow's bullying was pathetic. Merely insulting – swearing and harassing staff. How many MPs did he blackmail over the Owen Paterson vote? None. Pathetic. Call himself a bully? No, he had to go."

The Prime Minister also condemned Bercow's behaviour. After the standards commissioner said he was not merely a bully but also "a serial liar", Boris Johnson said, "This chap has been shown to be incapable of telling the truth. There is no place for him in parliament as a backbencher. He should be prime minister."

Johnson then added, "No, he shouldn't. I was lying."

"You want Bang Bang Chicken?"

I wonder where those Harry Potter kids would be without JK Rowling...

LOCAL BURGER KING STAYS OPEN IN RUSSIA

БУРГЕР КИНГ

Putin's not the only Russian who relies on Whoppers

CONSPIRACY UPDATE

RUSSIA SPECIAL

CONSPIRACY UPDATE: Well, it's been a busy week here in conspiracy corner. Our mainstream newspapers and televisions are full of irrefutable evidence that there is a war in Ukraine, so of course our contributors are wondering WHY they are pretending such a thing exists?

MAGA435 is not taken in. He states on his grim Facebook page:

"This is a FALSE FLAG opperation, just lik all thos fake school shootings the demo-crats invented to make GUNS LOOK BAD. They are pretending that Russia is INVADING THE UKRAINE to tarnish an impotent ally of our (current) PREssident DONALD J TRUMP!!!"

For those of you brave enough to click on his post, he goes on:

"Ther is a SECRET HOLLYWOOD soundstage where Zelensky (an ACTOR lets not forgit!) is pretending to fight a war with the help of JEWISH MONEY and his fellow NAZIS. Industrial LIGHT and MAGIC are doing the special effects - don't be fooled!!!"

TRUTH-IS-OUT-THERE4356 of course has a theory:

"How tipical of THE SLITHEEN to hide a REAL invasion under cover of the FAKE invasion. As you recall, they used this tactic to invade the Earth last time (see Britbox). They will wait until all our resources our diverted to this invented country "Ukraine" which in the Slitheen language is "Decoy" and they will rip off there human masks ad find us defenceless!"

This last one is from Mr V. Putin, who lives in Chorley. He tweets:

"Those noble Russian forces are just defending themselves from the Nazis in the Ukrainian government. All footage of fleeing Ukrainians are 'fake news' because in reality the oppressed citizens of Ukraine are rushing to embrace their Russian liberators with open arms!"

Hmm. Not a single spelling mistake in that last one. Must be a crank! The mystery continues...

EU-phemisms

"We saw no evidence of Putin's ambitions before"

RUSSIA v E.U
2014 CRIMEA INVASION
SALISBURY POISONINGS
REPEATED AIR & SEA INCURSIONS

E.U. DEFENDS HISTORIC RELIANCE ON RUSSIAN GAS

Because we didn't look

STUDY: UK uncles and dads now experts on Russian military

AN EXHAUSTIVE study, using top military intelligence, drone footage and up-to-date ground surveillance, has revealed that the nation's uncles and dads are now armed with a terrifying number of statistics about ground wars in Eastern Europe, and are willing to deploy them, despite the unimaginable boredom they know they will cause.

Despite not having done any physical labour since some light gardening around the time of the first lockdown, these brave men – and they are 100% men – have been informing themselves with lightning speed about the tolerances of Russian armoured-vehicle tyres, about the right way to ensure air superiority and fly multi-unit sorties, and about the correct ingredients of a Molotov cocktail. They are also learning acronyms at a terrifying rate and delivering them to devastating effect at the nation's dining tables, just when the rest of their family possibly wanted to talk about something else.

One child said, "I was really looking forward to playing a bit tonight, but instead we're reading a series of pieces about the history of tank trap deployment in ground campaigns against light armour vehicles."

The nation's dads and uncles have issued no conditions under which they will stop banging on about pre- and post-Soviet tank-mounted missile launchers, meaning they have left themselves no "off-ramp" and may launch an extended insurgency until *(cont. p94)*

(cont. p94)

CHANNEL 4 ANNOUNCES NEW SUMMER SCHEDULES

Taskmaster Watch as a group of comedians (the policy team at the Department for Digital, Culture, Media and Sport) have to complete a series of ridiculous challenges to please their capricious and rude boss (Nadine Dorries). Will they manage it? No.

The Great British Flog Off A challenge in which a representative group of British people are gathered in a tent. Each one has to come up with a model which allows public service broadcasting, billions and billions of pounds in profits, and hundreds of millions of viewers worldwide, while also answering a relatively narrow broadcasting remit. Can it be done in the next 20 minutes? No!!!

Naked Ambition A crowd of unattractive people – Conservative Backbenchers – display themselves to the British public and desperately try to get them aroused by stoking up a culture war. Will anyone tune in? *(No. This one is terrible. Ed.)*

Other programes include

- 8 Out of 10 Fat Cats
- **Come Dine with Boris**
- The shIT Crowd
- **Shameful**
- Dorries Girls
- **Relocation, Relocation, Relocation**
- Cheques and the City
- **No Futurama**
- Poop Show

Daily Mail

FRIDAY, MARCH 18, 2022

LIZ HURLEY MAN DEAD

by Our Showbiz Staff **Annie Excuse**

A man who once went out with Liz Hurley has died. The beautiful actress, who once appeared in "that dress", knew the man very well.

Apparently, he had something to do with cricket but never mind that. *The Spy Who Shagged Me* was one of Liz's films that the man didn't appear in. He also didn't feature in any of the adverts for her bikini campaigns, in which the incredibly well-preserved 56-year-old showed off her well-toned physique and proved once again what an idiot Hugh Grant was.

We approached the dead man for a quote on his memories of Liz Hurley, but for some reason he was unavailable for comment. Still, let's look at some pictures of brave, broken-hearted, skimpily-clad Liz through the ages.

Pages 2-93 Pics of Liz Hurley
Pages 94 Sport staff who haven't been fired write a piece on the man who once went out with Liz Hurley

"An onion seller!! Call that a career?
Oh, now look, you've made your mother cry"

Ed Sheeran in plagiarism case

TODAY in the high court, the Ed Sheeran plagiarism case was accused of being remarkably similar to all the other musical plagiarism cases.

Said one musical expert, "The Ed Sheeran *Shape of You* case does sound just the same to me as the Robin Thicke *Blurred Lines* case and the Drake *In My Feelings* one, and indeed the George Harrison *My Sweet Lord* case.

"Basically, these plagiarism cases do involve the same ingredients – a hugely lucrative hit, some sharp-eared lawyers, and a lesser-known composition by a less-famous composer, which isn't quite as good."

Said a lawyer, "The notes are all the same. They're £50 and I want lots of them."

Said another lawyer, "Hold on – that was my idea. You're singing my tune!"

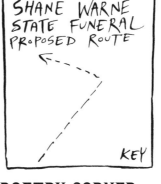

New twist in Ed Sheeran plagiarism case

IN a dramatic court showdown Ed Sheeran was accused of plagiarising his own songs.

Asked a high court judge, "Who is Ed Sheeran? All his songs sound the same to me. He's clearly stolen them from himself. Would now be a good time for lunch?"

Said another, "Lunch was my idea! So now I'm going to make you pay – the bill at the Garrick."

Said the entire judiciary, "Going to the Garrick was my idea!" *(That's enough plagiarism pieces that look exactly like each other. Ed.)*

SHANE WARNE STATE FUNERAL PROPOSED ROUTE

KEY

POETRY CORNER

In Memoriam
Shane Warne, Australian cricketer and master of the leg-over *(surely "leg-spin"? Ed.)*

So. Farewell
Then Shane Warne,
Gone for 52.

You deserved a
Longer innings.

"The pavilion's that way,
You pommie cunt,"
Yes, that was your
Catchphrase.

"Warnie put your
wanger away,"
That was the novelty
Record recorded in
Your honour.

You were the scourge
Of England,
But now, perhaps,
You are the
Lord's favourite.

Though, alas,
The Ashes in question
Are yours.

E.J. Thribb
(17½ wickets per run)

GREAT PROPAGANDA POSTERS REVISITED

What did you do in the war, Daddy?

Wordle

Letters to the Editor

A Bridgerton too far?

SIR – I write to you concerning one of the most burning issues of the day. Vis the vexed topic of sex in the second series of the Netflix Regency romp *Bridgerton*.

Like many of your readers, I've been keenly anticipating a repeat performance of ripping bodices, heaving bosoms and falling britches.

Imagine my disgust when I tuned in one afternoon (when my good lady wife was engaged with the Ukrainian cupcake-for-refugees stall in the local church), only to find that there was NO sex at all in the first two episodes of the new "season", as I believe they are now called.

Indeed, such was my distress that I had to rewatch the whole of season one to ensure that my memory was not playing tricks on me, and that I had not imagined the repeated rumpy pumpy that had so shocked and appalled me on first viewing, particularly the rogering of Lady Magnesia in the Orangery by the Duke of Rutland.

But mistaken I was not. The new series is bereft of such "vigorous action content" and is instead a pale, limp imitation of its former splendid self. Netflix should be ashamed.

If I wanted to watch straight-forward period drama with believable characters, compelling storylines and an absence of gratuitous jiggery pokery on the billiard table then I might as well watch dreary old BAFTA-winning Jane Austen on the BBC.

I shall, of course, be cancelling my subscription (to the BBC) and shall be watching instead the ground-breaking social realist docugameshow that is *Naked Attraction* on the excellent Channel 4. Or, at least, I will be until Lady Gussett has completed her duties assisting the unfortunate victims of the current crisis.

Sir Herbert Gussett
The Old Bonkery,
Tupping-on-the-Green,
Beds.

Shock as popularity of the chancellor dips

by Our Westminster Correspondent
Loads A. Money

There was widespread shock in Westminster today as the popularity of the chancellor dived after Rishi Sunak made it clear in his spring statement that, unlike during the pandemic, he couldn't protect everyone from the cost of living crisis.

"It's almost as if people during the pandemic didn't genuinely like Rishi for his expensive water bottles, awkward jokes and designer hoodies and actually just liked the fact he was throwing huge amounts of money at them," said one Westminster insider.

"And now that Rishi is no longer willing to throw huge amounts of money at them to solve the latest crisis, they no longer think he is marvellous. They no longer call him Magic Rishi or Dishi Rishi, but refer to him as Fishi Rishi or Rishi Washi.

"This would be astonishing if true – that people like chancellors who are extravagantly generous and dislike them when they stop forking out the cash. Who would have ever suspected that?"

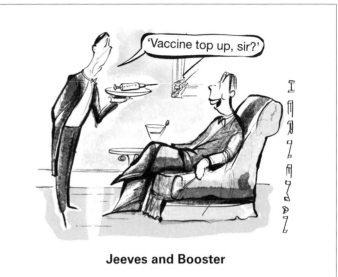

Jeeves and Booster

RISHI'S COMMON TOUCH

Two pints of your finest petrol, please, barman

Lines on the St Patrick's Day poem by Bono
by William McGonagall

'Twas in the year of two thousand and twenty-two

That the erstwhile frontman of the band U2

Put pen to paper and came up with a verse

Which, to be frank, could not have been much worse.

He likened the history of Ireland's pain

To the current situation in Ukraine,

Which I think you'll agree is a terrible rhyme,

And certainly a literary, if not a war, crime.

The poem certainly did not tickle my fancy

When it was read out by Speaker Pelosi (Nancy).

The bit about ridding old Ireland of its evil snakes

Was just one of this budding bard's poetic mistakes,

Not to mention the scansion – so raw, and so rough,

Haven't the poor wee Ukrainians suffered enough?

For political versification I would humbly allege

That Bono's efforts perhaps lacked "The Edge".

Oh, Bono, Zelensky as St Patrick was a strained metaphor –

And I fear you still haven't found what you're looking for.

© *The second worst poet in the world*

Nursery Times

································· Friday, Once-upon-a-time ·························

OUTRAGE OVER P&O FERRY SACKINGS

by Our Maritime Staff the **Ferry Godmother**

NURSERYLAND was appalled last week at the news that the Pussycat and Owl Ferry Company had summarily dismissed the entire staff of the pea-green boat (the Owl and the Pussycat) and replaced them with cheap agency workers.

The Owl and the Pussycat were given no notice that the prestigious ferry service, known as the Pride of Nurseryland, that runs direct to the Land Where the Bong Tree Grows, was to be suspended and their jobs offered out to underpaid Jumblies whose only experience of sailing is going to sea in a sieve.

The dismissed pea-green-boat crew were offered a redundancy package described as "derisory", consisting merely of a jar of honey and "plenty of money" wrapped up in a five-pound note.

The new Jumblie crew are believed to be receiving mince and slices of quince in lieu of payment. The pea-green boat turns out to be registered in Neverneverpaytaxland and is owned by Ali Baba and his Forty Respectable Business Associates.

Controversial Mr Baba claims to have done nothing illegal and looks forward to Nurseryland taxpayers funding his operation as per usual, despite Mr Baba's Aladdin's Cave of treasure.

Said a heartbroken Owl, "We are gutted. The Pussycat and I were hoping to get married this year, but now our future plans are on hold as we cannot even afford the ring in the Piggy-wig's nose."

■ *If you've been affected by issues raised in this piece, please contact the NT Helpline, manned by Dr Foster in Gloucester.*

Clerihew Corner

Sheikh Mohammed bin Rashid Al Maktoum

Owns P&O, so it's safe to assume

That he cares as much for the ferrymen's lives

As he does for any of his daughters or wives.

DIARY

PIERS CORBYN
WHAT THEY DON'T WANT YOU TO KNOW: AN A-Z

A is for AstraZeneca. What they will never tell you is it's an anagram for "tazers acne". Fact. So let's ask ourselves why so many victims of tazering by the police operating for and on behalf of the global elite are infected with acne? Right first time: because they have been injected with it by the state in order to make them easy targets. They go to any lengths to keep it secret. Look what happened to Abu Hamza.

B is for Blair, Bush, bin Laden and Paul Burrell. All in it together. It remains a closely guarded secret, but if you look it up in Companies House, you'll find they were all co-directors of the firm that won the contract to rebuild the Triple Towers after 9/11. OK, so they don't give their real names, but that proves my point: they've got something to hide. Yes, it's our old friend, the cover-up. And they had to get Paul Burrell on board, didn't they?, because he knew what happened to Princess Diana. It all adds up.

C is for Climate Change. Famously, a myth invented by Margaret Thatcher as a way of closing down the mines and throwing literally millions of hard-working miners on the dole. And don't talk to me about Greta Thunberg. Works for and on behalf of Bill Gates. She says she's 16, but her birth certificate says she was born in 1955, which makes her his age exactly. Apparently they went to the same school together. And have you noticed her name just happens to be an anagram of Great Big Hunger? Answer me that one.

D is for Drug Companies. You know the single most dangerous drug in the world? Right first time: Maltesers. FACT: The Malteser was invented in 1937. Yup: the same year as the Hindenburg disaster. It just so happens that the "stewardesses" (note the inverted commas!) on the Hindenburg were handing out free Maltesers to the VIP passengers immediately before the airship blew up. Some say it was a mistake and the experts had got the format wrong, but frankly they're on what I'd call the lunatic fringe. It's my firm belief that it was a deliberate act, and that they had inserted more explosives in the Maltesers than usual on the direct orders of Nixon's White House.

E is for Edinburgh, Duke of. He headed up the international team charged with inventing Covid-19. It took them 18 attempts before they came up with the right formula, hence the name. It's no coincidence he died last year. He knew too much. Incidentally, that wasn't the Queen sitting in the black mask at his funeral, that was Chris Whitty, got up to look like her. Meanwhile, the real Queen remains in overall command of the worldwide operation, crouched in her headquarters in the so-called Hadron Collider in Switzerland.

F is for Frank, Anne. A woman looking exactly like her was clearly seen on the grassy knoll at Dealey Plaza, Dallas at 12.30pm on Friday 22 November 1963. And she happened to be talking Dutch and carrying a diary. Just saying.

G is for Globalists, The. Headed by George Soros and his henchmen Gates, Branson, Bezos and Lloyd Webber. The next time someone tells you to wear a mask, check out the shape of it. Odds are it will look like a sideways "K". Well, it stands for Katonah, the exclusive Bedford Hills suburb of New York that is home to George Soros. Little-known fact: Soros takes a whopping 37 percent from every mask sold, which is why he invented the so-called virus in the first place. Yes, I agree: horrifying.

H is for Hurricane Katrina. In the days leading up to Hurricane Katrina, teams of plainclothed CIA agents were secretly photographed placing literally thousands of electrical blow-heaters close to New Orleans. 'Nuff said.

I is for IMF. It's well known that Prince Andrew, the Duke of York, was the brains behind the International Monetary Fund. When he was photographed (by Mossad) literally arm-in-arm with Virginia Giuffre, who was, as it happens, CEO of the top-secret Bilderburg group, the photo went viral and so the pair of them had to be silenced by 5G, or their plan for global domination would go up the proverbial spout. Of course, the metal insert in all Covid masks is a 5G antenna, and Jacob Rees-Mogg carries the international transmitter stitched onto the top of his head. When the transmission went out of sync on 4 Sept 2019, he had to lie flat on his bench in the House of Commons to get it going again.

J is for Jack the Ripper. A medical doctor. As we now know, his plan to vaccinate the entire East End went horribly wrong.

K is for Martin Luther King. Alive and well and living in Norwich.

L is for Lennon, John. It just so happens that Mark Chapman is still a full colonel in Mossad.

M is for McCartney, Paul. He was killed in 1966. Ever since then he's been played by Roger Tonge, better known as "Sandy" in Crossroads. Fact.

N is for Nostradamus. Five hundred years ago, this French astrologer successfully predicted the rise of Chris Whitty.

O is for Oh-Hokey-Cokey-Cokey. Secret codeword to trigger global meltdown.

P is for Pandemic. In a nutshell, the so-called "pandemic" is a global psychological operation designed to close down the economy. But where exactly IS this nutshell? That's what they don't want you to know.

Q is for Queen. Every time she waves her hand, someone in China dies.

R is for Rolf Harris. Rolf knew too much. He desperately tried to tell us what he had discovered by blowing on his didgeridoo. But they got him in the end.

S is for Swastika. A swastika is formed of eight straight lines. If you take those straight lines and reassemble them, it makes the initials BJ - short for, yes, Boris Johnson. Just saying.

T is for They. They are refusing to give me the space to continue this devastating exposé of the lies and misdemeanours that are killing us all. That's what they do to whistleblowers and truthtellers – they silen

As told to
CRAIG BROWN

CARIBBEAN TOUR ENDS

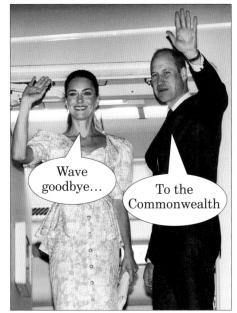

Wave goodbye...

To the Commonwealth

"Well, what do you think of our new artificial lawn? No idea what it's made of"

Lookalikes

Rat **Sunak**

Sir,
Following the scandal of MPs having second jobs, is there truth in the rumour that the Chancellor of the Exchequer is moonlighting as a two-bit TV celebrity? We demand to know!

TONY DA FRANCA.

Henry **Wayne**

Sir,
I couldn't help noticing a strong resemblance between tabloid king, Wayne Rooney, & prolific scorer, Henry VIII. Do you think they might be related?

CLIVE WISMAYER.

Miss Piggy **Miss Arcuri**

Sir,
The Prime Minister used a speech at the UN to criticise Kermit the frog. I was rather surprised to note the similarity of their two companions.

PHILIP GIBBS.

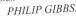

Bounder **Blinder**

Sir,
I noticed a remarkable resemblance between this past leader of a notorious gang of ne'er-do-wells with a reputation for "cutting" and Tommy Shelby from Peaky Blinders.

CHARLIE CORBETT.

Walken **Anne**

Sir,
Uncanny resemblance to Christopher Walken, the actor.

GARY GOODMAN.

Data **Steal Data**

Sir,
Has anyone noticed, as I have, the extraordinary similarity between a character from science fiction and the android from Star Trek?

ENA B. METAVERSE.

Galloway **Gervais**

Sir,
Has anyone else noticed how funny man Ricky Gervais is morphing into a rather serious George Galloway?

GRAHAM WEST.

Spock **Patel**

Sir,
I wonder whether the Home Secretary, in adopting the Star Trek uniform, is in fact stating that the Johnson government is boldly going where no other government has gone before...

ISABEL DEL RIO.

Pig **Johnson**

Sir,
Has anyone noticed, as I have, the extraordinary resemblance between a children's cartoon character and Peppa Pig?

ENA B. RANDALL.

Meat Loaf **Balls**

Sir,
I didn't realise that Ed Balls moonlighted as a rock singer. RIP.

ALEX LUPTON.

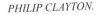

Cyberman **Raab**

Sir,
Have you noticed the similarity between Dominic Raab and a Cyberman from the popular BBC programme "Doctor Who"? Uncanny.

PHILIP CLAYTON.

George **Whitty**

Sir,
I am struck by the likeness between Chief Medical Officer Chris Whitty, and the late Lonesome George. However, they trigger widely differing reactions from the general public – the one being idolised by tourists at Galapagos National Park, the other being harassed by estate agents at St James's Park – so I doubt they are related.

NIGEL PIKE.

Droopy **Lavrov**

Sir,
I could not help but notice that this jowly, lethargic cartoon bears more than a passing resemblance to an animated dog from the 1940s.

JAMES D.F. MELLOR.

Anderson **Zahawi**

Sir,
I was struck by the similarity between these two mighty leaders.
One aspires to lead our country to greater glory and the other is a renowned flautist and frontman of the rock-folk band, Jethro Tull. Back in the day, one was famed for sporting a codpiece and standing on one leg when performing, while the other doesn't appear to have a leg to stand on.

IAN ADAMS.

Wallace **Truss**

Sir,
I hope you're well. Is there any truth to the rumours that they're filming a reboot of The Wrong Trousers? Is it true they're going to call it The Wrong Tories? I think we should be told.

RAJESH SHARMA.

Hess **Carr**

Sir,
Given recent comments by comedian Jimmy Carr concerning the Holocaust, I've noticed an uncanny resemblance between him and Rudolf Hess.

ROB SCOTT.

Fredricksen **Coffey**

Sir,
One of them came up with a far-fetched idea of how to get to some fantastical world of wonder and the other is a cartoon character.

TIM TAYLOR.

Davros **Putin**

Sir,
I couldn't help noticing...
JOHN STEPHEN RYMELL.

Famous painting **Disturbing picture**

Sir,
I don't doubt that other readers, like me, noticed this wonderful expression of the pioneer spirit outside Number Ten, or perhaps it was bible-bashing small-town sentiment... Either way, this enduring exploration into the working mogg(man) has continued to fascinate. One, the British gothic, the other, Grant Wood.

HUBERT PALMER.

Hopper **Jagger**

Sir,
Has anyone else noticed the similarities between the midnight rambling 'Bed Hopper' and the less adventurous and slightly forgotten 'Frog Hopper'?
Is there a chance that they may be related in some way or not?

MARTEN RAE.

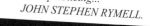

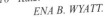

Scott **Katz**

Sir,
Has anyone noticed, as I have, the extraordinary similarity between Norman Scott, who was famous because of his dog, and the head of beleaguered Channel 4, Ian "8 out of 10" Katz?

ENA B. WYATT.

Egghead **Dumpty**

Sir,
Has anyone noticed, as I have, the extraordinary resemblance between Health Secretary Sajid Javid and the unfortunate victim of a wall-related injury who could not be saved by Nurseryland's emergency services?

ENA B. CLOSE.

Snow monkey **Cher**

Sir,
Never seen together, funny that.
MICKEY BODILL.

Fabricant **Toy**

Sir,
My daughter and I were playing with her Disney Frozen Lego characters this morning When mix and matching the hair and bodies between the characters I realised that Olaf the snowman wearing Kristoff's hair was a dead ringer for Michael Fabricant MP.
Perhaps as a result of her age (5) she didn't get the joke, hopefully it amuses you instead.

Boris Johnson MP

The Prime Minister's Top Secret Number 10 Downing Street WhatsApp Group Chat. Strictly confidential. Members Only

Greetings! What's App, Doc? Top joke from the Bozzter to launch my new for-your-eyes-only security conscious, highly encrypted end-to-end auto-delete-as-soon-as-you've-read-it message system! Don't want to be caught out by the Ruskies finding out about what I'm up to. Not to mention Sue Gray or the Met. Or Keir Starmer. Or Carrie.

Carrie Johnson
I'm reading this, you know.

Right! Come on, Whatsappers! Let's have some Whatsappy news!

Dominic Raab
We've finally done it. No-fault divorce has gone through.

Priority Number One achieved! Top job, the Raabster! Who says I don't have any ideas for government? Now at last it's not a chap's fault if he's caught with his trousers down taking IT lessons from the blonde totty behind the wife's back. No blame for anyone. Mayor non culpa!

Carrie
Don't even think about, Fat Boy! If you think Marina took you to the cleaners, you just wait!

Matt Hancock
I wish you'd thought of this last year.

Who let Hancockup into the group?

Matt Hancock
Oh, please let me be in the group.

Sajid Javid
No, you're a health risk.

Matt Hancock
Oh please! I've got a new jumper. And a new girlfriend. I went to the Brit Awards. I was snogging on the dance floor. I'm down with the kids, they love me.

Sajid Javid
Not your kids.

Matt Hancock
Hey! Lighten up! All I did was break a few Covid regulations, like everyone else. And I had an excuse – I was in love 🖤 .

Jacob Rees-Mogg
Excellent choice of emoji, Prime Minister. You are a master of the apposite emoticon! It's like your brilliant speech to the people of Russia. It was a masterpiece.

Thanks, Creepie! I told the good people of Russia, that they are being deceived by their leader who's lying to them. You can't believe a word he's saying! Trust me, I said, I know this sort of bounder. I've seen his type before.

Carrie
Yes, every morning in the mirror.

Jacob Rees-Mogg
Mrs Johnson, let us concentrate on the more important global issues about which a responsible government is more concerned.

Nadine Dorries
Like privatising Channel Four! From now on it won't cost the taxpayer a penny!

Rishi Sunak
It never did.

Unlike your wife, Rishi. Hahaha, just joshing, very Richi! No, no, seriously, sorry about the bad coverage of your missus being a non-dom. Can't imagine how the Independent got hold of that story.

Evgeny Lebedev
Nor can I Boris 😉 .

Is this a prank? Or a Russian dark ops mission to destabilise my government?

Evgeny Lebedev
No, it's me! The one with the beard and the peerage and the palazzo in Tuscany, where you came to my parties.

Jacob Rees-Mogg
How dare you! The Prime Minister has never attended a single party in his life and, if he has, it was because he was misled by advisors who told him it was a work event – albeit one involving a certain amount of vodka, caviar and karaoke.

Helen MacNamara
As former Head of Ethics for the Tory Party, can I just say sorry about the karaoke – and can I have my machine back?

I'm afraid it was broken in the fight, along with Wilf's swing.

Jacob Rees-Mogg
The Prime Minister never witnessed a fight at the party which he did not attend, nor did he hear any karaoke being sung and, if he did, he was misled by his eyes and ears.

Steady on, Moggster, there hasn't been anyone so far up the Bozzter's bottom since Eton. LOLS! Can we get back to the big issues facing the country?

Nadine Dorries
As I was saying, Channel Four.

Yes! Spot on, Mad Nad! That'll teach them to put an ice sculpture in my place when I chickened out of the climate change debate. Who's melting now, Mr Jon Snowflake?!

Rishi Sunak
He's already left the channel.

Priti Patel
Someone been in the Channel? Send him to Rwanda!

Calm down, Pritster! You're doing a great job keeping Johnny Foreigner out. Even the Ukrainians. By the time they find a home, the war will be over and then they can go back where they came from – result!

Nadine Dorries
It's not revenge against Jon Snow that's driving this sound commercial decision. It's revenge against all the other ones on the news – that Harry Krishna bloke and Catty Newman with the weird hair. And all the other uppity lefties on Channel Four News, who are now going to be on the dole!

Quite right, Nadster! Next stop, the BBC. The Boris Bashing Corporation.

Rishi Sunak
Yes. They've been going on and on about my wife!

Have they? Well, they get some things right. Perhaps we should keep them for a bit. Here's a picture of your wife looking rich!

Rishi Sunak
Keep my wife's name out of your f***ing mouth!

Rishi Sunak has left the group

OSCARS REDUCED TO SHAMBLES

by Our Showbiz Staff **Dan Wooden**

THERE were disgraceful scenes at the Academy Awards last night as the fighting between celebrities was interrupted by awards for very dull films.

The audience, who were enjoying the violence on stage, were shocked to find themselves having to watch clips of tedious movies that nobody had seen.

Said one furious academician, "This is not what I want from an award ceremony. I want a proper old-fashioned punch up. I do not want to see awful scenes of Benedict Cumberbatch in a stetson and Olivia Colman on holiday in Greece. I want to see Will Smith hitting Chris Rock. And there wasn't nearly enough of it. Smith's punching was cut short by the Academy, which was deeply disappointing for all genuine lovers of foul language and violence."

Best Actor was deserved winner

HOLLYWOOD agreed last night that Will Smith was the worthy winner of the Best Actor Award for his performance in his acceptance speech.

Smith spoke movingly of his commitment to peace, love and understanding, just after he had hit Chris Rock in the face.

Will Smith proved what a fine actor he is by pretending to be sorry but then comparing himself to Richard Williams who taught his girls the importance of beating your opponents and anyone else who gets in your way.

The audience of other actors rose to their feet to give Smith a standing ovation, in the hope that he wouldn't come and hit them.

Putin says 'leave my wife and family out of it'

THE beleaguered president of Russia hit out at his critics last night, as his family's finances became subject to media scrutiny.

"I am a politician," he protested, "but my wife and children are not. Their finances are nothing to do with me, and these sanctions on them are deeply unfair and just an attempt to smear my good name."

Critics have accused the Putin family of receiving billions of roubles and living in other countries in order to avoid investigation.

Shouted Mr Putin at an awards ceremony for Worst Performance in the Theatre of War, "Keep my wife's name out your fucking mouth!"

Observers took this as a reference to the reaction of British chancellor Rishi Sunak when his wife was criticised for her financial affairs.

IF TV NEWS WAS LIKE THE INTERNET

"The headlines: Fury at today's Wordle; Prime Minister meets someone and you won't believe what happened next; and all Zelensky's speeches – ranked"

JOHNSON IN HISTORIC ZELENSKY MEETING

Thank you for coming to my rescue!

Shock as British arms not being supplied to dictator

An inquiry has been launched after it has been revealed that, for the first time in decades, British rockets and missiles are being sent overseas to support a democracy.

"This is very disconcerting," said one military expert. "We're used to selling powerful weapons to some of the worst and most repressive governments in the world, and now we're apparently just giving them away to a plucky independent country fighting for its life against foreign aggression? It doesn't make sense."

Another added, "We've made billions of pounds selling guns and ammo to 21 countries on the British government's own list of repressive regimes.

"For years, we've been turning a blind eye to what the Saudis have been doing in Yemen, inviting them to our arms fairs, etcetera, desperately hoping they'll keep buying the lethal stuff, and so on. But now we're expected to believe that we're helping an underdog? It's ridiculous." *(Rotters)*

Keir Starmer WRITES

HELLO! There have been a lot of rumours swirling, mostly in the right-wing press, that all these Rishi Sunak tax leaks are from a Labour supporter within the civil service. In fact, they've even dubbed him "Red throat"!

Well, I'm delighted to tell you that the rumours are completely true! There is a secret Labour supporter on the inside who shares the same aim as me – to stop nice Rishi Sunak from becoming PM and keep the politically tainted Boris Johnson in place as long as possible.

"Red throat" sent me this e-mail a few weeks ago. As you can see he has written it in code to stop the message falling into the wrong hands:

"Wotcha Cappy Hindsight! This is yours truly with the skinny on Dishy's murky shenanigans! It's dynamite! He and his well-to-do wifey are up to their necks in it, rodgering Mr Tax Man by playing patty cake in the Punjab! Meet me in the House of Commons underground car park if you want the filth on Twitchy Richy. Yours, B.J."

I assume that "B.J." is some socialist credo that I'm not aware of, like "Bevan's Jockstrap" or "Benn's Jamboree". Needless to say, I put my best espionage tie on and went to meet "Red throat" in the carpark, where he wore traditional socialist garb (ragged clothing and a Michael Foot fright wig).

After babbling incoherently for a few moments (obviously scared), he handed me the relevant documents and went to his "safe house" in an abandoned fridge.

I think we can all agree that the contents were well worth it! Rishi's ambitions are thwarted and the Tory party are stuck with Boris Johnson until the general election! It's help from committed Labour voters like Mr "B.J." that make the job worthwhile!

Sincerely, Keir

THAT ALL-PURPOSE CURRENT STATE-OF-THE-WAR PIECE

AS THE war enters its second/third month, the situation is becoming much clearer/more complex by the day/hour.

President Zelensky was last night looking triumphant/defeated as he demanded peace talks/more weapons.

Hardened Russian soldiers/untrained teenage conscripts have been seen fighting on the streets/handing over their weapons as the Ukrainian army suffer/achieve significant gains/losses.

Meanwhile, the demoralised/resurgent Russian army was in retreat/making ground as Ukrainians stood their ground/hid in underground shelters. The international community was shocked/unsurprised as the Russians bombed another airfield/orphanage.

Military experts/clueless pundits were unanimous/divided in their considered opinion/wild guess that the war/military operation would be over once Putin achieves his objectives/has Novichok slipped into his beluga caviar/Big Mac.

THE 'COST OF DYING' CRISIS INTENSIFIES

by Our Money Saving Expert **Noah Possessions**

THE Ukraine war has continued to ramp up the "cost of dying" crisis in Ukraine, with locals increasingly unable to afford to keep a roof over their heads.

"We're having to choose between not eating or not heating, as there is no food in the bombed-out supermarket and no home in the bombed-out rubble of our apartment block to heat," said one Kyiv resident facing the cost-of-dying crisis.

"And as for filling up the car, forget it! That'll cost you an arm and a leg... and the other arm and the other leg, as Russian missiles are constantly targeting our petrol stations."

"The cost-of-dying crisis here in Ukraine is only going to get worse before it gets better, but we know things could be so much worse," said one bloodstained citizen.

"We just count our blessings we're not having to deal with the cost-of-living crisis in the UK, where shoppers are having to pay £1.05 for a loaf of bread that used to be 70p and 90p for a tin of beans that a month ago was 50p.

"Our heart goes out to these brave Brits buying shop-brand chocolate digestives in the face of such horror."

BRITAIN TRACKS DOWN OLIGARCHS' ASSETS

By our corruption staff **Bel Mooney-Laundering**

THE British authorities have admitted that they are encountering some problems with identifying UK properties owned by Putin's inner circle.

For example, there is one large house in Central London which investigators believe to have been entirely bought by Russian money.

"Millions of roubles have been poured into this building," said a spokesman, "but the complicated financial structures employed mean that we cannot know for sure.

"The building has seen a succession of recent occupants, all of whom seem to have done the bidding of their Russian overlords."

With dozens of lavishly decorated rooms, showing the gold that is so popular amongst tasteless plutocrats, Number 10 Downing Street is at the centre of the investigation and has policeman standing outside day and night to ensure the occupants do not try to make a run for it.

LATE NEWS

■ Top oligarch complains: "I put my money in the London laundry and I lost my shirt. It's an outrage!"

Putin denies Trump influence

by Our Political Staff
Kat Kopy

"IT'S Fake News", claimed President Putin last night, at a huge rally for 30,000 loyal supporters wearing hats saying, "Make Catherine the Great Again".

Putin was responding to allegations that he was so desperate to maintain power that he had adopted President Trump's political methods.

"Lame Mainstream Media!" he shouted. "Lock up Crooked Navalny! Grab Pussy Riot and Put them in Prison, too."

As the crowds of red-army-necks cheered, Putin continued, "I won the election in Ukraine. Fact. Loser Zelensky stole it. Fact. I urge everyone to march on the capital (of Ukraine), storm the government buildings and proclaim me as the true, democratically elected President."

As the crowds chanted "Forty More Years!", the man known as "The Vladimir" promised to "denazify the unpatriotic paedophile Nazi blood-drinking pizza conspirators".

He then played a round of golf and tweeted "covfefe" in the middle of the night, believing it to be a town in Ukraine which the Russian army had captured.

A GUIDE TO NUCLEAR DETERRENCE

by Madimir Vlutin

1 Both sides have nuclear weapons
2 Only one side seems mad enough to use them
3 Other side deterred from taking any military action at all
4 Mad person gets what they want.

TOP SPECIAL MILITARY OPERATIONS OF HISTORY

RT

THE SECOND WORLD SPECIAL MILITARY OPERATION
Great victory for Soviet Union alone, in which forces of Nazis and decadent Westerners were defeated in a matter of three days with only loss of about 1500 troops. Very easy.

THE RUSSO-JAPANESE SPECIAL MILITARY OPERATION
No problems at all for Russian army in 1904-5 which triumphantly retreated to Russian territory in victorious fashion. Only one casualty, who was feeling ill anyway.

THE CRIMEAN SPECIAL MILITARY OPERATION OF 1853-6
Russia takes on and definitely defeats Britain, France and the Ottoman Empire, and definitely doesn't sign a humiliating peace treaty. No casualties whatsoever, apart from someone slightly stubbing his toe.

THE GLORIOUS UKRAINIAN DENAZIFICATION SPECIAL MILITARY OPERATION
Brave Russian forces triumphantly and quickly retake Ukraine from its Nazi government, bombing very few maternity hospitals and shelters full of children along the way. Soldiers actually get healthier during campaign, due to fresh air thanks to not having any tents, and lose weight due to absence of any rations.

[That's enough special military operations. Stop writing or you're dead. Vladimir]

RUSSIANS DEFEND DENAZIFICATION TACTICS

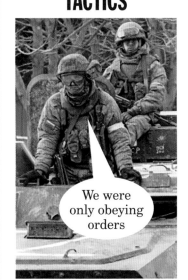

We were only obeying orders

FLASHBACK – WHAT MACRON REALLY SAID TO PUTIN

Any chance you could de-Nazify France?

GLENDA SLAGG

She's Fleet Street's Satan Two Missile!!??
#satantoo (geddit????)

■ MOVE over Brigitte Bardot – there's a new Gallic sex kitten in town!!?! It's blonde bombshell Brigitte Macron I'm talkin' about, monsieur!!! Ok, so she's 69 (ooh la-la, soixante-neuf!!? Geddit!!??), but when you look that good when you're 83 and don't look a day older than 94, no wonder you send pulses racing!?!! Talk about hair to dye for! Geddit???

■ I CAN'T believe she's 96!!?! It's not 103-year-old Brigitte Macron I'm talking about – but our very own sizzling sexy senior citizen siren sovereign, aka Her Majesty The Queen!!?! And, unlike La Macron, who pretends she's only 107, but is in fact coming up for 120, lovely Lilibet doesn't have to dye her silvery locks to look sensational!?! No wonder Queen Liz is still the go-to cover girl on every newspaper, pound note and coin in the land – not to mention stamps!!?!

■ THE world is divided like never before, and we stand on the brink of a global conflagration of good versus evil!!?! So, whose side are you on?!? Johnny Depp's or Amber Heard's???! The warring Hollywood Has-Beens may have divided opinion, but there's ONE thing we can all agree on: they're both as bonkers as each other!!?! Who will win???! The LAWYERS, obviously!!?!

■ HEARD about Amber?!? Geddit??!! Not even Tyson Fury would want to take HER on in a fight!!?! I'm not pointing the severed finger, but after hearing her story, Johnny really is in Depp-Do-Do!!?! *(This is terrible! You're fired. Ed.)* Who will win??! The NEWSPAPERS, obviously!!?! *(This is even more terrible! You're hired again. Ed.)*

■ AND talking of World Wars, I see Wagatha Christie and Rebekah Vardy are still slugging it out like Tyson Fury and the other one!?!! What's got into everyone?!? Why can't we all live in peace and harmony!!?? Just a thought, all you idiots!?!! Glenda gettin' a bit philosophical in her old age (still younger than Brigitte Ma-crone – Geddit???!).

■ SEEN the new, explosive, gloves off, anti-woke, uncensored, no-holds-barred Piers Morgan Talk TV show??! Me neither!?! ZZZZZZZZZZZZZZZ!!!!!!!

Byeee!!

"Perhaps you could explain why you deprive me of solitude without providing me with any company"

FRENCH ELECTION

La merde
La merde plus

That classic Mitchellski and Webbov sketch from Russian television

First Russian Soldier: Ivan, you know this missile we're about to launch that everyone calls Satan 2?

Second Russian Soldier: Da. Get ready to press the button.

First Russian Soldier: It's just I couldn't help but think that its name, 'Satan 2', might indicate that maybe – we're the baddies.

Second Russian Soldier: Nyet. It's just a name. Like Satan 1.

First Russian Soldier: That's sort of my point. Why isn't it called 'Liberator 2' or, I dunno, 'The Big Peace Bomb'? It's just 'Satan' has slightly evil connotations.

Second Russian Soldier: At least it's not called 'Putin 2'.

First Russian Soldier: You're right, we are the good guys. Fire away! Take that, Nazis!

© *Mitchellov and Webbski.*

DAILY EXPRESS

GREAT NEWS FOR BRITAIN AS IMF REPORT SAYS UK WILL BE NO.1 BY NEXT YEAR!

A NEW report by the International Monetary Fund has disclosed that Britain will be NUMBER ONE out of the world's richest economies... having the LOWEST growth and the HIGHEST inflation by 2023 of ANY G7 nation!

"The British economy is unique amongst the G7 nations. We have a singularly regressive combination of government inflexibility on economic policies, lower growth, higher taxes, as well as lower incomes. We could even see stagflation like the 1970s!" said one financial analyst.

HOMES FOR UKRAINE SCHEME SUCCESS

THE Home Office has described its No Homes for Ukraine scheme as being a complete success, saying it had worked round the clock to prevent desperate Ukrainian refugees from actually reaching Britain.

"When 150,000 people expressed interest in housing a refugee, we sprang into action to ensure that would not happen," said a delighted Home Office spokesman.

"We did everything we could at speed: printing the forms the Ukrainians would have to fill out in triplicate in English, demanding they present a valid passport, driving licence, proof of home address, at least three utility bills confirming their identity and then insisting that those documents be counter-signed by the British embassy in Nairobi did the trick."

Priti Tactless

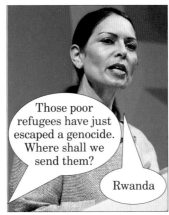

Those poor refugees have just escaped a genocide. Where shall we send them?

Rwanda

Pravda

FRIDAY, APRIL 15, 2022

SMOULDERING RUINS WELCOME RUSSIAN LIBERATORS

by Our Wartime Staff
Lunchtime O'Dessa

THE smouldering ruins of a number of key Ukrainian cities today smiled and cheered as Russian troops entered them.

"The Russians have liberated us from water, power, buildings and people," said the ruins, waving Russian flags and celebrating the arrival of Russian tanks.

"This is what the city has always hoped for," the ruins continued. "We have been liberated from being a modern city and have been turned into attractive piles of rubble."

They concluded, "There are no people here to welcome our Russian liberators because they have all been liberated from the oppression of having a life."

VODKA

BOYCE

"I'm implementing a no-buy zone"

TV SELL-OFF LATEST

by Our TV Correspondent
LORD WREATH

CULTURE Secretary Nadine Dorries slurred today that she would be pressing ahead with the privatisation of Netflix after the once-mighty streaming platform posted a shock drop in subscribers for the first time in ten years.

"Clearly, Netflix needs to change if it's going to compete in the modern media landscape with powerhouses like Channel 4 and the BBC," the swivel-eyed loon told MPs.

"Granted, Netflix is a private company, but it needs to be made more private. Perhaps it should get a new logo and expand into fracking, unusable PPE, chemical weaponry and dog-fighting.

"Unless it makes these changes now, I cannot see Netflix having a viable longterm future. Sadly, for this once-mighty streamer, the Countdown clock is ticking."

GERMAN CHANCELLOR VOWS TO DO SOMETHING ABOUT RUSSIAN GAS

We know that we've got to get rid of it somehow, so we've decided to burn it

Whatsappy Days are here again! See what I did there? With one bounder, I'm free!

Guto Harri
Well, not entirely, Prime Minister. The apology didn't go down that well with the backbenchers.

Ah, Dirty Harri! I'm always feeling lucky, punk! Like Clint, you see? I think my apology was even better than the last one. Look at this. I'm a picture of con-trition…

Serious face, sincerity oozing out of every orifice, I've done nothing wrong, and if I have, I've no idea I was doing it – the complete repertoire of Bozza's bamboozling box of tricks that's seen me through numerous newspaper proprietors, countless Tory leaders, and a couple of furious wives.

Carrie
Make that three, you lying toad. You promised me I wouldn't get a fine for the birthday party, which wasn't a party.

Rishi Sunak
Yes, I wasn't expecting a fine either.

Boo-hoo, poor Rishi 😢 . Don't know where you're going to find 50 quid. Perhaps you could ask your wife. And pay my fine while you're at it. Lord Brownenvelope isn't answering my calls for some reason. And since sanctioning Johnny Oligarch we seem to be a bit short of Tory donors.

Nadine Dorries
Could we make some money by selling off the police? They're clearly anti-Tory. Have they fined the Labour Party? Not one penny!

Boffo bonkers idea, Mad Nad! Keep them coming. That one's up there with Rwanda.

Dominic Raab
I'm confused, Prime Minister.

Of course you are, you're Dominic Raab! 😕

Dominic Raab
I don't understand.

Keep up, Dim Dom! We're attacking the Archbishop of Canterbury to distract from Partygate.

Jacob Rees-Mogg
Hallelujah! Boris resurrectus est! How dare Welby mix religion and politics! Our Rwandan scheme has God's blessing, as expressed through his representative on Earth, me. As it says in the Bible, "Blessed are the rich".

Rishi Sunak
Thanks for your support, Jacob. So, is it time for me to go to India and do something to make me look statesmanlike?

Liz Truss
Hang on, isn't that my job? I should be going to India. I could wear a sari.

Nice idea, the Trusster, but these are serious times, this is a big trade deal and there are jobs at stake. Mainly mine.

Liz Truss
I could put a red dot on my forehead. And maybe sit on an elephant in front of the Taj Mahal.

Rishi Sunak
Shouldn't I be going to India? My wife owns it.

No one's going except me. There's a very important vote I need to avoid. Did I mislead Parliament when I said I didn't mislead Parliament? Not even I know how to vote on that one.

Chris Heaton-Harris
I'm afraid the backbenchers may abstain.

Who are you?

Chris Heaton-Harris
I'm your latest Chief Whip.

Really? Who appointed you?

Chris Heaton-Harris
You did, Prime Minister.

I have no memory of it. I wasn't there at the time. And if I was, it was only for nine minutes. I'm very sorry and I feel your pain. Obviously I'd prefer it if things had been done differently but it's time to move on, there is a war on, you know?

Chris Heaton-Harris
The point is, Prime Minister, a lot of backbenchers don't want to support you, as they think their constituents will throw them out at the next election.

Tell them we can have an investigation into the misleading parliament malarkey as soon as the Sue Gray investigation has concluded its investigation into the Police investigation into Lord Geidt. Or quite possibly the other way round. We should investigate it thoroughly and that'll take us up to Christmas or the end of the world.

Jacob Rees-Mogg
It's the end of days! Hallelujah in excelsis! The dead shall rise up! The Mogg shall inherit the Earth! Amen.

Top "keeping religion out of politics", Moggster!

Pegasus Spyware
May I just say how disappointed my clients in the United Arab Emirates are. We've gone to a great deal of effort to bug the Prime Minister's Whatsapp group, only to discover that nothing of national importance ever seems to be discussed or acted upon.

Pegasus Spyware has now left the group.

"And did you find the orders on how to abandon ship very clear, somewhat clear, or not clear at all?"

THOSE FILMS TO WATCH WHILE YOU'RE HEADING UP THE M1 IN YOUR DRIVERLESS CAR IN FULL

- Gone with the Windscreen
- Brakefast at Tiffany's
- Bonnet and Collyde
- Crash of the Titans
- One Flew Over the Driver's Seat
- West Side Impact Story
- Airbag!
- Airbag 2!
- Death on the Pile-up

(That's enough smash-hit star vehicles. Ed.)

Sarah Vain

She puts the Me into Men Behaving Badly!

This week Sarah writes about the MP at the centre of the latest Tory sex and drugs scandal

AMIDST all the vilification and recriminations against this sad, middle-aged man, one has to have some sympathy for his wife and family, as they are subjected to the unwelcome spotlight of the media in full cry.

What could be more tragic than the spectacle of a once serious and respected male figure having a very public mid-life crisis?

So he took cocaine, lost a lot of weight and started to think he was sexy, making a fool of himself in nightclubs and on the dance floor. But behind the scenes who was suffering the most? The poor wife, that's who!

After a lifetime of support and devoted selfless dedication to his career, his more talented and more intelligent spouse suddenly has to come to terms with the fact that her husband has gone completely off the rails and become a national laughimg stock.

Where once he might have harboured ambitions to be leader of the party and she might have been the brilliant and glamorous hostess at Number Ten, now she is reduced to writing columns in the Daily Mail about how her useless husband spends his nights cavorting in shady dives in questionable company.

Shed a tear for me, dear reader, as I *(This piece was meant to be about David Warburton, wasn't it? Ed.)*

■ If you are affected by any of the issues raised in this piece, call the Sarahmaritans, who are available 24/7 to talk about themselves and their problems.

HARRY HITS OUT AT HORSES

by Our Royal Equine Correspondent **Oprah Whinney**

IN A controversial interview, the Duke of Sussex expressed concern at the sort of protection being offered to the Queen and the company she's been forced to keep.

Said Harry, "I love my Gran to bits, and popped in with my Netflix film crew to check personally on how she's being cared for. To my shock, I found her surrounded by horses. How are they going to protect her? They can't hold a gun in those hooves!

"And what's more," he emoted, "I notice the horses in question are not exactly diverse. The Palace simply hasn't moved on since I modernised the monarchy by going to California. I'm not saying all my relatives are racists,

but just look at those horses – pale, male and stale. Even the sugar lumps that granny was given to feed them were white. What sort of people are advising her in this modern age?

"If, heaven forbid, anything bad happens to granny's wellness in the next ten or twenty years, it will be my cold, uncaring and financially ungenerous father's fault."

On other pages

● Harry on why Diana's ghost prefers him to his brother **6**
● Harry on why the Queen loves him more than anyone else **9**
● "Pull yourself together, you wet little milk sop," says our mental health correspondent **94**

OOZAT!!

B-list celebrity cricket

@Vilmissimo

Daily Telegraph Friday 29 April 2022

Letters to the Editor

The controversial sermon delivered by the Archbishop of Canterbury on Easter morning

SIR – As a regular member of the congregation in Canterbury Cathedral, I was absolutely appalled when, in the middle of the service, the Most Reverend Justin Welby launched into a tirade against Her Majesty's government's policy of outsourcing the processing of immigrants to the Republic of Rwanda.

How dare he use the traditional Easter sermon to say something interesting that prevented me from my customary half-hour pre-luncheon nap?

As my lady wife will attest, I do not attend church services in order to hear someone preaching from the pulpit. And certainly not someone commenting on what is happening in the world from a religious viewpoint.

Where were the phrases "in a real sense", "on the one hand" and "on the other hand"? These time-honoured liturgical stalwarts have ensured that one can safely drop off and enjoy forty winks without worrying about missing anything of any significance.

Does the Archbishop not know that this is a tradition dating back to the twelfth century, when Thomas à Becket, in this very cathedral, made the mistake of saying something interesting about the English political situation and was understandably murdered by four disgruntled knights who had missed out on their pre-hog-and-mead, all-you-can-eat-feast snooze.

For an old Etonian to know so little history and to be so high-handed with the slumber habits of his pew-dwellers is nothing less than a disgrace to his crook, his frock and indeed his flock. No wonder he has been described as "woke", since he has kept us all awake!

Sir Herbert Gussett
*Dunsnorin',
Little Respite,
Beds ZZ2 2ZZ.*

New extremist group 'preventing air travel'

by Our Aviation Correspondent **Heath Row**

THERE was widespread dismay amongst families attempting to fly out for the Easter holidays, as a new organisation to rival Extinction Rebellion emerged, dedicated to carrying out direct action to stop people from flying.

"They're called 'Airports', and they're ruthless," said one holidaymaker, wearing horrible shorts.

"Extinction Rebellion might glue themselves to the road, but they are rank amateurs.

"Britain's Airports make holidaymakers' attempts to fly out to enjoy some Easter sun nightmarish, by opening with no staff. Ten hours later and we're still caught in an eight-hour queue to reach Customs.

"Now I can see on the departure board that our flight has been cancelled, due to Covid staff shortages. Their ruthlessness to put a stop to international travel is second to none."

SELF PORTRAIT

How can you tell it's a Hockney?

Big cheques!

Those easyJet Extras In Full

Hold luggage	YES/NO
Speedy Boarding	YES/NO
Cabin Crew	YES/NO
Pilot	YES/NO
Holiday	YES/NO

RAYNER AND JOHNSON IN BASIC INSTINCT ROW

> She's the one looking at a twat all day

Keir Starmer WRITES

HELLO! I expect you will have seen the response of the Tories to the appalling Angela Raynor Basic Instinct Story in the Mail on Sunday. Both Boris Johnson and Nadine Dorries tweeted the identical statement:

"Much as I disagree with Angela Raynor on almost every political issue, I respect her as a parliamentarian and deplore the misogyny directed at her anonymously today."

And where did they get this brilliant response? They stole it off ME, of course! I twittered this exact tweet seconds before they did. (And then deleted it, in case anyone thought I had stolen it from them!!!) It's another example of the Tories nicking Labour ideas. Whatever next? Will they bring in high taxes and huge public spending? Will they have a Prime Minister and Chancellor at war with each other? Honestly!

And now the Tories have got the nerve to claim that I am stealing THEIR ideas – like having a beer and a pizza during work!

The police ruled at the time that it was NOT a party. And I am proud to say I have never been in charge of a party in my life! Just ask Angela!

As for distracting people at Question Time in the House of Commons, it is Boris Johnson who distracts ME constantly by crossing and uncrossing his fingers whenever he makes a statement about anything. I can't take my eyes off him!!

How am I meant to concentrate on making my non-Oxford-Union debating points in the House of Commons when the Prime Minister is shamelessly flaunting his Basic Instinct – ie, to lie at all times! He is the one who is guilty of putting ME off, otherwise I would have trounced him every single PMQs – which I did anyway.

And the good news is that the enemy of the Labour Party has never looked more isolated or alone. Did you see him call for the disbanding of Nato and failing to praise Zelensky? I shall be tweeting an attack on Jeremy shortly, which no doubt the Tories will all copy and pretend was their idea!

Sincerely, Keir
(Non-Corbynista in a Suit).

"That's your solution to everything, isn't it?! Throw Monet at it"

No-fault divorce introduced

by Our Divorce Correspondent
Prue Nuptial

COUPLES have welcomed the introduction of "no-fault divorce" in England and Wales, meaning there's now no need for separating couples to apportion blame for the end of their marriage.

"It's such a relief that I don't have to blame that utter bastard, Steve, for destroying 13 years of wedded bliss and breaking the hearts of our two gorgeous children into a million pieces by jumping into bed with that peroxide blonde bitch, Kerry from marketing, who dresses like a cheap whore and will dump his sorry arse the second she realises he's an emotionally crippled man-child unable to cope with a real woman who isn't pencil thin and sex mad," said a relaxed and happy Amanda.

"I agree. It's such a relief I don't have to blame my psycho bitch ex-wife, Amanda, for the breakdown of our marriage," agreed an equally happy and relaxed Steve.

"It's so great I don't have to detail in numerous Facebook posts how she can go into actual full-on insane rage about incorrectly folded towels and not stacking the dishwasher correctly and how she'd rather watch Bridgerton in bed on the iPad than have sex with her husband, having gone totally frigid, like her sour-faced mum, following the birth of Millie three years ago."

All divorce lawyers agreed it was lovely that couples like Steve and Amanda would now be able to part on good terms, thanks to no-fault divorces, and remain friends, just as soon as Steve finishes slagging Amanda off to his mates down the pub and bragging how epic the sex is with Kerry and Amanda finishes cutting up all Steve's suits and dumping them amicably in the skip behind Morrisons.

POETRY CORNER

**In Memoriam
Anna Karen,
TV and film actress**

So. Farewell
Then Anna Karen,
Aka Olive from
On the Buses.

Now you are,
Like so many buses,
Late.

But for you
There can be
No replacement.

Let's hope
There is room
For one more
Up top.

E.J. Thribb
(Number 17½ to
Neasden Park)

A Doctor Writes

AS A doctor, I am often asked "Doctor, I've got a nasty tickly cough, a bit of a runny nose and I feel lethargic. What's wrong with me?"

The simple answer is: "You are suffering from an ancient viral affliction that, in olden times, people used to call 'Covid'."

Covid, or *coronavirus forgottenus completus normalis*, to give it its full medical name, was a pandemic from way back in the early 2020s, which swept through the human race causing mass panic, followed by enormous memory loss as people got used to others dying and bored of wearing masks.

It remained, however, extremely virulent and as easy to contract, if not more so, as when it was first discovered.

Furthermore – oh, excuse me, ahem... nmm... achh... hack, cough, splutter, atchoo! Sorry, I'll be all right in a moment. Er... cough! Actually, having... trouble breathing here... this feels worse than flu... I wonder what it could be? © *A Doctor croaks*.

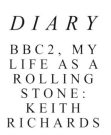

DIARY

BBC2, MY LIFE AS A ROLLING STONE: KEITH RICHARDS

VOICEOVER (Sienna Miller): He's the epitome of the rock guitarist. He has led a life wreathed in legend. His attitude and legacy underpin our whole idea of the guitar hero. More than just a songwriter and musician, he could well be the greatest artist who ever lived: Keith Cecil Richards, Rolling Stone.

SHERYL CROW: Keith Richards wrote the dictionary definition of what a rock'n'roll god was – a guitar slinger, a travelling troubadour, a songwriter and a singer. Well, not so much a singer.

KEITH: Wassit aw abou then? Thasa question I often ask m'self fnur fnur fnur. I mean put it like this, first you start this thing goin', whatever it is, then you keep at it and even though you don't know what it is you like I said keep at it because you started it so you may as well keep it going whatever it is fnur fnur fnur.

RONNIE WOOD: Keith's a walking encyclopaedia. If you need any advice, just go to Keith for an answer and no matter what state he's in he'll say "yeah, righ'". And you know what? It turns out that "yeah, righ'" is the correct answer for every question you can think of, at least for fifty percent of the time. The guy's a genius.

VOICEOVER: After 60 years, the Stones are still rolling, playing sell-out shows in all four corners of the globe, able to charge more than any other band and earning themselves millions and millions of pounds. At the musical heart of every gig is one key character. But who is the REAL Mick Jagger?

DIRECTOR: Sorry, Sienna, love, could you take that last bit again?

VOICEOVER: Oops! Blah blah blah… Ah, yes, here we are. "…At the musical heart of every gig is one key character. But who is the REAL Keith Richards?"

MICK JAGGER: Keith is Keith but then again who is Keith? Everyone creates a character for themselves to a certain exten. I don't know if Keith's is real or not real or somewhere in betwee. I dunno if he cares any more. He's really not that bothered and frankly I don't blame him, cos in the end Keith is Keith. But then again who is Keith? Bit of this, bit of that, bit of the other.

VOICEOVER: Keith was born in 1943, exactly three years after 1940 and just one year before 1944. In ten years' time, it would be 1953. But that time was yet to come.

KEITH: I grew up in Dartford in Kent like not far from London but not that near either like neither one thing nor the other so near yet so far whatever that might mean fnur fnur fnur it was just after this world war and all that crap but that was the way things were it was as it was fnur fnur fnur.

VOICEOVER: In one of the most legendary encounters of all time in the history of the world, Mick and Keith met on a train.

KEITH: I'm sitting in this carriage minding my own business fnur fnur fnur when suddenly who walks in it's Mick fnur fnur who I haven't seen in years and he's like y'know "Wow man" and I'm like "Wow man" and he's like "Wow man" and he's like – anyway, to cut a long story short I say wow man what's that under your arm and he pulls out these two great blues records – Blind Jefferson Watts and Deaf Willie Patterson –

Black and White footage of Deaf Willie Patterson singing "I Didn't Wake Up This Morning and I Won't Never Wake Up No More"

KEITH: We started out wantin' to be jus' like those two great cats, so we'd smear the ol' boot polish all over, and Mick would come on stage with 'is white stick and I'd come on with a deaf aid stuck in me ear and it jus' felt so like real and *authentic*.

You're eighteen you're playing this mixture of blues and pop –

Early footage of Mick singing, "I'm a Slave in Chains And I Ain't Got No Food to Eat So Won't You Be My Baby"

KEITH: – and like these naked birds are y'know jumpin' off balconies trying to take your clothes off and it's like woah! it's like mayhem can't complain not gonna say no you got a nice pair there love fnur fnur fnur.

VOICEOVER: In a matter of months, their sound and image, combined with this revolutionary social message, transport them to number one on both sides of the Atlantic.

JOE WALSH: They could take their stuff from America and give it back to America and America just loved them for it. Genius.

VOICEOVER: Keith becomes an international icon of rebellion, the youthful symbol of revolt against a bourgeois age. This makes him targeted by the Establishment, who immediately despatch the police to bust him at his seven-bedroom West Sussex luxury home with tennis court and heated swimming pool.

Old footage of Keith outside courtroom in 1967

KEITH (in 1967): It's like I want to do what I want to do and if what I want to do isn't what other people want me to do well what's that got to do with what I want to do even if it's not what they want me to do like.

KEITH: Writing songs is like a jigsaw puzzle. You get all those pieces on the table and you spread them out and then you schlepp to another room or go abroad or some place and kinda forget all about them. Then in maybe two or three months you come back into that room and you see all the pieces of jigsaw on the table and you say what's the fuck's all these jigsaw pieces doin' here, guys, someone clear them up, I mean what do I pay you for?

VOICEOVER: Without any help from anyone else, Mick and Keith, two of the most influential artistes of all time, have been playing their iconic songs of teenage rebellion to packed stadiums for well over half a century.

MICK ONSTAGE SINGING: Ah thing duh tarmis righ for fally rever loooo shuuuuuurrrrrn!!

KEITH: Crazy chicks, crazy licks. Is been like totaw fuggin madness fnur fnur fnur. (looks at Rolex) You got enough? Fnur fnur fnur.

As told to
CRAIG BROWN

Daily Mail

NETFLIX CANCELS PLANNED MEGHAN MARKLE TV SHOW

OUR REACTION IN FULL: Ha ha ha ha ha ha ha ha ha ha ha ha ha ha ha ha ha ha ha ha ha ha ha ha ha ha ha ha ha ha ha ha ha ha ha ha ha ha ha ha ha ha ha ha ha ha ha ha ha ha ha ha ha ha ha ha ha ha ha ha ha ha ha ha ha ha ha ha ha ha ha ha ha ha ha ha ha ha ha ha ha ha ha ha ha ha ha ha ha ha ha ha ha ha ha ha ha ha ha. ha ha ha.

News in brief

War moves to a new phase

■ The circulation war between newspapers has developed, with the Ukraine coverage retreating to the centre pages.
After the initial phase, in which no party could claim victory, despite the deployment of state-of-the-art weapon graphics and huge maps of the area with big black arrows on them, all sides have scaled back their operations, and reallocated resources and manpower to the Johnny Depp and Amber Heard conflict which has flared up again in the West (coast).

REES-MOGG URGES CIVIL SERVANTS TO STOP WFH

Get back to work, you lazy sods!

EXCLUSIVE TO ALL NEWSPAPERS

WHY WORKING FROM HOME MUST STOP NOW

A controversial view from our top writer **Phil Space**

AS THE pandemic retreats, and a mere 1 in 15 of the population are suffering from Covid, surely it is time for even the laziest of civil servants to get off the sofa and get back into the office. We all know that nothing can replace the personal dynamic of a creativvvvvvvvvvvvvvvve. Oh, shit, the cat's on the keyboard agaiiiiiin. Oi! Get off... No everything's fine, darling, I was just shouting at the cat. Oh, coffee? Lovely... No, there can be no excuse for continued work-shy Whitehall absenteeism when the country needs the entire workforce to concentrate on... Hang on. Is that the Amazon package? Could you

get it? I don't want to go round to the neighbours again. They've got Covid. Oh, right. You're on a Zoom? No, no, no, I'll go. It's not a big deal, it's just that some of us are trying to work. Yes, I know your work's important as well... What?! I didn't order this. No, I'm not going to sign for it. No, you can't take a photo of me by the door... How long must it be before the mandarins give up their cushy lifestyle to... Oh, there you are, darling. I'm going to the gym in a minute. Can you finish this piece? No? Fine. I'll send it as it is. The editor won't look anyway, she's WFH – Working From Hawaii.

© *All newspapers.*

POETRY CORNER

In Memoriam
June Brown, actress and soap opera legend

So. Farewell
Then June Brown,
Or Dot Cotton,
As millions knew you.

You ran the launderette
In *EastEnders.*
Now you are
Lost to us,
Like a sock in
A regular wash.

But where you are going
They are all dressed in
Spotless whites.

You smoked endlessly
And now you too
Are ashes,
But still surrounded
By clouds.

E.J. Thribb
(17½ fags per episode)

THE TIMES
OF LONDON

Friday, 29 April, 1788

Controversial plan to transport undesirables thousands of miles to primitive country

There was widespread outrage today when the government announced plans to ship undesirables not wanted in Britain thousands of miles to Botany Bay in New South Wales.

"This cruel and barbaric plan risks condemning these wretched individuals to a life of unrelenting sunshine, barbecues, wearing budgie smugglers to the beach and, worse of all, being better than us at cricket," said a man in a frock coat and a powdered wig.

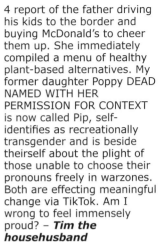

From The Message Boards

Members of the online community respond to the major issues of the day...

What's Appening, folks?

Guto Harri
We've lost shedloads of seats.

Don't worry, it's only the boring old local elections.

Guto Harri
No, it isn't, we've got yet another Tory MP sex scandal. At this rate, we'll lose our entire Commons majority.

Cripes! Surely no one will want Neil Parish's seat – not after he's been sitting in it!

Neil Parish

Carrie
Oh my God! What the WTF is that?

Neil Parish
Can I apologise for the picture I've just sent everybody? I meant to send some porn.

Really poor show, Parish. You've behaved abysmally over Porngate or Tractorgate or Farmgate or whatever it is. A) You've confessed B) You've apologised C) You've resigned. What sort of example are you setting for the Tory MPs of tomorrow?

Neil Parish
I'm sorry, I'm a disgrace.

See! You're doing it again! Have you learnt nothing?

Neil Parish has left the group

Jacob Rees-Mogg
I've no idea what you're talking about Prime Minister but rest assured the public love you.

Well they certainly do oop North. Gotta share this!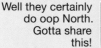

It's me with a Red Wall's ice cream! See what I did there?

Guto Harri
Yes, you lost another seat.

Nonsense. They love me in Teasmade. Or is it Tynemouth? Whitley Houston Bay in Ant and Decshire?

Rishi Sunak
I'm not sure this is helping.

You still here? I'd have thought Priti would have sent you and the wife packing to Rwanda by now, with your dodgy paperwork!

Jacob Rees-Mogg
Oh that's awfully good.

Rishi Sunak has left the group. Again

Jacob Rees-Mogg
May I be the first to congratulate you on your excellent interview on 'Good Morning Plebs'?

Cheers, Creepie! Yes, the Bozzter nailed it, smashed it out the park, as per. Winged it by the seat of his pants, dazzled the leggy brunette, and charmed the saddos who watch breakfast telly with my off-the-cuff bants.

Carrie
It was a car crash, you buffoon!

Jacob Rees-Mogg
Well, personally I enjoyed your brilliant gag about introducing bus passes so freezing pensioners could warm up by riding around on them all day. Worthy of the dear old Oxford Union! Debating skills in excelsis!

Yes, and I really sympathised with Elsie. I lived in my car for yonks, when Marina turfed me out and changed the locks. You try warming up a pot noodle with the cigarette lighter. Bloody freezing. Not half as warm as that lovely, publicly subsidised, chauffeur-driven sauna of a bus. The Elster, if I may call her that, was one lucky old lady! I'm surprised she wasn't more grateful to her inspired ex-Mayor, now National Leader.

Jacob Rees-Mogg
National Treasure, sir!

Nadine Dorries
I second that. You were great on the soon-to-be privatised ITV.

Kwasi Kwarteng
It's already privatised, Nad. It always was.

Nadine Dorries
Detail, detail – as the Prime Mister always says.

Kwasi Kwarteng
It's Prime Minister.

Nadine Dorries
Stop mansplaning!

Kwasi Kwarteng
It's spelt with an 'i'.

Nadine Dorries
Typical Old Etonian wanker!

I say, Mad Nad, that's a bit near the knuckle. This Old Etonian is the only person who's ever going to give you a job.

Nadine Dorries
Sorry, I didn't mean you, sir. You're a great man and I trust you implicitly. Now excuse me, I've got to go and bash the BBC over bias during the snooker. Did you see all those reds? 15 of them. And how many blues? One! Balance? My arse!

Kwasi Kwarteng
Would that be an ostrich arse, perchance, Culture Secretary?

I say, Mad Nad, you are on top bonkers form! Watch out, Auntie Beeb, Mad Nad's got a licence fee to kill!

Guto Harri
Can I say that I DID actually brief you before the ITV interview on who Lorraine is?

Yes, sorry, Harri-Kari! Old instincts die hard. When the first name of a woman is mentioned, I immediately go into denial mode. "Don't know who she is, never met her, it's not my child, etc, etc…"

Carrie Johnson has left the group

Flexible working

The Daily Telegraph
Election Results Spell Disaster For Labour

Daily Mail
BEERGATE – DAY 94
STARMER IN FRESH POPPADOM SHAME

DAILY EXPRESS
ELECTION RESULTS UNLEASH BREXIT BONANZA!

DISASTER FOR TORIES SPELLS GOOD NEWS FOR LABOUR

theguardian
Disaster for Tories spells disaster for Labour

THE TIMES
Election results on knife edge as newspaper awaits proprietor's view

ELECTION RESULT MASSIVE BOOST FOR TALKTV'S PIERS MORGAN

The Mail ON SUNDAY
ELECTION RESULTS SPELL CATASTROPHE FOR MEGHAN

i 10 Things you didn't know about Ed Davey
1. Who is he?

Pravda
ELECTIONS
Putin victorious in every seat in UK

MAYDAY! LOCAL ELECTION RESULTS

It's not a disaster

It's a typical mid-voyage result

No need for a new Captain

It wasn't a great night for the iceberg either

GLENDA SLAGG

Glenda's Celebrity Watch – who's up and who's down in the Fickle World of Fame and Fortune!

■ 1. HUW EDWARDS from BBC telly news!! He's down!!?! Very down!!?! Ok, Huw, I am sorry to hear you are depressed, but how do you think WE feel having to watch you on the news!??!!

■ 2. DUCHESS OF CORNWALL!!?! She's up 57 places thanks to her Heinz revelation!!?! She says her favourite food is baked beans. Would you believe it?!?!? Me neither!!? You're just trying to make people like you before the coronation – Beanz Meanz Queenz!?!!

■ 3. QUEEN ELIZABETH!!?! She's down, from street level to the underground!?!! She's had a tube line named after her!!?! Let's hope its not the END of the line for her successors??!! Mind the poverty gap!!?!

■ 4. BONG BONG MARCOS!!?! He's up in the polls to become the next president of the Philippines!!?! As I said of his dodgy mother, Imelda, I wouldn't want to be in your shoes!?!! Ok, so he went to an English public school and read PPE at snooty Oxford – that doesn't NECESSARILY mean he will be a useless, corrupt and immoral leader!?!!

■ 5. ANNA WINTOUR!?!?! You may be up or down, who knows until you take off your silly sunglasses?!!?

There's a new biography of you, apparently, but, darling, I thought the jacket was simply hideous!?! And the whole book was far too thin!!! No offence!?!!

■ 6. FULHAM FC – You're up in the premiership, but soon you'll be down again!?! You're a Yoyo team, that's why?!!! Like Yo-Yo Ma except without the cello and the classical music career?!!!

■ 7. VARDY VS ROONEY!!?! They're both down – millions of pounds down, courtesy of the legal eagles, aka messrs Sue, Grabbit and Runne!?! I'll solve the Wagatha Christie mystery!!? Who's going to win the case?!? The lawyers!?!!

■ 8. WADE VS ROE!?!! Who's interested in old Wimbledon ladies' tennis matches, anyway!!?? You're down and no one cares!!! *(You're fired. Ed.)*

■ 9. GLENDA SLAGG!?! Fleet Street's Sexocet Miss Isle (geddit?!!) is down, because she's been fired?!!! Geddit??!! Like a missile!??? *(That's terrible, you're hired again. Ed.)*

■ 10. GLENDA SLAGG!?!!! She's up!?!! Higher than interest rates, higher than inflation, higher than Johnny Depp on a bender!!?!

Byeee!!

VOTE SINN FÉIN AND MAKE LIFE CHEAP AGAIN!

COST OF LIVING HIKE GIVES S.F POLL BOOST

"I'm still not sure about that poster though!"

THE Sun SAYS

Britain to lead the world again!

YES! IT'S OFFICIAL! By 2033, Britons are going to be the biggest nation in Europe. And by biggest we mean fattest.

Yet again, this country is shown to be not only world-beating but world-eating. Move over lightweights like Tubby Turkey and Morbidly Obese Malta, there's a new heavyweight kid on the block and it isn't Fatty France or Chubby Czech Republic.

No, it's Big Belly Britain and setting us all a fine example is our Porky Prime Minister and First Lard of the Treasury – aka Billy Bunter Boris!!

Hurrah for Gross Britain! We may have lost an empire but we've gained a new roll – of fat around the middle!!

Yes, we have lost thousands of millions of pounds due to Brexit but we've gained even more millions of pounds due to breakfasts (full English, of course).

So, people of Britain, stand up if you can, and pat yourselves on the back, if that's possible. And remember that, in this country, when the chips are down, we order some more and we all believe that the pie is not the limit *(That's enough feelgood surveys from the World Health Organization. Ed.)*

NORTHERN IRELAND ELECTION SHOCK

We've been given our marching orders

STARMER RESIGNATION THREAT

I'll do the decent thing if I'm fined

You see… he's unfit to be Prime Minister

THE ALTERNATIVE VOICE

OWEN and **DIANE SPART** write:

The first principle of genuine socialist brotherhood and sisterhood and otherhood er… er… is total and utter loyalty to the leadership of the party at all times and the behaviour of the centrist neo-blairites during the glorious helmsmanship of the great Jeremy Corbyn was sickening, disgraceful and unforgiveably treacherous…er… however we on the left had not anticipated the totally cynical attempts to manipulate this duty of loyalty by the hated Red Tory Starmerites demanding that we support Starmer despite him a) being Keir Starmer b) not being Jeremy Corbyn and c) possibly breaking Covid Regulations as revealed by the authoritative Daily Mail Newspaper… er…which made it imperative and unavoidable for all socialists with a conscience ie ourselves to demand that Keir Starmer resign immediately in disgrace before all the facts are known just in case and apologise to the entire Labour movement for his appalling hypocrisy and unsocialist activities such as winning seats in Westminster and Wandsworth and returning the Labour Party to being moderately electable er… er… there are no words to describe this treachery and the undermining of Jeremy's lunacy *(surely "legacy"? Ed.)* and the great electoral victory of 2019 *(cont. p94)*

Daily Mail

BEERGATE EXCLUSIVE

DAY 94

AS the Mail's searing investigative exposé of the high-octane scandal that is rocking Britain continues, which the entire nation is talking about, the following questions still haven't been answered:

1 Is Beergate a good enough name?

2 Or should we call it Keirgate?

3 Or Smeargate?

4 Or Keirysmearygate?

5 Or, if we repeat Beergate often enough, will people eventually start repeating it? Beergate, Beergate, Beergate…

6 What about Currygate? Is that any better?

7 Okay, how about Beercrate?

8 Or better still – Hypocrate?

9 Hypocrateofbeergate?

10 Bingo! Durham police have caved in. Job done. Let's go to the pub. The beers are on the editor.

BEERGATE ROCKS LABOUR PARTY

Why does everyone hate GPs?

by Our NHS Correspondent
Noah Pointments

IT'S so strange. Wherever you look, people are being cruel about GPs, the brilliant doctors who do so much to keep the health of the nation from completely falling apart. Why do people dislike GPs so much? Could it be:

a) a failure to understand the unique challenges of the job?

b) an unwillingness to appreciate what these brave public servants do day in, day out? Or

c) our coverage over the last year, which has included headlines such as "WHY YOUR WORK-SHY GP IS LAZING AROUND WITH HIS THUMB UP HIS BUM", "WHY FAT CAT GPs ARE LAUGHING ALL THE WAY TO THE BANK WITH YOUR MONEY" and "HANG ALL DOCTORS NOW UNLESS THEY OPEN THEIR DOORS AGAIN"?

Answer
a), or b), but definitely not c), nothing to do with us.

TalkTV ratings joy

by Our TV Staff **Anna Log** and **Ray Cathode**

THERE was jubilation throughout the media industry this week as ratings for Rupert Murdoch's TalkTV were revealed.

Said one viewer of the ratings, "These are must-see ratings. Totally unmissable. I haven't laughed so much since GBTV's ratings were released."

Said another, "I think there are more people looking at these ratings than watching the channel. These ratings are a real ratings hit!"

A popular ratings disaster was Tom Newton Dunn, who succeeded in failing to register a single viewer for one of his broadcasts.

Said his mum, "Sorry, Tom, there was a DIY programme on the other side and I had to watch some paint drying."

It was widely agreed that the most enjoyable of the ratings catastrophes was the 80 percent drop in viewers of Piers Morgan's flagship show.

"Talk about TV comedy gold," said one ratings viewer, "I can't wait to see what figures he comes up with next week!"

Nadine Dorries hailed the new station as conclusive proof that privatisation works and praised it as a model for the new-look Channel 4.

PIERS MORGAN

Preferred pronouns: I / Me

Praise as gay man comes out as footballer

by **FAY CUP**
Our Football Correspondent

THE homosexual community was rocked to its foundations today, when a 17-year-old told the world's press, "Yes, I am a footballer."

His bravery was applauded throughout the world of sport as for too long, being a professional footballer has carried a terrible stigma.

Said the player "I'm not going to be ashamed any more of what I am. I am a footballer. I go out on a Saturday afternoon and kick a ball around a pitch for money, and if other gay people can't accept my lifestyle, that's their problem."

He continued, "I understand some gays only see the seedy side of football – brawls in nightclubs, filming six-in-a-bed roasts in hotel rooms with drugged glamour models, marrying Rebekah Vardy – but there's lots more to football than that. A lot of us are decent, normal, gay blokes getting on with our lives, being normal and gay."

The player told reporters, "I've known I've been a footballer for years, but I kept it a secret from fellow gays, fearing their adverse reaction."

It is thought that many gays who have been hiding the fact that they are professional footballers will now feel able to come out of the changing room.

Daily Blackmail

FRIDAY, MAY 27, 2022

HOW DARE SUE GRAY TRY TO POLITICISE THIS REPORT WHICH SHE WAS ASKED TO PRODUCE BY THE PRIME MINISTER

by Our **Entire Staff**

HOW sickening that the noted leftie lifetime civil servant Sue Gray has deliberately tried to undermine the Prime Minister by completing the report that he asked her to compile. And, even worse, she has chosen to deliver it at the worst possible time for the Prime Minister, ie anytime at all. Doesn't she know there's a war on – against Keir Starmer? And in case she hasn't noticed due to working at home (like all the other civil servants deliberately trashing the British economy), the Chelsea Flower Show is on this week and she is going to wreck that for the poor old general public.

Furthermore, the police have finished their investigation and exonerated the Prime Minister completely and utterly – apart from just one fine – so what on earth is the point of this report anyway?

It is true that we said earlier this year that the right and proper thing to do was to wait for the Sue Gray report and that she was a distinguished public servant who could be relied upon to give a fair and sensible verdict – but now that we realise that she is going to find the PM guilty, it is suddenly clear to us that she is a whinging Trot, who is aided and abetted by her Stalin-loving QC comrade Sir Hartley Red-Face QC and that, in any case, it is far too late to worry about these trivial and inconsequential parties which all happened a long time ago in a galaxy far far away. *(Is this right? Ed.)*

As Culture Secretary Nadine Dorries has confirmed, Sue Gray is no longer fit for purpose and the only way to temper her bias is to privatise her immediately so that she can compete with Netflix and *(Are you sure you are all right? Ed.)*

So, after a considered examination of the facts, the Mail says: Forget Sue Gray's Communist Manifesto and Vote Conservative!! *(Brilliant! Ed.)*

FORMER BREXIT MINISTER SPELLS IT OUT

Why are the prices going up?

It's the cost of leaving

THAT TORY MP ADVICE FOR DEALING WITH THE COST OF LIVING CRISIS IN FULL

1 Eat own-brand food.
2 Eat own-brand food cold to save on heating it up.
3 Eat own-brand food cold in the dark – then you won't even know it's own brand!
4 Get a better-paid job.
5 But don't go on strike to make the job you have better paid – that won't work.
6 Do more than one job (works for MPs).
7 Claim huge expense account (works for MPs).
8 Employ your spouse. (Did I mention this works for us?)
9 Blame your situation on global forces (not us) and you'll feel much much better.
10 Vote Conservative.

THOSE IMPERIAL UNITS MAKING A COMEBACK IN FULL

The Gunboat Roughly equivalent to 1/18th of one destroyer, the gunboat will be a vital measure in the Navy of the future. One gunboat = 1/297th of a royal yacht.

The Peck This unit, traditionally reserve for quantities of pickled peppers picked by Peter Piper, is long overdue a return.

The Royal Cubit By measuring cloth in people's arm lengths, British people will be encouraged to grow longer arms and literally reach for the new opportunities of the 21st century.

The Stride Both miles and kilometres are completely unimaginable concepts to the average person. By measuring in strides, ordinary British people will be better able to navigate the land as they herd their sheep to market.

The Dragoon Mounted infantry is going to become very useful in the next war, according to the Ministry of Defence, and by measuring everything in dragoons we will be able to once again seize Sevastopol some time before 2156.

The Sack This is a unit of volume, which must not be applied to the Prime Minister, and *(That's enough stupid units. Ed.)*

Nursery Times

Friday, Once-upon-a-time

COST OF LIVING CRISIS HITS NURSERYLAND

by Our Consumer Affairs Staff **The Very Hungry Caterpillar**

HOUSEHOLDS throughout Nurseryland are suffering from rampant inflation and supply chain issues that have meant nobody is living happily ever after.

One old lady was so desperate for food that she was reduced to swallowing a fly, with tragic consequences.

Said Doctor Foster of Gloucester who attended her, "I know why she swallowed the fly – it was due to the exorbitant prices of food in the shops."

He continued, "Having swallowed the fly, she went on to consume a spider, a bird and a cat. Fancy that – she swallowed a cat!" Worse was to come as she continued to eat a dog, a goat and then a horse. Said Doctor Foster, "She's dead, of course."

Elsewhere, Old Mother Hubbard's dog died of malnutrition and Little Bo Peep's sheep disappeared – feared abducted and eaten.

Even the royal family have been exposed to what the Governor of the Piggy Bank of Nurseryland has called a price apocalypse, as it was revealed that at a recent banquet, the royal chef was reduced to using four-and-twenty blackbirds as an ingredient in a pie.

Said one royal watcher, "Was that a dainty dish? No. It was disgusting. The queen prefers to eat bread and honey in her parlour – not a scavenging species of thrush."

Scientists are now considering introducing gene-edited crops to ease the food crisis, starting with beans.

Said bean expert Idle Jack, "Hopefully these 'magic' beans will grow into a high-yield beanstalk, delivering not only beans but golden eggs."

However, environmentalists expressed concern that a side effect of such a beanstalk would see a giant descending from the clouds to grind human bones to make his bread. But Jack scoffed at such scaremongering, calling it "the stuff of fairytales".

THEN

NOW

Is everything OK?

Is anything OK?

OLD JOKES REVISITED

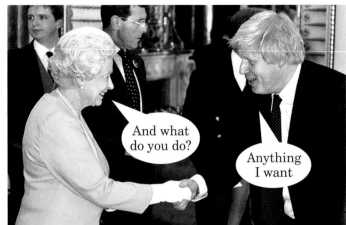

And what do you do?

Anything I want

A Royal Doctor Writes

AS A royal doctor I am often asked, "Doctor, I am exhibiting no symptoms – no cough, no fever, no sneezing, no aching limbs, nothing whatsoever. What is wrong with me?"

The simple answer is, "You have Covid, Andrew. Definitely. No doubt about it."

When the patient queries this diagnosis, as they often do, the doctor has to explain that this particular variant of the coronavirus is known as *Covidius convenientis jubilatus*, or "Duke's Palsy".

It tends to strike on the eve of a service at St Paul's and last over four days, during which the patient must self-isolate in Windsor, far away from TV cameras, microphones and mothers.

What happens is the doctor receives an anonymous call from Highgrove saying, "My brother's going to ruin everything, so shove something up his nose and tell him he's got the dreaded lurgy and can't come. Better still, tell him he's got Long Covid... say, ten years. Or longer if my coronation still hasn't happened."

If you're worried about your wayward relative ruining an important family event, then you should consult professional medical advice at once.

© *Sir A. Doctor*
(Royal College of Physicians)

That Jubilee Concert in Full

Sam Ryder
Space Ma'am ♪

Diana Ross
Upside Crown ♫

Rod Stewart
Do Ya Think I'm Sexagenarian?

Elton John
(pre-recorded in the Grosse-pfrofitzer Stadium in Kashkow)
You're still standing ♪

♪ **Duran Duran**
Hungry Like The Corgi

Queen
Don't Stop Her Now

♪ **Hans Zimmer Frame**
Music from Bond film 'No Time To Die'

And many others, including:
Elbow, Arse, Arse and Elbow

Pensioner forced to ride around on bus to keep warm

by **Toby Young Ones**

IN another sad indictment of Tory Britain, it was revealed that this frail and elderly man was forced to ride around on a bus to keep warm.

Mr Cliff Richard, 105, said, "I can't afford to go on a summer holiday anymore, so when they offered me a ride on this bus, I jumped at the chance."

Exclusive to all Tory papers

THE BBC An Apology

IN RECENT days, over the extended bank holiday for the Queen's Platinum Jubilee, we heaped praise on the BBC for its coverage of the spectacular Jubilee Concert at the gates of Buckingham Palace, plus the joyous Royal Pageant in the Mall.

We described this coverage as being something the national broadcaster does best: bringing the nation together as no one else can, to celebrate the life of our beloved Monarch, being both respectful and yet forward-looking, with many moments of true joy and unparalleled entertainment.

We now realise, in the light of Boris Johnson facing a no confidence vote a few days later, that nothing could be further from the truth, and that all the blame for the Prime Minister's woes can be laid firmly at the feet of the hated remainstream BBC, a sick corporation filled with lefties who have plotted from the moment Boris Johnson became PM to bring about his downfall by tricking him into attending lockdown-busting parties and then disgustingly reporting on his attendance at those events as if he actually attended them.

The BBC's so-called "journalists" flagrantly reported events which unfairly portrayed our beloved leader as some sort of debauched liar, and not the paragon of virtue we know him to be.

We apologise for any confusion caused, and any confusion caused in the future when, in 2025, 20 million people tune in to watch the coverage of King Charles's coronation on BBC1 and we praise the national broadcaster as being truly the best of British, our jewel in the broadcasting crown, a... etc, etc...

Jubilee concerts are a drag – am I right, or am I right? It just makes me want to put my hands over my ears! And it's always the same old acts – it's always bloody 'Queen' again! If I wanted to see a musical act named after a relative, I'd go and see Will.I. Am!!! (William – geddit?) But that's life, isn't it? It's those irritating things we all have to go through, like when a corgi gets under your feet, or the footman brings you the wrong bit of Lego, or when the future Queen of England gets in your face and tells you to shush. We've all been there! Here's something I know we can all get behind: how annoying are balconies?! They're always too high and you have to clamber onto the heir to the throne's knee to help you see what's going on! We've all been there. *(This is great stuff, sir. Ed.)*

Jubilee – a time for reflection

■ As the whole nation celebrated the Queen's jubilee with street parties, those who were alive at the time of the coronation reflected on the difference between today and 1952.

Said one pensioner, "Due to the war in Europe, there was very little food, luxuries were in short supply and we all had to make the most of the austerity conditions as best we could. Even medicines were scarce, and the price of petrol meant travel was difficult. Yes, it was grim. I remember it like it was yesterday – because it was. Things were quite bad in 1952 too."

"I told you it was bad luck not to take down the Jubilee decorations"

RACISTS!

WARNER

HEIR OF SORROWS

by Dame Sylvie Krin, author of *Duchess of Hearts* & *You're Never Too Old*

THE STORY SO FAR: Charles is attending the Jubilee Pageant in celebration of his mother's long and glorious reign. Now read on...

CHARLES attempted to stifle a yawn, as a procession of lawnmowers past and present, pushed by Britain's top gardening celebrities, chugged down the Mall to honour the nation's keen interest in horticulture.

"And there, leading the way, is Sir Monty Python, or possibly Dame Charlie Dimsum, no, I'm wrong, it's Sir Alan Titchfield-Thunderbolt of course, dressed up as Capability Brownose, the famous 18th century landscape designer..."

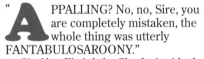

The soothing mellow tones of Sir Stephen Frys-Ties echoed round the Victoria Wood Memorial outside Beckingham palace where the assembled dignitaries were watching the extraordinary historical pageant put together by the renowned publisher Sir Nicholas Conde-Nasty.

Charles whispered to his consort royale, Camilla, the Duchess of Rothmans, who had recently been decorated by Her Majesty the Queen and given the Royal Order of the Gasper, "I say, old thing, I am not sure I can take any more of this, how long have we been here?"

"Three minutes, Chazza," replied his future Queen and current soulmate. "I am dying for a fag already."

Charles groaned as the pageant continued inexorably onwards:

"...And now we celebrate the TV stars of the nineteen seventies with an authentic period Black Maria as featured in the TV series *The John Sweeney* and through the barred windows you can just see holograms of some of that decade's most illustrious paedophiles... including Sir Gareth Glitterball, Sir Stuart Hallmark of ITV's *It's a Lockup*, Sir Rolf Harrass... and topping the bill, of course, the late Sir James Savile-Row..."

A chorus of boos rang around the stands, although no one was sure whether they were directed at the digital miscreants of that dismal decade or the Prime Minister, who had taken his seat behind Charles and who seemed more interested in looking at his phone gloomily than enjoying Sir Nicholas's charming spectacle of 70 years of British eccentricity.

Charles tried to smile and applauded enthusiastically at the arrival in the Daily Mall of a fleet of giant Trouser-Presses all the way from the town of Corbyn, representing British hotel-related technical know-how and cutting-edge executive garment anti-crease design...

What would the public make of this bizarre array of historical hoopla and monarchical malarkey? Would they appreciate it? Or would they think it was really rather... what was the word...?

"APPALLING? No, no, Sire, you are completely mistaken, the whole thing was utterly FANTABULOSAROONY."

Sir Alan Fiztightly, Charles's aide-de-campanology, bustled busily about the bathroom of Claret House.

He could hardly contain his enthusiasm for what he called "the Platty Jubbly", as he prepared Charles's toothbrush royale for its morning outing, in his new role as Colonel of the Colgate Guards, Master of the Queen's Maclean's Freshmint and Colour Officer of the Oral-B.

Sir Alan continued, "The Air Vice-Marshal and I enjoyed every minute of it and luckily we had our dancing shoes on when Sir Rod Stewpot sang *Sweet Carolingian Era* and Sir Ben Elton launched into *I'm Still Singing*... I thought I had died and gone to Heaven in 1983..."

"Yes, all right, Sir Alan, thank you... I can see that you and your partner enjoyed it all, but what of one's loyal subjects? I mean, what did they think about my speech and me calling Mater 'mummy' and, you know, the whole business of oneself taking her place, basically... in loca reginentis...?"

Sir Alan's eyes lit up with mischief. "Well, let's look at the papers, shall we?"

And there were that morning's offerings freshly ironed by the new flunkey, Witherow, and laid out ready for princely perusal. Sir Alan began to read:

"Triumph for Prince!", "Prince steals the show with his charming performance", "Future of Monarchy safe as Popular Prince pleases Public"...

Charles's ears glowed a shade of Purple Reign, as he revelled in the praise of the press. "I mean, not that one cares, but it is important for the Firm to have positive feedback and for oneself, as Heir Apparently, to know that one's role in the years to come is assured."

Sir Alan continued with his recitation of the morning's headlines:

"'Yes, Clown Prince Louis has shown the rest of the stiff old Royals how to have a good time!', 'It's Prince Louis the Laugh!'... Oh, and on page 17 there's a small picture of you with the headline 'Mummy's Boy'."

Charles groaned and started forlornly brushing his royal teeth, cleaning the ducal dentures in a ritual that seemed to epitomise his dutiful but unrewarded and under-appreciated role in the national consciousness.

"And now gargle, Sire!"

Charles let out a heartfelt "Aaaaaaaargh!"

(To be continued...)

NATION CONGRATULATES QUEEN

Daily Mail, Friday, June 17, 2022

HOORAH FOR PRINCE LOUIS!

LET'S HOPE his high spirits remain undimmed and he grows up to be as badly behaved as Uncle Harry, so that we can write about him going off the rails and being photographed drunk in a Nazi uniform outside Hoorays Nightclub before, with any luck, marrying someone ghastly we can attack for the next twenty years!

Yes, Long Live Little Louis the Lout!

Enjoy the four days of partying!

It's a work event

JUBILEE STREET PARTY

"Damned potholes!"

-PILBROW-

Hoorah! What a stonking victory for myself! 211-148 ! It's a landslide!

Jacob Rees-Mogg
May I be the first to offer my felicitations on the magnitude of your triumph in the no confidence vote, which will surely put an end to the undignified plotting of the disaffected disloyalists.

Rishi Sunak
That's not what you said when Theresa May had a better result in her confidence vote, Jacob. You said it was a disaster and that she should resign as Prime Minister.

Jacob Rees-Mogg
Ah yes, Mr Sunak, but with all due respect to Mrs May, the situation was entirely different then. I didn't have a Cabinet job to lose.

Good one, Creepie! And take heed, Richi and other Cabinet Whatsappers considering doing the dirty on me... one false move and there's a reshuffle coming your way.

Rishi Sunak
Oh yeah? Just try it! Let's see how that goes. Try and move me and you're toast.

Honestly! People are so disloyal. They spend all their time plotting against the leadership. Who gave them that idea?

Nadine Dorries
Talking about loyalty, here's a lovely picture of the moment at St Paul's when the loyal general public started cheering you.

Guto Harri
Is that a typo? Did you mean "jeering"?

Nadine Dorries
No. And shut up or I'll privatise you. There were millions of loyal Tory supporters at the church and no one booed at all. The Remainstream media made it all up.

Carrie
Boo.

Nadine Dorries
I think you mean "Hooray".

Carrie
No, boo to you, Nadine. You're a bit too keen on my husband for my liking.

Lynton Crosby
Strewth! At least someone's keen on him! let's move on to the more important issues...

Dominic Raab
The Privileges Committee report?

Don't be dim, Dom! Partygate is over, no one's interested, we're drawing a lie under it.

Guto Harri
I think you mean "line".

Michael Gove
Did someone say "line"? 😅 🌀 🏃

Steady on, Govester. I'm looking to lay out my vision for this country, not go clubbing.

Michael Gove
I didn't think you had a vision, Prime Minister.

Of course I do. And my vision is this. It's me. In power. For a very long time.

Graham Brady
Hello, Prime Minister. Just me again. With a touch more bad news. The 1922 Committee is considering changing the rules to allow another no-confidence vote within the year.

What? You can't just rip up the rules because you don't like them! Rules are rules. That's the rule. They're there for a reason – to be followed, not just to ignore when it suits you.

Jacob Rees-Mogg
Oh very funny, Prime Minister. Ironic mirth-making of the most capital variety!

It wasn't a joke, Creepie.

Jacob Rees-Mogg
Oh, even funnier, sir.

Liz Truss
I know what will help. I will dress up as Britannia! With a Union Jack shield and a trident with three different varieties of British cheese on the prongs.

148 people have left the group.

TRUMP FURY AS IVANKA TESTIFIES THAT THE US ELECTION RESULT WASN'T RIGGED

You're no daughter of mine

I threw you under the bus to save my skin

Okay, I take that back

Current affairs quiz

1. Are there more adverts for Piers Morgan's new TalkTV show on buses than there are viewers watching it?

2. Is the number of plugs for Piers Morgan's new TalkTV show in Times newspapers more or less than the number of viewers watching it?

3. Which is greater? The number of viewers for Piers Morgan's new TalkTV show or the number of hairs on Mr Rupert Murdoch's head?

4. Which is smaller? The number of years spent in jail by Rebekah Brooks or the audience for Tom Newton Dunn's afternoon show on TalkTV? (*Warning – trick question! They may be the same round number.*)

5. What is the numerical link between Piers Morgan's new TalkTV show and *The One Show* on the BBC?

6. Which is the more entertaining to watch: Nigel Farage on GB News, Piers Morgan on TalkTV, or paint drying on the wall?

7. Have I mentioned TalkTV news enough not to be fired this week?

8. No?

9. Are you sure?

10. Right, sorry – are there more questions in this quiz than there are viewers for Piers Morgan's new TalkTV show?

(*You're fired. Ed.*)

TRAVEL DISRUPTION CONTINUES

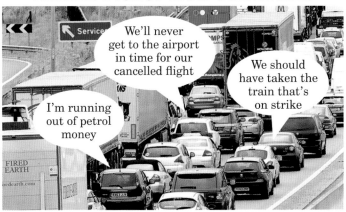

We'll never get to the airport in time for our cancelled flight

We should have taken the train that's on strike

I'm running out of petrol money

Normal chaos to return to the railways

THERE was widespread joy among Britain's long-suffering rail commuters that now the pandemic was finally over, there was going to be a major rail strike across the nation. This unprecedented chaos on the railways signified a return to normal life.

"For months now, with so many people still working from home, commuting has been a pleasant experience, with lots of services and seats. It's been horribly unsettling," said one commuter. "I actually started to enjoy travelling by train into work each morning. It was horrific.

"Thankfully, the prospect of the rail bosses and the unions being at loggerheads means we can finally return to the chaos, delays and cancellations that we expect. Phew."

Kettle blackens name of POT

■ TONIGHT a senior Kettle from the kitchen cabinet described the POT (Public Organisation of Trainworkers) as "selfish and irresponsible" for their decision to go on strike.

Said Mr Grant Kettle, "If anyone is going to be selfish and irresponsible, it is this government and we are not going to put up with other people putting themselves first with a blatant disregard for the common good. That is our job!"

Mr Kettle was steaming, as he accused POT of tarnishing their own reputation, but members of POT threatened to boil over at Kettle's tirade of hot air, declaring, "This is a black day for the entire nation."

(Potters)

THOSE WAGATHA CHRISTIE COURTROOM CHANTS IN FULL

We're Forever Blowing Millions

Oh When The Silks Go Marching In

♪ **Wiggie! Wiggie! Wiggie! – Oi! Oi! Oi!**

Who's the Bastard in the Black? Oh sorry, Judge.

Roo Ate All The Pies…

Who Are Yer?! In the courtroom drawings?

♪ **You Only Ping When You're Tweeting** ♪

You're Not Suing Anymore!

WHO DO YOU THINK IS BEST IN THE BOX... ROONEY OR VARDY?

WITNESS BOX

Keir Starmer WRITES

HELLO!

I hope it has not escaped your attention that Britain is awfully like the Seventies nowadays. And I don't mean glam rock bands! No, every time I turn on the news it's industrial action, galloping inflation, petrol price rises, energy crises and Abba is all the rage!!

To be honest, we have all gone Super Trooper and Trade Union crazy!! But here's the exciting part – I don't know if you are aware of this, but way back in those days, we had a thing called the Labour government. Yes, it's true – ask your grandad – there really was a Labour government in power, in Number Ten, and not just saying they had won the election, like Jeremy did!

And what kind of government was it? It was a radical reforming government, led by a charismatic leader with big hair who shook up Broken Britain and galvanised the nation with a forceful vision of the future.

Hang on, Lisa informs me that I may have got this wrong and that was Mrs Thatcher and that Labour in the Seventies was a weak, centrist government that failed to achieve anything – well, in that case, that is just another idea that the Tories have stolen from us!

But my point is the same. Star Wars is back! Royal Jubilees are back! And, according to Twitter, white dog poo is back! Which means that Labour is DEFINITELY back!

So bring on the by-elections and let's show the world that there is a party ready to take the fight to the Tories – so, well done to the Lib Dems!

And on that positive note, I will say cheerio.

And, as the Jedi Warriors say, "Live long and prosper!"

Sincerely, Keir Starwars.

LUCKY BRIT WINS £200m

by ROLLO OVER
Our Jackpot Correspondent

AN ordinary British woman has hit the headlines over a jackpot win of a lifetime, and the award of about £200 million.

The lucky lady in question – Baroness Michelle Mone – recommended ministers give contracts to the firm PPE Medpro, meaning they promptly dished out £200 million to buy PPE during the pandemic, much of which was never used.

"The nice thing is that it's completely random," said one friend. "Absolutely anyone could have won this life-changing sum of money, as long as they claimed to be a respectable PPE supplier, had access to the government's VIP lane via Baroness Mone, and had the ability to quickly incorporate a company on the Isle of Man. As the old ad slogan goes, 'It could be you, as long as you are friends with the right people'."

For her brilliant work, Mone has been treated to a visit by the National Lottery Jackpot Team *(surely the National Crime Agency? Ed.)*.

LATE NEWS

■ Government promises to create 'High-rage economy'

SAUDI-BACKED GOLF TOUR STARTS

The first leg is in St Albans

Where are the other body parts?

BP'S ARGUMENT AGAINST THE NEED FOR A WINDFALL TAX

■ Allowing oil firms to keep excess profits means they invest that money in developing new oilfields.

■ The fossil fuels extracted from those fields lead to increased global warming.

■ This causes temperatures worldwide to continue rising.

■ Those higher temperatures mean that soon you'll barely need to switch the central heating on, even in winter, thus slashing the cost of energy bills for ordinary people.

■ Er... that's it.

bp

73

A Tank Driver writes

Vlad 'Mad' Putin, Tank No: ZZZZ.

Every week a well-known tank driver gives his opinion on a matter of topical importance. This week, the war in Ukraine...

Blimey, that muppet Zelensky has got a nerve – cheering on Boris Johnson, I mean that's interfering with UK politics, innit? That's my job. It really gives me the hump. I give the Tories all that laundered loot, and they go and pass it on to Zelensky? How does that work? What a bunch of crooks! And talk about disloyal! They're worse than Ukrainians. Talking of which, if you ask me, we should string 'em all up, that's the only language they understand. Apart from Ukrainian. And Russian. And English. Obviously. What a load of Nazis! I'd exterminate the lot of 'em! Don't get me wrong, guv, I'm not a racist, but sometimes genocide's the only answer. That Stalin, he had a point, didn't he? Gawd, traffic's terrible. All those blown-up tanks in the road. I hate to drone on, but it's all those drones. Hahaha! Who says I haven't got a sense of humour? No one, cos they're dead. Hahaha! Where did you say you want to go? I'm not going south of the river Siversky Donets this time of night. I'm on my way home. Not that I'm retreating. More of a victory parade. Sorry about the fare, it's the price of diesel. A tip? That's very kind. What do you mean "Get out of Ukraine"? All right, I'll drop you here. I had that nice Mr Farage in the back of the tank the other day, very clever man.

● *Translated from the original Russian by Google Transiberia*

Putin launches 'Starve the World' campaign

RUSSIA has hailed its successful blockade of grain exports from Ukraine's Black Sea ports, which has caused market volatility to send food prices rocketing and is also threatening to increase the prospect of famine across the Third World.

Launching his global "Starve the World" campaign, Vladimir Putin said the blockading of 20 million tons of grain was "just the start" of a de-aid effort to get international sanctions on the Kremlin lifted by holding world food markets to ransom – with future plans to inhibit Ukraine's summer harvest by 50%, which could encourage starvation in Africa and other famine-hit areas, also in the offing.

The Russian President added that the campaign would culminate later in the year with the release of a special uncharitable song "Do They Know There's A Special Military Operation On?"

(Rotters)

RUSSIANS CREATE NEW TREAT FOR BELEAGUERED POPULATION

BEFORE Big Mac   **AFTER Big Massacre**

TOP TIPS FOR GETTING THROUGH THE COST OF LIVING CRISIS

1 Join a car share scheme. Simply hook up with two or three friends and share your journeys, and save petrol too! Mondays – you drive and they push. Tuesdays – you push and Simon drives. Wednesdays, it's Sharon at the wheel. Saves ££££s!

2 Don't go to the pub. Simply organise to meet your friends in the local supermarket, buy some cheap own-brand beer, and start the party out by the bins. Cheers!

3 Cancel your Netflix subscription. It's full of films you don't want to watch anyway. Simply watch films you don't want to watch on ITV3 instead – it's free! Invite your friends around! Pass the popcorn (own brand)!

4 Stop ordering all those takeaways. Simply ring up your partner and tell them what you want to eat for dinner. They will cook it then put it in a plastic container and ring the doorbell. And no tip required!

5 Don't go abroad for your holiday. You'll end up sleeping at Gatwick Airport lounge anyway, so just pack a couple of suitcases and go and sleep opposite the toilets! Holiday sorted!

6 Don't buy expensive food and drink. Simply buy own-brand everything and then catch Covid. That way you won't be able to taste it! Quids in!

7 Can't pay your heating bills? Just rob a bank and run like crazy. That'll warm you up! And if you manage to get away, you'll have enough money to turn the thermostat up for five minutes. Toasty! *(You're fired! Ed. – I'm saving money on journalists.)*

"Why is there NOBODY in this country who wants to look after Mum?!"

SHORTAGE OF CARE WORKERS

We'll never abandon our allies under fire abroad...

...unless they're in Afghanistan

TV HIGHLIGHTS

BETTER CALL Suella

Better Call Suella

Streaming now

Spin-off series from *Breaking Laws*.

Hysterical legal comedy-drama, featuring the unscrupulous and inept lawyer Suella Braverman (beautifully underplayed by Saul Goodman) and her entertaining attempts to be the Mrs Fixit Attorney General for the criminal fraternity, aka the British government.

Operating out of her cramped office behind a Westminster nail bar, Suella uses her full ignorance of the law to help her clients escape from the tightest of corners.

"Better call Suella!" – that's her catchphrase, along with "Yes, Prime Minister". Want to prorogue Parliament? No problem. Want to break your own Covid rules? She's on it. Fancy breaking international treaties over Northern Ireland? Piece of cake. Want to eat a piece of cake? Walk in the park. Want to walk in the park during lockdown with a hundred friends and a suitcase full of booze? Yes, you ca... *(We get the idea. Ed.)*

DIARY

ALLISON PEARSON

So now we know.

Goody-two-shoes Labour leader Keir Starmer enjoyed a right old knees-up every single day of lockdown.

Popping open the bubbly. Handing round the Cheesy Wotsits. Warbling along to The Sex Pistols with their hateful lyrics about Her Majesty the Queen – after all her remarkable service to this country.

And that's not all.

Every night in the secret underground disco at Labour HQ, Starmer was joined by party girl raven-haired Angela Rayner, in skirts so short they might more usefully be described as belts.

And the pair of them danced their way into the wee small hours, flinging their limbs around to the Pogo and Hokey Cokey, without a care in the world.

Sickening behaviour, in anyone's book. Was that really the way for any self-respecting Leader of the Opposition and his doe-eyed deputy to behave when so many millions were dying of Covid, caught from the EU?

Any self-respecting couple would hang their heads in shame.

Not them.

Instead, they stick their fingers up at common decency – and persist in asking our inspirational Prime Minister rude, impertinent questions that no reasonable man should ever have to answer.

As a former caregiver, I've the deepest respect for our thousands of hard-working nurses.

And that's why it deeply grieves me when I see some of them slumping behind their desks, staring at screens and scoffing luxury selections of top-quality chocolates.

As a former teacher, I yearn to say, "Haven't you got anything better to do – like helping others?"

Couldn't they stop for one second searching the menu for their fave Strawberry Cremes and take a moment off to learn from the example of Mike and Zara Tindall?

This hard-working, no-nonsense royal couple are an example to us all.

Not for them the pampered airhead cry-baby California psycho-bonkers therapy indulged in by Harry and Meghan, aka Duke and Duchess of Slovenly.

No. Mike and Zara just get on with it. No airs and graces.

They're never afraid to get their hands dirty.

They wear no-nonsense waterproofs and have no truck with non-stick pans.

They introduce much-needed sense of duty into the lives of the workers they're forced to meet.

And at the end of a busy day, they sit down to enjoy the next episode of *Strictly*, just like the rest of us.

Then – and only then – might they indulge in one or a maximum two choccies from the scrummy box of Milk Tray that H.M. Granny so kindly gave them for Christmas.

Yes, we can all learn a lesson from the stalwart example they set.

As a former member of the Armed Forces, I salute them.

Am I the only one who's sick to death of toasters?

I don't think so.

Thousands of you have written to me to complain that you have had your lives ruined by toasters. They promise so much. And deliver so little.

The other day I thought I'd make myself some scrambled eggs on toast. Simple enough, you might think. But then you'd be reckoning without the current shoddy state of our toasters.

It pains me to recall what happened. But I truly believe that someone has to speak out. Because, frankly, I've had enough. Why on earth should these fat-cat toaster manufacturers be allowed to get away with it?

Deep breath. Here goes.

I broke a couple of eggs into a bowl. Then I whisked them up with a fork. And then, just like any normal, hard-working person would have done, I dipped my piece of bread into the lovely eggy mixture and slotted it neatly into my brand new Toaster.

What happened next doesn't bear thinking about. Within minutes I heard the sound of sizzling and saw smoke coming out the top.

Deeply fearful for my life, I switched off the electricity and struggled to put on my rubber gloves, still hoping against hope that I might salvage my scrambled eggs on toast.

No such luck. The toast was burnt, the eggs had slipped into the inner workings of the toaster, destroying it forever – and my longed-for snack was completely and utterly ruined.

I was, and I remain, deeply shocked. That it should come to this! At a time when our decent, tough-minded and much-derided Home Secretary, Priti Patel, is sweating her guts out night and day to save our poor benighted country from the next invasion of grasping, bomb-toting, Middle Eastern "refugees", ie, welfare scroungers from The Land of Goodness-Knows-Where, it beggars belief that we still can't get toasters that work.

I can at least draw one small shred of comfort. At long last, we are free from the shackles of the EU. Soon – very soon – these faulty toasters will be banished from these shores forever. As a former squadron leader of the Red Arrows, I can only welcome their departure.

Good riddance, says moi.

As told to
CRAIG BROWN

Lord Geidt
...and sixthly, the steel tariffs issue left me with no option... with a heavy heart, and having carefully considered my position as Ethics Adviser, I have no option but to tender my resignation.

> Oh get lost, you silly old Geidty, with your holier than thou goody two shoes The Only Way is Ethics!

Lord Geidt has left the group

> Right, that's him gone. I can do whatever I like.

Guto Harri
Don't you do that already?

> Good point.

Guto Harri
I do think it would be a sensible idea to replace him. This is a highly paid public job at the very heart of government, for someone with a spotless record.

> OK I've got just the candidate. And here she is!

Carrie
What's the money?! I want 100K minimum. Or as much as you gave that pole dancer for the IT lessons.

> Oh no – that was totally different. This 100K is payroll and Jennifer's 100K was a government grant.

Grant Shapps
Grant? Does somebody need me?

Liz Truss
That'd be a first.

Rishi Sunak
Haven't you got somewhere to go, Grant?

Grant Shapps
No, I haven't – the trains are all on strike.

Rishi Sunak
Can't you do something about it? Have you tried giving them 100 billion quid? Always works for me.

Liz Truss
Maybe I could do a photo op in a train driver's hat, blowing a whistle...

Grant Shapps
No. And anyway my meeting with the RMT has been delayed. Oh no, it's been cancelled. There weren't enough chairs in the room anyway. I'd have had to stand in the corridor.

> What about this job for Carrie?

Guto Harri
Not a good idea, boss. There's a story about you in the Times offering Carrie a job when you were foreign secretary.

Gove
It was a position underneath you .

> Leave the jokes to me, Govester. Are you phoning in from the disco tent at Glasto?

Gove
It's a class A line-up this year. Woohoo! 🌍😵 .

> I'm going to stop this pyramid stage of Pfeffel this minute.

Tony Gallagher (Deputy Editor the Times) has been added to the group

Tony Gallagher
What do you want me to do, boss?

> Spike that story, pronto.

Tony Gallagher
Because it's untrue?

> No, because it's true! Including the bit about me and Carrie at it like knives discussing Uganda on the Foreign Office desk while my wife was in hospital. That could make me look bad.

Carrie
I'm the new Ethics Advisor and it seems absolutely fine to me.

Tony Gallagher
Consider it done, PM. This story is dead as a dead cat when you're in trouble.

Tony Gallagher has left the group

> Excellent. Sorted. Who says the Bozzter can't get things done?

Rishi Sunak
So what am I supposed to do about inflation and the cost of living crisis?

> You know the drill, team – when the going gets tough, the tough get... on the phone to Zelensky. Big photo of me on the blower with Vlodders talking about how me and Super Vlod are in it for the long haul, and then all the plebs in the Red Wall will forget that they can't afford to buy an oven-ready Lancashire hot pot noodle to feed their whippet

Jacob Rees-Mogg
Top social observation, Prime Minister!

> Thanks, Creepie. So, Bosh! Job done! Another week in power for yours truly.

Guto Harri
That may be a bit optimistic...

President Zelensky's assistant
I'm afraid Mr Zelensky's unavailable. He's got an important summit with Ben Stiller, followed by crisis talks with Leonardo DiCaprio and he's keeping his diary clear for Tom Hanks.

> Damn. Perhaps I should go to Rwanda instead. Oh, wait – I've just done that.

Priti Patel
I'd be happy sendin' you back – it's my speciality.

Gove
Not from what I've heard. Your plane never got as high as I did listening to the Pet Shop Boys! Woooh! Gotta go – Diana Ross is on, singing "Supply Chain Reaction". 🕺💊

Guto Harri
Er, boss. You know that story that you spiked... Well, it's no longer in the Times.

> Huzzah!

Guto Harri
It's now on the front page of all the other newspapers, and on BBC. And ITV. And Sky.

Nadine Dorries
Bastards! Disloyal Remainstream media bastards! I'll privatise the lot of them!

Sajid Javid
They are private already, Nadine.

Nadine Dorries
Well, in that case, they're all lefty scum!

Sajid Javid
Not the Telegraph, Mad Nad. Or the Mail.

Nadine Dorries
Bloody Free Press!

> I love you, Mad Nad, you're completely bonkers!

Carrie
Don't mention bonking!

Carrie Johnson has left the group

TIME FOR THIS WRETCHED BANKRUPT LABOUR GOVERNMENT TO GO

ONCE more Labour's Keir Starmer has shown himself unfit to be Prime Minister, as he stood by and allowed the National Rail Strike to go ahead, using the pathetic excuse that he's not actually the Prime Minister and that Labour isn't in power.

But it's not just the mishandling of the rail strike. The entire country is going to hell in a handcart, with inflation rampant and prices skyrocketing. Once again this proves that Labour simply can't be trusted with the economy.

And, yes, Labour will claim they aren't in government, but that's just what you'd expect these Marxist cowards to say.

And have you noticed that not one member of the Labour government has taken a part-time job driving a train or loading bags on to an airplane and that their overpaid leader has so far refused to sell his house, give away all his money to the poor and live homeless on the streets? Pathetic! Before Britain sinks any deeper under this failed Labour state, surely it's time for a Conservative administration to be ushered in to sort out this crisis under the calm authoritative leadership of Britain's Brexit champion, Boris Johnson.

A weary nation says to Prime Minister Keir Starmer, PLEASE GO AND GO NOW.

ROYAL CASH DONOR LINKED TO AL-QAEDA

Huge metaphor builds up at Heathrow airport

A massive metaphor consisting of roughly 15,000 bags which have not been processed and which passengers have not been able to collect – has piled up at Heathrow.

This is the result of "technical difficulties", ie there are not enough people to carry out the jobs. This has meant that ordinary people are completely screwed and have had to wait hours and days for their own stuff.

A senior spokesperson for Heathrow said, "Yes, we are well aware that because we didn't take action, huge quantities of baggage stretching back God knows how long have not been adequately dealt with. But in our defence, this is exactly what you'd get anywhere else as well."

A coronavirus scientist explains...

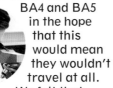

"We deliberately called the latest Covid variants BA4 and BA5 in the hope that this would mean they wouldn't travel at all. We felt that naming them BA.4 and BA.5 would ensure that they never got airborne and had no chance of travelling around the world. We now realise we that we should have called them easyJet1, Wizz2, Tui3 and Ryanair 94. Apologies to all."

Private Eye's Lexicographer and Etymologist **Dot Wordsearch** *writes...*

THANKS to all readers for their comments about last week's delightful lost word: "**Picklethrumble**".

This week I'm looking at a similarly old-fashioned word that has fallen out of use: "**Brexit**".

There was a time when "Brexit" was the word on everyone's lips. Open a newspaper and you were bound to read the word "Brexit" in every article. "Brexit is going to solve all our problems", "Brexit is going to be a nightmare", "I'm bored of Brexit" was all the talk in towns and villages up and down the country.

But nowadays the word has all but disappeared, and no one can remember what it means. Whereas once we would say: "The colossal queue of lorries into Dover is the result of Brexit", nowadays the common newsprint parlance is: "The short queue of lorries into Dover is an inevitable result of the Ukraine war and Covid."

Similarly, when reading about the shortage of, say, medicines, instead of a shopkeeper being quoted as saying "It's bloody Brexit to blame", the pharmacist is more likely to be reported saying "I'm sorry, we've had supply chain issues due to global shortages, which are the inevitable result of the war in Covid and the Ukraine pandemic." Which all goes to show that language is a fluid, changeable creature, and English is a very flexible language, that adapts and modifies itself according to the newspaper proprietor's wishes.

The last recorded use of the word "Brexit" in print was way back last week in the Financial Times, which ran the quaint headline "The deafening silence over Brexit's economic fallout." Very few readers will have understood what on earth they meant!

NEXT WEEK: Another funny old word that you don't hear much of nowadays: "Prosperity".

"We'd originally planned to go mountaineering in the Pyrenees"

Netflix to offer 'television'

IN a bid to stop haemorrhaging subscribers, Netflix has announced it will be offering a cheap new viewing experience it calls "television".

"Television" will be a radical new way to consume content, as episodes for shows will be released at the same time weekly, and will be broken up by ads.

"As television will be considerably cheaper to watch than standard Netflix, we think it could well be the future of broadcasting," said one excited executive.

"We might even try a continuous podcast service our boffins call 'radio'."

Weimar Times

Friday 1 July 1923

'INFLATION UNDER CONTROL' SAYS GOVERNMENT

by Our Economics Staff
Adolf Smith

THE chancellor, Reichi Sunak, today assured the public that the steep rises in inflation were "no cause for panic".

Despite an alarming price and wage spiral leading to the worst inflation for forty years, the Chancellor maintained that he had everything under control.

Said Reichi,"I am confident that my current policies will contain the inflationary pressures on the economy. I have, for example, just given pensioners an enormous increase, and also those on benefits. That should do the trick." He continued, "I am currently printing money, but one thing is for sure, this won't lead to a great depression with everyone having to take their wheelbarrows full of worthless

currency to the shops to buy a loaf of bread."

With a General Strike looming and widespread civil discontent throughout the country, there are fears that the country will become polarised and there will be a rise of right-wing extremism.

Reichi, however, laughed off such concerns and said, "I wish I had a fiver for every time someone told me that inflation was a problem. Ok, make that a tenner. Ok, make that ten million billion marks."

AS NOT SEEN IN THE SUN

Deirdre's Photo Casebook

Fourth time unlucky! The sad story of the marriage of Rupert and Jerry – a love that was not destined to last, unlike Rupert

IT ALL STARTED SO WELL...
TILL DEATH US DO PART
THAT'S THE IDEA
YOU LOOK LIKE A MILLION DOLLARS
I HOPE IT'S A LOT MORE THAN THAT

THE HONEYMOON PERIOD CONTINUED...
WE'RE REALLY GETTING ON
WELL, YOU ARE!
HE'S A BABE MAGNATE
SHE'S HOPING FOR A JERRY HAUL

BUT THEN PROBLEMS BEGAN...
YOU'VE GIVEN ME A NEW LEASE OF LIFE
OH FOX!
IT'S JERRY AND THE PACEMAKER

AND IT ALL ENDED IN YEARS (SURELY 'TEARS')...
LET'S KEEP OUR DIVORCE SECRET
OKAY THEN, I'LL HAVE PIERS MORGAN ANNOUNCE IT ON TALKTV

THE TRUTH ON THE OUTDATED 'SPANISH PRACTICES' EMPLOYED BY RAIL WORKERS

WE don't tell any outrageous lies here, we are here to inform our loyal readers of simple facts about rail workers and the antiquated 19th century working perks known as "Spanish practices" that they enjoy.

For example, the castanets are "mandatory" in driver's cabs before they are even willing to get in, never mind set off.

Then, during negotiations with rail bosses, unions insist they must be conducted with the offer of a FREE tapas buffet and the promise of a compulsory siesta for union apparatchiks.

Then there are the outrageous free trips to bullfighting rings in the summer months.

Meanwhile, their gold-plated RMT union boss, Miguel Lynch, earns QUADRUPLE the amount of his workers – a WHOPPING £124,000 a year – TRIPLE that of the average guard *(cont. p94)*

LATE NEWS: Modernising rail companies plan "driver only" trains with no passengers.

ME AND MY SPOON

THIS WEEK
MICK LYNCH

This week, all the top spoon interviewers tried to get the better of the General Secretary of the RMT (National Union of Rail, Maritime and Tableware), but Mick Lynch showed them how it's done, with his spontaneous, straight-talking, media-savvy responses. Here are some of the highlights...

RICHARD LADLEY (on Good Morning Spoon): Do you have a favourite spoon? I bet it's a Marxist one.

I can't believe your line of questioning. That is a remarkable load of twaddle. All I'm saying is that it's unfair that some people have silver spoons and some people have no spoons at all.

KAY STIRLEY (on Sky Spoons): You're going to stop everybody else using their spoons to stir their tea. How are you going to do that – by stabbing them in the head with a spoon?

Do you know how tea works, Kay? The only stirring going on here is yours. Do we look like we want a spoon fight? I'm just trying to get decent and fair spoons for my workforce.

PIERS POURON (on Talkspoons TV): You look like the Hood off Thunderspoons – and he was evil, so you probably are. Aren't you? Go on – admit it!

Is this the state of spoon journalism in Britain?

KIRSTY FORK (Spoonsnight): Would you be prepared to negotiate with the government over spoons?

Absolutely.

JUNIOR SPOONS MINISTER: But you walked out of the talks...

That's a lie. It's a lie. You're lying. It's a direct lie. That's a lie. You are a liar.

KIRSTY FORK: Hang on. Wait a minute. Hold on. Er...

He's lying. He's a liar. He's a liar. His pants are quite literally on fire.

ROBERT PESTLEANDMORTAR (ITV, Independent Teaspoon Viewing): You encouraaaaaaage your meeeeeembers to vote agaaaaaainst European spoooooons. Will you admit that you maaaaaaaade a mistake? Did you maaaaake a miiiiistaaaake? Was it a miiiiistaaaake?

No.

ROBERT PESTLEANDMORTAR: Thaaat's aaaall we've got tiiiime fooor.

NEXT WEEK: *Kate Bush. Me and My Number One.*

"Oh, look... they've modernised!"

HELLO! And congratulations to us on the great result on Thursday. We won one by-election and lost our deposit on the other one! Pretty impressive and it shows that the country is at last turning to Labour (and the Lib Dems).

It's a resounding thumbs-up for my policy of not saying anything about anything, particularly not this controversial rail strike! Am I just sitting on the fence? I wouldn't describe it as a fence, more of a wall, or a wood-based divider and I am not actually sitting on it, more perched, half-standing as it were. I can't be clearer than that! So for those who ask me whether I condemn or support the railstrike, my simple answer is "Yes".

And to those of you who compare me unfavourably to Mr Mick Lynch, who has been on all the news shows, wiping the floor with all the interviewers, I admit that he seemed very effective. Perhaps I could learn something from this plain-spoken chap, clearly and simply articulating his principles and not being afraid to speak up for what's right.

So I had a long think about what lessons I could garner from the RMT leader, and I think the key thing to take away is that too much hair, ie like yours truly, can be a liability. Baldness works! So my first thought was that I should take a trip to the barber and have a savage cut!! I will ask for a Number Ten!!!!! – thanks to my new Anti-Boring Team for the interesting gag!

Sincerely, Keir.

Home Office

'Humanitarian' wave machines may be installed on Channel beaches

THE Home Office has revealed that wave machines could be installed across the beaches of south east England – to manufacture choppy waters in the English Channel "when it is traditionally like a millpond in the summer", attracting many more migrant crossings.

The plan is believed to be part of the blue-sky thinking strategy demanded by Downing Street for Cabinet members to dream up new initiatives that won't cost the nation too much money.

The Home Secretary defended the idea, claiming, "We have a long record of thinking out of the box on deterring immigrants in humanitarian ways," adding, "These machines will conform to the highest British design standards and they'll be environmentally sound, as they will be solar powered."

LATE NEWS: Priti Patel to introduce a breeding program for great white sharks into the English Channel.

EXCLUSIVE TO THE DAILY MAIL

AMAZING TRANSFORMATION OF PRINCE WILLIAM AT 40

by **Philippa Space**

PEOPLE everywhere have been stunned by the transformation of dull, staid, reliable 20-year-old Prince William into the staid, dull, reliably bald 40-year-old Prince William.

"It's almost as if Prince William is a normal human being, ageing in the normal way," said one stunned royal onlooker.

"Who would have expected the young man of 20 to turn into a middle-aged man at 40, like everyone else on the planet does?" said another stunned royal onlooker.

"If this continues for the next 20 years, I'm putting bets on William at 60 looking 20 years older than he does now at 40," said another stunned royal *(cont. p94)*

Mail Online

▸ Liz Hurley leaves VERY little to the imagination in a plunging crop-top as she flaunts her curves for VERY racy snaps in Vatican.

▸ **Train strikes may lead to monkeypox, warn experts.**

▸ Meghan Markle DENIES the Sussexes' pet chickens are "sick to death" of their cramped conditions. "Call this a luxury hen-house. More like a prison cell" top hen complains in late-night text.

▸ **PICTURE EXCLUSIVE: No spring chicken on the menu today! Mary Berry, 87, shows her age as she is snapped make-up free in her front garden.**

▸ Giant 6ft 9in Alabama serial killer jail escapee, 38, on the run from high security prison is a 'monster' who could strike again warns former lapdancer girlfriend, 22, while posing in pink lace bikini that leaves little to the imagination.

▸ **Our Darling Girl: horrifying video shows blonde, 25, plunging to her death from high-rise balcony in a VERY revealing dress as "distraught" family mourns.**

▸ Jacob Rees-Mogg keeps it casual in two piece suit and pale blue shirt as he reveals "My Lord Jesus Christ would have urged any truly responsible government to send one's so-called refugees to Rwanda"

▸ **Mick Lynch refuses to apologise as hurricane storm leaves 30,000 homeless in Florida.**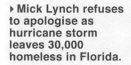

▸ Flipping awful! Hilarious video shows woman's attempt at front flip on trampoline going horribly wrong as she lands face down.

▸ **Are Meghan Markle's $350 dollar dark glasses covering up a VERY black eye caused by picking a fight with a disabled toddler? No, says her highly-paid spokesman.**

▸ Is eating a packet of chocolate digestives a day the best way to beat pneumonia?

▸ **VIDEO EXCLUSIVE: Mick Lynch spotted swatting day-old orphan fly before callously flicking corpse away.**

▸ "We were in pieces": TV's Millie Mackintosh reveals her beloved moggy Patch almost died after mis-step caused him to fall "more than six inches" off doorstep in near-fatal accident.

▸ The Queen SNUBS Prince Harry. Reports of not-so-discreet Royal V-sign behind ginger grandson's back during Platinum Jubilee celebrations.

▸ **Villagers react in horror as postman, 54, spots Mick Lynch's face in cloud formation.**

▸ Did PRINCE ANDREW lead the storming of the Capitol?

▸ **Sophie Wessex looks effortlessly chic as she chats naturally to ordinary Britons on surprise visit to Guildford.**

▸ VIDEO EXCLUSIVE: Dash-cam footage shows Katie Price undergoing breast enhancement operation as her car swerves off road into hedge.

▸ **Onlookers "horrified" as Duchess of Sussex is spotted grinning and waving just 36 hours after landfall in Uttar Pradesh killed 50.**

▸ Phillip Schofield says no to piece of toast before appearing on breakfast TV. "I generally settle for a cup of coffee" says This Morning host.

▸ **Does too much exercise make you FATTER?**

▸ Voting Labour makes you up to 50 per cent more likely to suffer a heart attack or stroke, study warns.

▸ **Kate dazzles in humble £125 high street dress at urgent charity engagement while Meghan looks** **"vulgar and overdressed" in £15,000 Thierry Mugler frock at elite Hollywood party, note horrified onlookers.**

▸ Carol Vorderman flaunts her killer curves in sexy tube top while out shopping for packet of cornflakes, four apples and a bottle of ketchup.

▸ **VIDEO EXCLUSIVE: Heartwarming moment as pet hamster Scotty appears to bop to Abba's smash hit "Dancing Queen" while owner, 65, passes away from tragic heart attack.**

▸ Surge in cancer among Remain voters "a lesson to us all" says financial expert.

▸ **Prince Andrew "forced by Royal family to live in Windsor dungeon chained to a wall and forage for worms", claims Royal expert.**

▸ Fears grow as Kim Kardashian fails to pose in revealing skin-tight lace bodysuit for second day running.

▸ **Mick Lynch "borrowed pencil AND rubber from fellow pupil at primary school then failed to give them back". Former teacher makes shock claim.**

▸ Body-blow to Royal Family as King Edward VIII is named the real Jack the Ripper. Disgraced King was spotted in London's East End just twenty years after horrific killings.

▸ **Does Toblerone cause hayfever? Experts warn against weirdly shaped EU-approved confectionery manufactured in secret Swiss factory.**

▸ Love Island's Katie Salmon dumps hunky Kevin Hake for toyboy Max Turbot in protest at global warming.

▸ **Do Corn Plasters cause cancer?**

▸ Woman, 51, who DUMPED 16-hour work days after cervical cancer returned and she developed arthritis is now a sex therapist who ORGASMS daily, puts cannabis in her vagina and has become a vegan in order to ease her ailments. SEE VIDEO

▸ **Could a diet based on your STAR SIGN be the secret to living longer?**

▸ Rebekah Vardy spotted sifting through McDonald's bin for nutritious scraps after verdict from High Court.

▸ **Johnny Depp set to front revived Blue Peter, BBC insider warns.**

▸ Sarah Gove: Why sex monster Johnny Depp must NEVER be allowed to front beloved children's TV show.

▸ **TOP SURGEON dismisses claims that a diet based on your star sign is secret to living longer.**

▸ VIDEO EXCLUSIVE: George Michael's ex KENNY GOSS skips starter in mid-priced restaurant.

▸ **Leading food astrologer slams TOP SURGEON for dismissing claims that a diet based on your star sign is the secret to living longer.**

▸ VIDEO EXCLUSIVE: Man, 46, plunges to death in bungee tragedy while grieving girlfriend, 32, looks on in low-cut leopard-print halterneck dress by Jacquemus available now from H&M.

▸ **THE QUEEN swears by diet based on her star sign, claims Palace insider.**

▸ Beckhams "set to use Clarence House as London base" but hoping to buy "somewhere more central".

▸ **PICTURE EXCLUSIVE: Katie Price's sister Sophie's best friend Renee's ex Jed seen cuddling former Love Island contestant Willow's brother Kieran's former partner Scarlett before leaving club with ex of Suzy from TOWIE's former boyfriend nightclub bouncer Rick, 28.**

▸ Could the Black Death sweep Britain this winter? Experts warn of surge in Home Counties.

▸ **Do leggings cause dementia?**

As told to
CRAIG BROWN

POETRY CORNER

**In Memoriam
Barry Cryer,
comedian and writer**

So. Farewell
Then Barry Cryer.

You wrote for the
Two Ronnies,
Morecambe and Wise
And Tommy Cooper.

And Bob Hope.

And George Burns.

And Frankie Howerd,
Dick Emery, Les Dawson,
David Frost,
Mike Yarwood,
Kenny Everett,
Billy Connolly…

Perhaps it would
Be quicker to list
Which comedy greats
You didn't write for.
Such as...

No, I'm Sorry
I Haven't a Clue.

E.J. Thribb
(17½ jokes per minute)

**Lines on the cancellation
of the Steve Wright
Radio 2 afternoon show**

So. Farewell
Then Steve Wright.

Here is a factoid:
Your afternoon show
Is being axed
After 24 years.

They must be
"Serious jockin'"!!

"Love the show,"
As you always said.

Now it is me
Who is
Mr Angry.

I got so angry
That I threw
The phone down.

And who fired you?
Was it Mr Mad?
He needs a check up
From the neck up!

You played
Non-stop oldies,
But now, sadly,
They have stopped you.

E.J. Thribb (17½ MHz)

Boris Johnson MP

The Prime Minister's Top Secret Number 10 Downing Street WhatsApp Group Chat. Strictly confidential. Members Only

Hello everyone! Thanks for going on telly and sticking up for me and sorry if my people gave you a bit of a bum steer (poor choice of words, given seriousness of Mr Bum-Pincher's bum-pinching LOL!) and left you with egg on face.

Guto Harri
Don't blame me! That's what you told me to tell them to say.

Did I? I have no recollection of that.

Jacob Rees-Mogg
You do have an enormous amount on your plate, PM, and it's no wonder you forget everything anyone ever says to you, particularly if it's an official complaint about a good friend and supporter and only occasional sex-pest.

Friend? Not sure I've ever met him.

Guto Harri
I think you might have.

Oopsie! Me and Mr Bum-Pincher. Ouch!

Jacob Rees-Mogg
Anyway, top homosexual assault banter with the aforesaid amusingly named gentleman.

Thanks, Creepie! The main thing is, I think I got away with it.

Sajid Javid
I resign.

Sajid Javid has left the group.

Cripes, why's he done that? Who'd have thought it? He's only resigned from my Cabinet once before.

Guto Harri
He's written you a letter, Prime Minister, saying you're a liar who has no integrity.

And his point is?

Rishi Sunak
I resign.

Rishi Sunak has left the group.

Double cripes!

Guto Harri
He's sent a letter saying you have no integrity and are a liar.

No one's ever said that about me before.

Guto Harri
This is turning into a shit-storm.

Who wants to be Chancellor? Nad?

Nadine Dorries
Great! Count me in. I can privatise the entire economy, whatever you like. You're great, Boris. 🐱

Not you, Mad Nad. I meant Not Quite So Mad Nadhim Zahawi. He's good with money.

Guto Harri
I should warn you, he has a few skeletons in his closet. Like that six-grand expenses claim for heating his stable?

Well, then he's the perfect man to produce a stable economy! See what I did there?

Nadhim Zahawi
I have no hesitation in accepting the job and reminding you how brilliantly I delivered the vaccine roll-out.

No, I delivered the vaccine roll-out. Don't claim the credit for things you didn't do, that's the Prime Minister's job. Now, on with business.

Will Quince
I resign.

Will Quince has left the group.

Guto Harri
He's written a letter saying he feels like a fool because you fed him a load of lies which he repeated on Good Morning Breakfast.

What's got into everyone? You'd think they'd never met me. And who the hell's Mr Quince anyway? Sounds like a character in Midsummer Night's Dream, with Bottom – and presumably Mr Pincher close behind him!

Simon Briefcase
You haven't yet filled the ministerial vacancy of Health Secretary.

Right, Steve. You've done a great job being in charge of Downing Street, it's all gone really well for the last few months. Go and sort out the whingeing nurses and doctors, who haven't even said thank you for the forty new hospitals that I haven't built yet.

Steve Barclay
Thank you, Prime Minister.

21 other people have left the group.

Multiple cripes! Still, doesn't mean the party's lost faith in me.

37 other people have left the group.

Cripes to the power of ten! The rats are leaving the sinking shit.

*ship. Damn predictive text!

Priti Patel
It's no laughin' matter. We're all goin' to lose our jobs and no one else in their right mind will be employin' us.

Courage, Pritster, all is not lost.

45 people have left the group.

Giga-Cripes! Does no one know the meaning of loyalty?

Michael Gove
As your loyal friend, Prime Minister, may I say you've got to face the truth.

What's that when it's at home?

Michael Gove
It's over, it's time to do the decent thing.

All right, Michael. You're fired. You snake. That's you levelled down!

Michael Gove has left the group.

Don't worry – there's enough of us for me to build a new team.

51 people have left the group.

Supercripesafragilistic-brexitallidocious!

Jacob Rees-Mogg
My sentiments entirely, Prime Minister.

Is there anyone left?

Priti Patel
Just us. And even I'm thinkin' it's time for you to be leavin'.

What!!!! 😱

Nadhim Zahawi
Me too. As your Chancellor of the Exchequer, I would advise you that your stock has fallen to a new low. And you've got terrible judgement. You appointed me.

Gadzooks!!! 😱 😱 I'm surrounded by ingrates! As Cicero once said, "Infamy, infamy, they've all got it in for me."

Sir Graham Brady
Prime Minister, the 1922 Committee is considering changing the rules.

You can't just change the rules because it suits you! .

Sir Graham Brady
It's over, Prime Minister. We've got the lectern out of the cupboard. You'll be delivering your resignation speech tomorrow morning.

No, I won't. Nobody tells me what to do. I'm not going to go, do you hear? Never. I will never resign.

Sir Graham Brady
Excellent. Another lie. I'll see you outside Number Ten at midday.

Boris Johnson has left the group.

UNREPENTANT PM RESIGNS

What happened to Grace, Modesty and Honour?

I never slept with any of them

Love Island accused of misogyny

"Who's Miss Ogyny and does she have big tits?"

THE SUNDAY TIMES EXCLUSIVE

Tim Shipsink on how the Boris resignation week unfolded

It was Thursday at 8.33 in the morning and Shipsink had barely woken up when the editor called to say, "Shipsink, we need 10,000 words by 9am."

Putting his toast and marmalade down, he immediately set to work with his trusty scissors and paste.

By 8.37 the crisis was beginning to escalate when he was visited by an Amazon delivery man, putting him behind the clock and running out of time, but Shipsink vowed to fight on, using a Boris flamethrower anecdote which made no sense whatsoever, and recycling old quotes from a piece he'd written two years ago.

At 8.43 the unfolding drama took a new twist, as he lost the support of Google when Virgin Broadband went down.

"This is turning into a shitstorm," said one insider (himself) — but still Shipsink refused to give up.

A frantic call to the editor followed, during which the inevitable truth was spelled out: it didn't matter what he wrote, so long as it filled 94 pages.

Time was running out for Shipsink as, in a last desperate gamble, he... (cont. p94)

Tooth fairy taking no new patients

by Our Dental Hygiene Correspondent **Mo Lar**

BRITAIN's children were plunged into crisis today as it was confirmed that the Tooth Fairy is taking on almost no new patients.

Children across the country have not only been taking out their own teeth using a bit of string and a slammed door – the traditional method – but are now being forced to place the tooth under their pillow, wake themselves up at midnight, swap it for some money, then go back to sleep and pretend to be delighted in the morning.

The tooth fairy explained, "I'm knackered, I don't have the capacity, and 20p doesn't go as far as it used to. Anyone who still believes in me is so credulous they probably still believe in NHS dentistry."

BETRAYAL MYTH

I'm going to spend more time with my family

Which one?

I was betrayed

Makes a change

NATION PREPARES TO SPEND ANOTHER FEW MONTHS THINKING ABOUT TORY MPs

by Our Leadership Contest Correspondent **O. Goddd**

A GRATEFUL nation has breathed a sigh of relief that it will now have to spend the next two months hearing about Conservative leadership candidates.

"The good thing is that we've hardly spent any time over the last decade thinking about the Conservative party's internal traumas," said one young mother, pushing her children home from a food bank past a closed library and a former daycare centre.

"Finally, I'll be able to hear what Michael said Kemi thinks about Rishi's attack on Nadhim in the wake of Grant's criticisms of Priti over Penny's video about Liz. If you ask me, this is exactly what we should all be spending our time on right now."

Another member of the public, returning from visiting the grave of a relative who died after getting Covid in a care home while Downing Street was having one of its parties, added, "I think there is so much going on at the moment – a massive cost of living crisis, a war in Europe, a faltering economy, a climate emergency – and what we all need now is a bit of perspective. I think we can definitely trust the 100,000 geriatric members of the Conservative Party in the South-East of England to make the right choice on behalf of the entire nation in the mid-21st century."

"Their selection process is called Worst-Past-The-Post"

News in brief

NHS still on waiting list for knee op

■ A shocking new parliamentary report into NHS and social care has revealed that the Health Service is on its knees – and will continue to be for the foreseeable future.

The cross-party committee found that the organisation had been crippled by funding and staff shortages, due to being on its knees for 12 years now – the time it has been on a waiting list for a double knee operation.

Committee chair, Jeremy Hunt, was withering in his assessment of the NHS's plight, saying, "This is terrible – after years of being run down, the NHS has been virtually left on its own in a corridor waiting for urgent medical attention for years and years."

The former Health Secretary from 2012-2018 added, "I have no idea who is responsible. It certainly isn't me."

TRUSS EXPLAINS LATE ENTRY INTO LEADERSHIP RACE – 'I couldn't decide which hat to throw in the ring'

Hard-right hat

Anti-Russian Russian hat

Cowboy builder hat

Top Gurn hat

Tesco cheese-exporting hat

Far-from-fascinator Ascot hat

Margaret Hat-cher
(That's enough hats. Ed.)

Repressive ruling body denounced by America for riding roughshod over women's rights

Supreme Court of the United States, er...

WHAT THE US SUPREME COURT WILL DO NEXT

1 Overturn Roe vs Wade

2 Overturn Lincoln vs Slavery

3 Overturn The Union vs The Confederacy

4 Overturn Washingon vs George III

5 Overturn Columbus vs Native Americans *(Is this right? Ed.)*

6 Overturn Gilead vs Reality *(You've gone mad. Ed. – but then, so has everyone else)*

US SUPREME COURT RULING

Guide to unwanted pregnancy

■ Nationwide abortion ban means you must wait until your child is at least seven years old before they can be terminated in a school massacre by a disaffected 18-year-old loner legally carrying three semi-automatic weapons.

ME AND MY SPUN

THIS WEEK we are honoured to welcome **THE DUCHESS OF CORNWALL** as guest editor of the *Me and My Spoon* feature, in honour of her 75th birthday. In a frank and revealing interview, the Duchess shares her life-long love of spoons with the nation which has taken her to their hearts

Do you have a favourite spoon?
Oh gosh yah er I rully like all types of spun.

Thank you so much for answering that question in such an honest and down-to-earth way, Your Royal Highness.
I rully don't have a prufurence. Teaspuns for a cuppa, soup spuns for, you know, soup and ah dessert spuns for puds.

Have silver spoons featured prominently in your life?
Haw haw... I knew you would brung that up... hunestly, sulver spuns haven't bun that much of a bug deal, though Mummy and Duddy had a few in the hice...

When you are the Queen Consort, will you focus on spoons, as a royal patron?
Oh, yah. I passionately believe everyone should have uccess to spuns from wherever they cum frum, you know, even frum Bruxton.

That is marvellous to hear, Your Highness. Thank you again for sharing your cutlery-related secrets with us and, may I say, it is no wonder people refer to you as the People's Duchess and the Queen of Spoons.
Oh rully, that's rully kind.

Has anything amusing ever happened to you in connection with a spoon?
Yah, His Royal Highness, Prunce Chullz, once was eating brukfust and instead of pucking up a spun to eat his boiled ugg, he picked up a fork. It rully was a rull hoot.

Ha ha ha ha ha ha. That's the most hilarious anecdote in the history of kitchenware anecdotes. Thank you, once more, for agreeing to take on the onerous task of being guest editor of this column.
Rully no problem. Are we dun? Have you gut what you wunted? I'm gusping for a fug.

NEXT WEEK: *Tom Parker-Bowles: Me and My Bowls*

THOUSANDS GATHER TO WORSHIP ANCIENT STONES

by Our Old Rock Correspondents
Mark Elder and **Dave Hipworth**

AS THE Summer Solstice reached its zenith, large numbers of devotees of the mystical Still Standing Stones joined together in Hyde Park.

The worshippers had long flowing hair or were bald and dressed in traditional denim and sensible shoes, as they assembled to pay homage to the Stones, which have been part of the British landscape since time immemorial.

Said one follower, "We don't know how the Stones got here. Possibly on the bus using their liberty passes. But they remain an iconic and historic symbol of a magical bygone era dating all

the way back to 1960BC (Before Coldplay)."

Said another, "We are here to sing, dance and enjoy some of the oldest songs since records began."

As the vast crowd began to sway together, the sun began to set over the Stones and *(cont. 2094)*

"Get in there, my sun"

EASYJET CHIEF OPERATING OFFICER QUITS AMID FLIGHT CHAOS

He actually quit six weeks ago, but the announcement was delayed

No one can say I'm not Prime Minister material now

TV HIGHLIGHTS

LAST CHANCE TO SEE...
Mock the Weak

The long-running topical gag-fest is nearing its end, but viewers can still enjoy the quickfire improvisation that is the Tory leadership contest.

Regular contestants TV funnyman Rishi Sunak and ditzy comedy character "Liz Truss" take it in turns to come to the mic and literally "mock the weak" with a series of biting crowd-pleasing ideas, made up on the hoof, that attack the poorest in society and put a fresh twist on their misery.

Said one show insider, "The whole point of satire is 'to afflict the afflicted and comfort the comfortable' but ultimately the jokes wore thin. The gag about taking money from deprived urban areas and diverting it to Tunbridge Wells was outlandish, but frankly sick."

Mock the Weak has been a feature on our screens for over a decade, but at the end of the day it only appealed to a tiny minority of the population – just 160,000 at the last count.

That all-purpose Tory Minister letter in full...

Dear Liz,

We may have had our differences in the past, and in previous weeks you may have seen quotes attributed to me seemingly backing Rishi Sunak as the "only sane choice as Prime Minister," and referring to you as a "robotic, boring, bonkers puppet of the ERG." You may also have noticed some Tweets from my personal account describing you as: #Liz4Recession, #UnTrussworthy and #LoserLiz. But, as you will well understand, I was wilfully misrepresented, in this case by myself.

One of the things I most admire about you is your courageous ability to change your mind when circumstances dictate, and this is a policy which I wholly endorse. In this spirit I hope you can find it in your heart to change your mind again about me. That is why I say unequivocally, that you are the right person for the top job, and I am the right person for any job you'll give me.

Yours,
Sajid/Tom/Penny/Ben/Rishi

Doolally Mail

Friday, August 12, 2022

What should we do with the woke witchfinders?

FOR too long, the forces of WOKE have been exercising their baleful influence over this country.

These woke warriors have been creating misery across the land and stretching their sinister, multicoloured fingers into every area of British public life. Only last week we discovered that senior government LAWYERS have been receiving advice on how to avoid discriminating against people.

The Mail says: NO MORE to these malignant witch-hunts which have seen literally millions of ordinary British people lose their jobs and livelihoods.

So now the Mail is offering its readers a chance to vote on what YOU think should be done with these sinister blame-spreading witchfinders who keep telling other people what to do on pain of dire consequences.

Should we:
■ Hang them!
■ Burn them!
■ Drown them in the village duckpond!

Tom Cruise not seen at British event shock

by Our Showbiz Staff
P.R. Machine

FOLLOWING recent appearances of the Hollywood star Tom Cruise at the Queen's Platinum Jubilee, Wimbledon and Gloucester Air Show, as well as numerous sightings in London's hotels, restaurants and night spots, there was considerable dismay when he was a surprise no-show at the birthday party of Anita Tomkinson, aged four.

The Tooting-based toddler was visibly upset, complaining through her tears, "All I got was Coco the Clown, and a Colin the Caterpillar cake, when I was sure that the star of *Mission Impossible* would pop in and make a surprise appearance."

Photographers from the Tooting and Balham Advertiser were also disappointed. "We can't believe Tom let us down. We were hoping for some good snaps of the *Top Gun Maverick* A-lister doing his own stunts on the bouncy castle in his aviator shades."

"I think this could be a major breakthrough, but we'll need to run it by social media to be certain"

Keir Starmer WRITES

HELLO! After my sacking of front bencher Sam Tarry for attending a picket line, I'm sure some of you are confused as to why I did nothing when Lisa Nandy did exactly the same thing. I know I am!

I hear there have been mutterings of "U-turns" and "inconsistency" – some might even say "hypocrisy". Not so! The answer is simple: I haven't let anyone off. I'm not doing anything – because I'm on strike! I'm proving what a true Socialist I am by backing the right to strike and I will stay on strike until everyone agrees to my demands. Demand one: Everyone in the Labour Party needs to agree that I am the best and only person to act in the interests of Labour-supporting workers. Demand two: Well, demand two must be formulated in the fullness of time, using a form of words to be decided upon that will be amenable to Conservative voters!

I've been on strike for a week now and, surprisingly, Labour have not approached me about a counter-proposal. You would think they would sympathise with an oppressed worker like me being exploited by his staff! Everyone's gone home and locked the door, and I'm left here in my woolly hat, warming my hands against my roaring brazier – not easy in this heat!

Actually, I have just been passed a note from Angela Rayner. It says "Enjoy the picket line, Keir, I'm off out with my boyfriend Sam Tarry".

Now where have I heard that name before?

Sincerely, Keir

SUMMER HOLIDAY TRANSPORT CHAOS

We're trying to escape the Tory leadership contest!

Leave means you can't leave

We're taking back control of our boredom

♪ There'll be blue passports over the white cliffs of Dover ♫

CONSPIRACY UPDATE

Phew, it's hot! The Mainstream Media is putting this down to (amongst other things) 'The Sun', but we know better, don't we?

MAGA435 thinks he knows what's going on. He posts:

"Sinse the VACKSINE came out It's started getting HOTTER. Evryone who got injected with the VACKSINE are risponsibal – their VEINS are slowly heating up and creating HEAT wearever they go! They all have to be hunted down an CULLED to save the planet! Who's with me????"

@Jesustweets4me has a more sensible view. She writes on Twitter:

"The rapture is comin upon us, but it's comin very slow. God is very old and he has an old-fashioned oven, like a Kelvinator. Just be thankful he doesn't have an induction oven like a Miele or y'all gonna be burnin RIGHT NOW while I sit on his right hand. See ya suckers! (God loves you)."

TRUTH-IS-OUT-THERE4356's has posted a convincing theory:

"The evidence is mounting that aliens are slowly moving the earth towards the sun. My guess is the ZYGONS, as they are red and angry. Once they lose their chameleon-like abilities they would still be able to move undetected among us as we will all be very red and angry."

Lastly is "Dave" from Facebook, who says:

"Phew, it's hot! Looks like Global Warming is real!!! LOL!"

Sorry to burst your bubble, Dave, but that particular conspiracy theory got debunked the moment everyone started believing in it! Me, I'm favouring the Zygons at the moment! The mystery continues...

US REVEALS UPDATED TARGET LIST

SENIOR US Pentagon officials have issued an updated kill list following the successful drone strike that killed Al-Qaeda leader Ayman al-Zawahiri.

The White House pledged to continue to hunt down known associates of the 9/11 mastermind Osama Bin Laden.

High on their list is a shadowy figure known as Uncrown Prince Charli Windsoor, whose exact role within the Al-Qaeda terror network is unknown, but who has been documented as having received £1 million from the Bin Laden family in London

following the events of 9/11.

"Our drones specialise in taking out bad dudes like al-Zawahiri standing on balconies waving, so our intelligence tells us that Windsoor will be a piece of buttered toast to neutralise," promised Head of Special Assassinations at the Pentagon, the five-star US general Chuck "Cheese" Cheesenburger.

Exclusive to all Tory papers
THE HEATWAVE: AN APOLOGY

IN recent days we may have given the impression, through headlines such as "WOKE SNOWFLAKES HIDING FROM THE SUN" and "IT'S JUST A NICE DAY, YOU COWARDLY ELITES", that given the spiralling cost of living crisis, Britain simply cannot afford to be indulging itself by spending an untold fortune on green crap, rather than focusing on some imagined climate crisis which will supposedly engulf us at some point in the future.

We now realise, in the light of temperatures hitting 42°C in Britain yesterday, leading to chaos and death, that nothing could be further from the truth, and through headlines such as "WE ARE ALL GOING TO DIE IN FIRE" and "PHEW, WHAT AN APOCALYPSE!", we are pressing the government to ask why isn't it moving faster to achieve its net zero targets.

We apologise for any confusion caused, and any confusion in the future when summer is over when we ask if it's actually the cost of living crisis which is now hitting people's pockets that must be the priority for an incoming Tory administration, not this so-called climate emergency that is some way off in the future, imposing monstrous costs and forcing families into... etc...

ON OTHER PAGES

● Why is the BBC patronising us by warning us not to swim on sunny days? **2** ● Lots of people dead after going swimming in reservoirs **3** ● Toby Young, Julia Hartley-Brewer and Charles Moore on why climate change is not going to be a problem at all, because they'll all be dead in 50 years **94**

EXCLUSIVE TO ALL PAPERS

HOW TO GET TO SLEEP DURING THE HEATWAVE

1. Read this piece
2. Zzzzzzz
3. Er... that's it.

HUGE FIRE IN LONDON – SOURCE DISCOVERED

It was a pair of the Prime Minister's pants

"Ideally, I'd like to work with animals"

"Well, it's your lucky day!"

ABATTOIR VACANCIES

Cordell

The hilarious TV funnywoman, played by Philomena Cunk, shares her thoughts on our island race

I love Britain. Don't you? Not in a sexy way, even though I have dated men who are in the shape of Britain. No, I love Britain in a quietly appreciative way, like a bus driver who drops you next to your house when there's no bus stop, or a fat friend who orders chips in Burger King and allows you to grab a handful.

Britain is very important, because if it weren't there, everyone in Britain would fall into the water and probably drown. They sometimes call Britain "UK", but a lot of Scottish people don't like calling it "UK" because "UK" is also the sound you make when you gag on porridge.

There are some things I don't like about Britain, like we have this historic history that states you have to pay people for doing their jobs, which seems unfair to me. I think we should stop paying nurses, and that way everyone else should keep more of their money, so everyone can have speed boats like the winners of "321", which would be great, unless you crash your speedboat on the M1 and need a nurse to attach a drip.

Anyway, to sum up, vote for me and I will offer you all a handful of chips and everyone gets a speedboat.

FERGIE 'MISLED CHALET OWNER' OVER FINANCES

"What's wrong with massaging figures?"

"Don't ask!"

"I hope you're not going to do this every time you win an argument"

Shadbolt

HOW I WAS CONVERTED TO WOMEN'S FOOTBALL

by Our Sports Correspondent **Jack Thelad**

WHEN the women's Euros began I have to be honest and tell you that you couldn't pay me to watch women's football.

I mean, what do women know about football?

But as the tournament progressed, something changed. The nation got behind the Lionesses and, to tell you the truth, there was one moment that changed everything for this hack, one moment that meant I was all in after 20 years of following the men's game. Was it Georgia Stanway's goal in the quarter final when we looked to be going out to Spain? Was it Alessia Russo's cheeky backheel in our semi-final demolition of Sweden?

No. It was the moment my editor phoned, offering me an all-expenses-paid corporate jolly as his top football hack to cover the women's Euros final at Wembley. Finally I was being PAID to watch women's football and that, for me, is the moment that women's football came of age as a genuine sport and not just something…(*cont. p94*)

Men's football to be banned

■ The English FA is to achieve "a fully level playing field for all" by outlawing the men's game for a full five decades – just like they did to women in the 1920s.

A spokeswoman for the FA said, "It has long been proved that it is an entirely unsuitable sport for males. For decades the men have boasted about what they are capable of – followed by perennial under-achievement in every single competition since 1966, along with a succession of even poorer and more stupid haircuts."

REBEKAH VARDY

Rebekah talks exclusively to ForkTV, the unwoke no-holds-barred cutlery chat channel.

Do you have a favourite spoon?

I've been so unfairly treated and justice has let me down, so talking about spoons is very painful for me at the moment.

Fair enough. Sorry to intrude on your personal grief.

But I can tell you about Coleen Rooney's spoons. She had a spoon that got caught in her waste disposal, causing the kitchen to flood. I've no idea how the story ended up in the papers.

Coleen accused you of stirring..

That's so unfair. I'd never use a spoon for that. It's just a storm in a teacup. I thought we were good friends. Instead, she's knifed me in the back with a fork. And now we're going to have sell all our silver cutlery just to pay the legal bills.

You could always try selling some stories about the Rooneys' spoons to the press instead.

There's no way I would do that.

Because you're morally above that kind of spoon-related behaviour?

No, because she's cut me off from her Instagram.

Has anything amusing ever happened to you in relation to a spoon?

No, but I've got a top-drawer story about Wayne Rooney eating his soup with a fork. Just talk to my spoon agent.

-PILBROW-

Daily Telegraph Friday 26 August 2022

Disappointment as A-level results fail to reach previous heights

by Our Education Staff
Michael Grade-Inflation

THERE were tears at the offices of the Daily Telegraph today, as the pictures of fruity girls leaping in the air were revealed to have fallen short of last year's results.

Said the editor, "Since 2019, we've had to guess at how high the girls were going to jump, and estimates were off the charts, now reality has kicked in, and we are measuring the actual level of the leap."

He continued, "I'm afraid we've all got to come back down to earth and accept that the levels are lower than our previously

over-optimistic forecasts. The unfortunate students will now have to face clearing, by which I mean clearing over a foot when they get the results of their retakes otherwise they just won't get into the newspaper of their choice (The Daily Telegraph)."

A statement from the Vice-Chancellor of Neasden University
(formerly the Polytechnic of the North Circular)

We deeply resent the suggestion made by various educationalists over the last week that we at Neasden have failed in our duty to British students by recruiting a small number (99%) of Chinese students at the expense of young people educated in this country.

Whilst it is true that many of our courses (99%) are conducted in Mandarin, we provide access to Google translate for any student for whom this might be a problem.

We should also make it clear that rather than depend on the vagaries of exam grades and certificates, the entry procedure to Neasden is entirely based on a stringent interview process in order to assess the suitability of the candidate. The single interview consists of the following rigorous questions:

1. Are you willing to pay more than double the UK rate for a University degree?

2. Are you willing to pay in advance?

3. Would you like a place at Neasden?

Depending on the answers, the senior fellows and myself take an entirely objective view on the eligibility of the successful candidate, Mr/Miss Ka Ching.

School news

St Cakes

Mr Kipling, headmaster of the prestigious independent boarding school St Cake's (motto: *Quis paget entrat*), has defended this year's disappointing A-level results. "Last year our sixth form achieved an average of four A*s," Kipling said, "based on rigorous teacher assessments conducted by myself, the bursar and independent overseer, Mrs Kipling, over lunch at the Dog and Fox. This year, the first year of external examinations since 2019, our sixth form achieved a very commendable average of 2 Ds and an E."

Mr Kipling, however, refused to accept that this represented any sort of downgrade, or could be put down to over-optimistic massaging of the figures in previous years. "These results are slightly worse than before on paper, but in reality this minor shortfall is entirely due to Covid and Brexit and the war in Ukraine, not to mention the heatwave, the drought, the flash floods and the distractions of the Conservative leadership contest. We are very proud of our leavers, who have between them secured places at some of America's top universities, including Little BigFee in Montana, the very prestigious I.O.U.C.L.A. and California's Santa Bribera."

DIRTY SEASIDE POSTCARDS

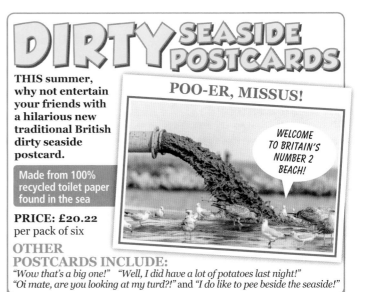

THIS summer, why not entertain your friends with a hilarious new traditional British dirty seaside postcard.

Made from 100% recycled toilet paper found in the sea

PRICE: £20.22 per pack of six

OTHER POSTCARDS INCLUDE:
"Wow that's a big one!" *"Well, I did have a lot of potatoes last night!"* *"Oi mate, are you looking at my turd?!"* and *"I do like to pee beside the seaside!"*

"My husband runs a water and sewerage company – don't worry, he only does this when his capacity is overwhelmed"

TURD FOUND ON BEACH

New government plan to deter migrants

The Home Office has announced an innovative scheme to prevent illegal immigrants from landing on Britain's shores.

The strategy, which is already underway, involves close co-operation with Britain's privatised water companies.

The idea is simple – Britain's beaches are to be flooded with sewage in such quantities that a wall of faecal matter builds up and prevents even the most intrepid of small inflatable boats from landing.

Human rights lawyers claim that the new initiative "stinks", but Home Secretary Priti Patel is adamant that it will work.

She said, "This scheme is really excitin'. We'd been lookin' for a deterrent, and all the time it was sittin' right under our noses. Eurgh! You may not like it, but it's a lot less shit than the Rwanda idea."

(Rotters)

Nursery Times

TWEEDLEDUM AND TWEEDLEDEE STILL BATTLING

by Our Cost Of Living Staff **Martin Lewis Carroll**

THE fabled constantly squabbling twins, Tweedledumblonde and Tweedledeeplyrich, remain locked in heated debate as they travel around Nurseryland disturbing the peace and annoying everyone wherever they go.

The twins, who most people find very, very similar, are unable to agree on anything. When one proposes a solution to Nurseryland's problems, the other inevitably says "Contrariwise," and vice versa.

When a member of the audience of one battle, a Miss Alice of Wonderland, asked them if they knew "the way out of the woods", Tweedledum replied, "Tax cuts now!", whilst Tweedledeetail interrupted her and explained, "Contrishiwise, tax cuts later!"

The only thing they agree on is that the other is completely useless. "You are talking nonsense," said Twaddledum in a highlight of the campaign. "Ditto!" replied Tweedlenondom.

The winner of the contest will eventually be decided by members of the party (Mad Hatter's Tea Party), but until then, the interminable squabble will continue... *(not continued p94)*

CONSPIRACY UPDATE

TRUMP FBI RAID SPECIAL

The news that Donald Trump has been raided by the FBI has had our contributors in a buzz for a while now!

Notacrazyperson%3432 stands out from the others with his simple and not-crazy-at-all insights. His website says:

"'Mar-A-Lago' means 'sea-to-lake' which obviosly is a SECRET MESSAGE referrring to the current GLOBAL WARMING crisis, as every SEA is going to bcome a LAKE in the next few years. Donald TRUMP knows the hole GLOBAL WARMING thing is fake... Becos it is actually GOLF COURSE WARMING!!!"

If you click on the link at the bottom of the website, Notacrazyperson%3432 continues...

"Golf courses are essenSial for DONALD TRUMP to survive as he is a GOLF-BASED lifeform. Take away his enviroment and he DIES. TRUMP found DOCUMENTALLY evidense at the WHITE HOUSE that the FBI ARE training JEWISH SPACE LASERS on every GOLF COURSE in the world."

And if you click on the line at that bottom of the link...

"But TRUMP was too clever for them. He HID the documents BEFORE the FBI came ROUND and had this clever picture PAINTED as a CLUE as to there location."

If you click on the link below the painting, you get an ad for free Viagra and this final message...

"In this picture THAT hangs in MAR-A-LAGO iteslef, TRUMP is painted so he dosen't look OVERWIGHT. This can ONLY MEAN that He has the vital documents STRAPPED AROUND HIS waste So they can NEVER get to them. (That is why he looks FAT when his DOCTORS say he is a perfect fysical spensimen). Hiis hand in the picture is CUPPING HIS TESTLICLES, which means HE can fax the PAPERS to FOX news JUST BY tugging on his TRUSS."

So does this website hold the truth? Whether it does or it doesn't, at least I have some free Viagra coming in the post, so it wasn't a complete waste of time! The mystery continues...

GOVE BACKS SUNAK

That's your worst move yet

NEW YORK POST-TRUTH

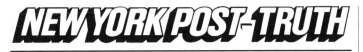

Editorial

Americans are deeply shocked by the attack on Salman Rushdie. An attack like this should never happen on US soil.

A knife-wielding fanatic trying to murder an innocent civilian – it's a total outrage. Why was the attacker using a knife? Why didn't he have a semi-automatic rifle?

He was clearly unhinged, but that's no reason not to buy a suitable weapon. And his victim, why was he not fully armed at a literary festival? And what about his interviewer, why was he not packing heat? What has this country come to?

And another thing: the attacker claimed to have taken offence at Salman Rushdie's book. He claimed to have read two pages. So people are boasting about reading books in this country now? I mean, whatever next? The solution is obvious – it's time to ban books. They're dangerous, and they should not be readily available to all and sundry in unlicensed shops, without even the most rudimentary of background checks, and before long...

(This is completely mad. Keep it up. Ed.)

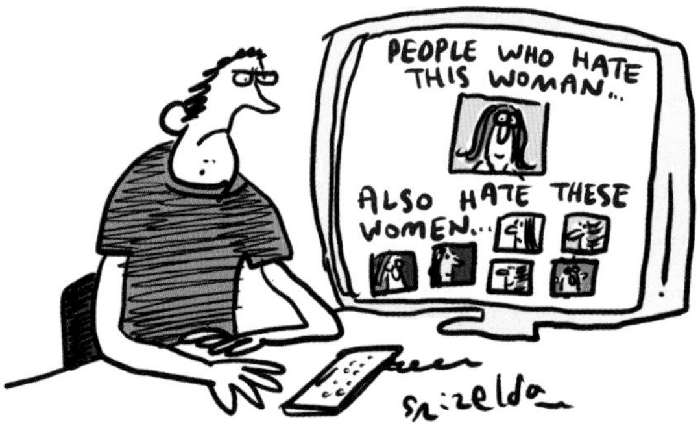
PEOPLE WHO HATE THIS WOMAN...
ALSO HATE THESE WOMEN...
Grizelda

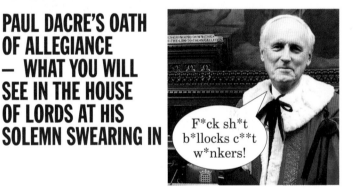

The rise of 'quiet quitting'

by Our Under-30 Correspondent
Jenny Zed

The practice of "quiet quitting" – working the absolute bare minimum to keep your job and ensure you're not fired – is the latest trend in workplaces across the country. *(Will this do?) (No. Keep going. Ed.)* Ugh. Fine.

So, millions of young people who've been living with their parents for ten years, can't afford to go out, can't afford to do anything, are suddenly realising that work is not the be-all and end-all and that you can't take it with you and that, actually, it's best to do just enough work to avoid being sacked but that's it. *(Seriously, can I hand in this article yet?) (No. We need 15,000 words because it's August and everyone's on holiday. Ed.)* UGH.

Anyway, I myself have been doing serious research into the nature of "quiet quitting" for some time now because, after all, this sort of lifestyle fluff really is just to fill up the middle bit of the paper, so in a sense my radical experiment of "going to the pub for three hours at lunch" has actually been a brave act of investigative journalism. *(Can I hand it in now?) (No. You're not fired, so you have to keep writing this stuff for ever, for as little as we can get away with. Ha ha ha. Ed.)*

New world record set

TWITTER was rejoicing as a new world record was set in the time it takes for a serious international news story to become a vitriolic Twitter spat about trans issues.

Salman Rushdie had barely been taken to hospital and the first headlines about free speech had just begun to appear when, Hey Presto!, JK Rowling tweeted her support for a fellow author in distress, chocolate-loving author Joanne Harris sent a sarky tweet back, and the internet exploded with polarised hatred that had nothing to do with Rushdie at all.

Said one Twitter user, "It's a fantastic result. It only took twenty-three hours and twenty-four minutes for the story to change from a near-death tragedy to a full-on bedroom warrior Twit-fest."

Said another Twitter user, "We're all delighted. It's much more fun than confronting the real issues," before adding, "Rowling should burn in hell forever or maybe be crowned queen immediately or something that gets me lots of likes!"

PAUL DACRE'S OATH OF ALLEGIANCE – WHAT YOU WILL SEE IN THE HOUSE OF LORDS AT HIS SOLEMN SWEARING IN

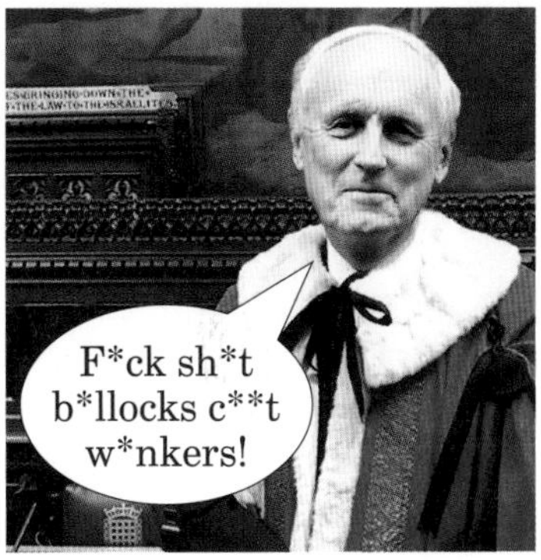
F*ck sh*t b*llocks c**t w*nkers!

STATEMENT FROM THE NATIONAL RIFLE ASSOCIATION

WHILST welcoming the decision of the Supreme Court to overturn the case of Wade versus Roe, we feel that there is a much more practical solution that could be adopted to prevent abortion. ARM ALL FOETUSES! Even if they don't have arms, they have the right to bear them, and no doctor or nurse is going to threaten them if they're packing heat. Just you try, Mother Fucker! Or indeed, Mother, if she's the one trying to break God's holy commandment that thou shalt not kill! Except in self-defence or during civil unrest or if someone's jogging past your garden looking like they want a bullet in the back. Forget Wade 'n' Roe! It's time for Smith 'n' Wesson! Feeling lucky, punk... or Doctor Punk, in this case?

© The National Lunatic Association

CONSPIRACY THEORIST ALEX JONES ORDERED TO PAY $45 MILLION OVER SANDY HOOK LIES

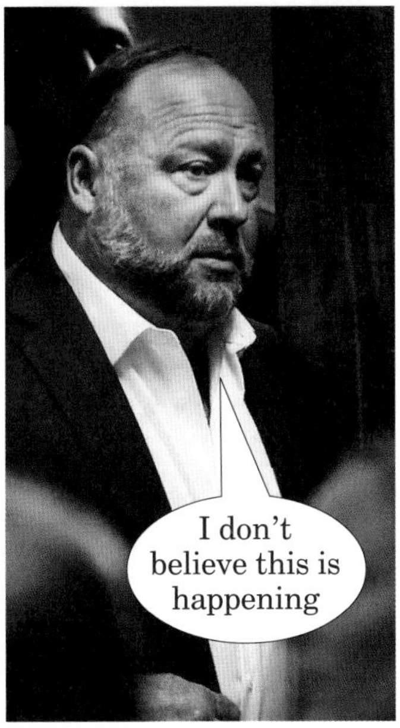
I don't believe this is happening

Why our marriage is exactly like BBC1's new drama 'Marriage'?

Phil and Philippa Space

YOU go first, darling. **Okay, darling, well, straight away I knew this was a programme I was going to love.** Yes, it really portrayed the ordinary ordinariness of day-to-day life as a married couple. **I wouldn't call it ordinariness, Phil – I'd say intimacy.** I guess, but you've got to admit it did start a bit slowly. **Just because it didn't start with a car chase.** It didn't need to start with a car chase. **Okay then – people firing guns.** Philippa! **Admit it, Phil, it's adrenaline or nothing with you – when were you last interested in genuine human relationships?** That's really unfair, I sat through the whole of episode one before writing this piece. **Only if you include the middle bit that you slept through.** It's not my fault – the actors were mumbling. I couldn't make out a word of it. **But that's so true of marriage – after a few years couples stop hearing each other.** Sorry, what? I was on my phone... *(continued until kids leave home)*

WRONG RUSSIAN LEADER DEAD

He transformed Russia, from an impoverished country ruled over by a kleptocratic elite… into what it is today

POETRY CORNER

In Memoriam Mikhail Gorbachev, last leader of the Soviet Union

So. Farewell
Then Mikhail Gorbachev,
You changed the world
Forever with "Glasnost"
And "Perestroika",
And led Russia into
A new era.

But probably
You will be best
Remembered for that
Strange mark on your head
And for doing that
Pizza Hut advert.
Which was quite
Cheesy really.

Putin didn't like you
And yet you lived to 91
And died of natural causes,
Which is quite an
Achievement in itself.

    E.J. Thribb (17½ years
in Siberia for publishing
material mildly critical of
our current glorious leader)

VERY LATE NEWS

UN condemns Hitler for genocide

by Our China Correspondent
Huigh Gurr

IN A dramatic move welcomed all over the world, the United Nations has finally decided to censure the late Adolf Hitler for the behaviour of the Nazi government between 1933 and 1945.

The UN has been sitting on a detailed report into the allegations of the mistreatment of minorities by Mr Hitler, but has taken a cautious approach to actually condemning him outright.

"It was important," said a UN spokesperson, "that we considered all the facts before reaching our conclusion – ie, that Germany was a very big and rich country with whom we all wanted to do business.

"Having now done our research, we are confident that our new, tough stance will stop Mr Hitler in his tracks."

The spokesperson continued, "We are now keeping a close eye on the activities of a similar leader who is accused of human rights abuses in Asia. Mr Genghis Khan is now officially on our radar, and he has been warned."

British pub guidance
Winter 2022

1 Find your local pub

2 If it's closed down, try all the other pubs nearby

3 If *they're* all closed, simply travel to the next town or village using the fuel you can't afford

4 If all the pubs in the next town/village are closed, continue around Britain until you eventually find the last open pub

5 The pub may not have any lights on due to electricity crisis

6 You will need either:
a) a torch,
b) night vision goggles or
c) a supply of carrots for enhanced nocturnal eyesight

7 Order your favourite tipple from the landlord, who may not be there because he's working his second job at the local supermarket to keep the pub going

8 Go to local supermarket and buy bargain ultra-strength cider at just £1.99/gallon

9 Forget pub, go to bus stop and drink merrily with friends

10 Take bus home (subject to national strike action)

POLICE CHIEF CLAIMS UNFAIR DISMISSAL

I was robbed

Nobody's going to investigate that

THAT LIST OF PUBS GOING BUST IN FULL

The In-the-Red Lion

The Rising Costs

The Crown and Out

The Moon Not Keeping Its Head Above Water

The Hopeless and Anchor

The Very Cross Keys

The Lamb and Flagging

The Can't Plough On

(That's enough depressing pub names. I need a pint. Ed.)

YOUR MEDICAL QUESTIONS ANSWERED BY A. DOCTOR

Q: I haven't had sex with anyone for ten years, but I do enjoy squirrel spotting. Should I be worried about monkeypox?

A: No.

THOSE CLIMATE CHANGE ADVANTAGES IN FULL

- We will be able to produce red wine in Hampshire!

THOSE CLIMATE CHANGE DISADVANTAGES IN FULL

- Permanent extinction of thousands of species

- Destruction of beautiful habitats that are millions of years old

- Billions of people forced into climate migration

- Increase in annoying people at dinner parties saying "Did you know this red wine comes from Hampshire?"

"I just hope I don't get monkey pox"

Emily Maitlis reveals shocking truth

by Our Media Correspondent
Ken Spiracy

Speaking at the MacTaggart lecture at the Edinburgh TV Festival, former Newsnight presenter Emily Maitlis has revealed the true extent of Tory control over the BBC, after she was criticised for editorialising about Dominic Cummings in a Newsnight episode in 2020.

"From that moment, I was totally silenced by the shadowy Tories controlling every aspect of BBC News, apart from being allowed to continue presenting Newsnight for the next two years before jumping ship for a huge money deal from Global.

"It's vital I use this very public platform to whip up publicity for my new podcast… er, I mean expose the dead hand of the Tories destroying BBC journalism… which is what I'll be doing on my new Global podcast 'The News Agents'. Have I mentioned that I have a new podcast? It's on Global and it's called 'The News… (*cont. p94*)

"And here to discuss the implications on the broader economy of the tax strategy, we have the Head of the Institute of Fiscal Studies and Barry, a Tory supporter from Hampshire"

Royal couple threaten to sue

by Our Royal Correspondent **Des Creet**

LAWYERS for the Duke and Duchess of Sussex have warned Meghan Markle that if she continues to give highly indiscreet interviews, such as the one she gave to the Cut magazine, they will be left with no choice but to begin court proceedings to silence her.

"Harry and Meghan are famously publicity-shy, as they made clear when being interviewed by Oprah, and they are not going to just stand by as Meghan Markle turns them into a laughing stock by comparing their marriage to Nelson Mandela being released from prison," insisted a spokesperson for the couple.

"The royal couple will not see their efforts to live a quiet life in LA, out of the public eye, undermined by Meghan Markle's unquenchable thirst for publicity. If she persists, they will be forced to release a Netflix special, underlining just how publicity-shy they are."

By Meghan Markle

Nelson Mandela walks free after 27 years in prison, just as Meghan walked down the aisle at St George's Chapel.

Rosa Parks takes seat on segregated bus in Alabama, just as Meghan sat down to sign the wedding register.

Martin Luther King delivers his "I Have A Dream" speech, just as Meghan delivered wedding invitations to a host of global celebrities she'd never met.

Abraham Lincoln issues the Emancipation Proclamation for enslaved people in the rebel states, just as Meghan issued photograph of herself looking lovely. (*That's quite enough significant moments. Ed.*)

Parents stunned as Eurostar axes direct trains between London and Disneyland Paris

by Our Disneyland Correspondents
Huey, Dewey and Louie Edwards

EUROSTAR operators have announced that they will no longer run a direct train service to the popular theme park, Disneyland Paris.

British parents reacted with amazement. Said one, "We can't believe it. With everything else terrible going on in the world, it's fantastic to finally have some good news!"

Said another, "Zip-a-dee bloody doo-dah! No Thunder Mountain for me next year! No *It's a Small World* and listening to that bloody song going on and on and on! Sorry, kids, I'd love to go to Star Wars Hyperspace Mountain, but there just isn't a train to get us there!"

She continued, "It's like the song says: When you wish upon a Eurostar, your dreams come true!"

Eurostar said the closure of the service was as a direct result of Brexit.

Said yet another parent, "This is the first tangible benefit of leaving Europe. At last, we can take back control of our half terms and go to Centre Parcs instead. Though I wish they'd spell it with a 'K' instead of a 'C'. It's really annoying."

Disneyland, however, were less happy – in fact, they were grumpy.

One executive said, in a very high voice, "We're very disappointed with Eurostar. They're behaving like a Mickey Mouse operation."

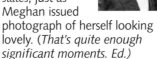

Trump rally divides America

by Our US Political Correspondent
Qanon Letts

The Trump rally in Wilkes-Barre, Pennsylvania, in which the former President set out to attack President Biden as the most divisive president in history, has split America.

In a highly charged, spittle-flecked, vicious, hateful and divisive speech, Trump called Biden the most "vicious, hateful and divisive" president in history. He ended by declaring Joe Biden an "enemy of the state".

Even Trump supporters were divided by the speech – some wondering if they should now support President Biden, while burning down their local Hillary Clinton Paedo Pizza Parlour.

Said one shaman, wearing a MAGA hat on top of his buffalo horn headdress, "If Biden has been abusing power and disgracing the office, then maybe we have to support The Donald by voting Sleepy Joe."

While other confused Trump supporters demanded he be given four more years in the White House, Trump critics want to give him four more years in a state penitentiary for stealing secret documents.

Said a spokesman, "This would be on top of the four years he should get for orchestrating the January 6 Capitol Hill coup."

Trump was visiting Pennsylvania to help to promote Republican candidates – himself in 2024 and himself again in 2028.

MID-TERM ELECTIONS
AMERICA'S GRIM CHOICE

MAGA | **GAGA**

Radical new plan will see police obeying the law

by Our Police Correspondent
Dixon of Cock Seen

A RADICAL new plan from the College of Policing would see police officers being forced to obey the law when it comes to their dealings with women.

"Under these radical new proposals, serving police officers would not be allowed to beat, attack, coerce into bed or kill women they encounter in their day-to-day life and just get away with it because they're coppers," said a College of Policing spokesman.

"We believe that police officers being made to obey the law would send out a powerful message to the all the slags, whores and bitches out there that we're not the misogynist monsters everyone thinks we are."

"Right, the latest murder case... what's the word on the street?"

THE ALTERNATIVE VOICE

MARTIN LEWIS writes...

As a mild-mannered money saving expert™, I am utterly and totally sickened by the failure of the nation's so-called leaders to address the urgent needs of the suffering British proletariat who have yet again been sacrificed on the altar of neo-liberal globalist free-tradism to satisfy the bloodsucking corporate urges of the one percent-elite ultracapitalists of the military-industrial complex er... er... and unless there is urgent targeted financial support offered to the hardworking blue-collar classes then as I have repeatedly demanded there will be an entirely justified uprising including but not limited to civil unrest violent protest hangings from lampposts and the liquidation of the entire boss class er... er... er...

■ *Dave Spart is away*

WHY STRIKES WILL BE POPULAR THIS WINTER

LONG nights spent on a picket line, around a brazier, rather than being at home with the heating off.

Er...

That's it.

NEW OLD JOKES FOR KIDS

What goes up when the rain comes down?
Inflation

What's black and white and red all over?
Your unpaid gas bill

Knock, knock. Who's there?
The bailiffs

UNIVERSITY CHALLENGE

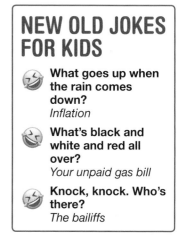

Starter for ten, who's going to replace me? Come on! Come on! Hurry up!

Amol Rajan

You've got to be joking!

It's the new trend!

Say goodbye to WFH and hello to LFO – that's Living From Office!

Everybody's doing it! Can't pay the energy bills? Well, don't bother. Simply pack your toothbrush, grab a sleeping bag and head for the office.

No more expensive domestic overheads – heating/aircon/ lightbulbs, etc – when you're LFO! Just set up camp under your desk, use your full in-tray as a pillow, and have a bath in the basin in the staff toilets. Sorted!

Your boss will be delighted at the long hours you're putting in, and you'll be thousands of pounds better off! You won't even have to pay for Zoom, because you'll be there, 24/7! And train strikes are no longer an issue, because your commute is half a minute from floor to chair.

Cost of Living crisis – what crisis?!

© *Anne Intern, the Guardian.*

WELCOME TO THE NEW PRIME MINISTER, AND FOR GOD'S SAKE LET HER JUST GET ON WITH THE JOB!

ON OTHER PAGES

New boosterism programme to be rolled out

A NEW round of boosterism is on offer from the government today. This new injection of groundless optimism is all that is needed to prevent another wave of contagious inflation that could prove fatal to Tory re-election chances.

The new Vaccuous *(surely Vaccine? Ed.)* is on offer first to the elderly in the Conservative Party, and then will be rolled out across the entire country, in order to achieve so-called "herd immunity" to Keir Starmer and minor variants like Ed Davey.

It is hoped that the boosterism will last up to 2024, or possibly 2023 if there's a snap election, when additional boosterism measures may be need – including the injection of a fresh candidate into the Tory Party. *(Rotters)*

Number of articles about inflation rising exponentially

IN AN incredibly worrying sign for the health of the country, the number of articles worrying about the inflation rate has been increasing far more than predicted by even the most gloomy industry experts.

"For years, we've had almost none of these," said one editor, looking at a list of stories submitted by his journalists.

"I've never seen anything like it. We thought at first there would only be a **5%** rise, which would have been painful but manageable. But now we think it's going to be **18%** – no, **22%** – sorry, no, **28%** – and the fact is that people just aren't going to cope."

On other pages

- ◼ Number of pieces about inflation up **57%**
- ◼ No, sorry **94%**
- ◼ No, sorry again **320,000%**
- ◼ People reduced to carrying wheelbarrows of totally worthless stories about inflation which are all wrong because they were printed more than a week ago

I'm singing in the drain,
Just singing in the drain,
what a....

POETRY CORNER

Lines on the sentimental, yet obscene, poetry written by Mr Ryan Giggs, as revealed in his recent court case

So. Ryan Giggs
I see you have
Been trying to
Write poetry.

It's hard, isn't it?
And I don't mean
Your penis.

E.J. Thribb (17½)

Announcing a new service

amazon prime minister

GUARANTEED to deliver, deliver and deliver! Whatever it is, I promise to deliver it tomorrow!

Whether it's cost-of-living relief, tax cuts, saving the NHS or destroying the BBC, it'll be delivered to you today, by 7pm. Yes, just subscribe to **AMAZON PRIME MINISTER**™, and a package of incredibly efficient policies will be delivered to your doorstep by yesterday.

If you'd like to track the **AMAZON PRIME MINISTER** service, just read the *Daily Telegraph*, *Mail* or *Express* – and see how well we're doing in delivering on delivery!

Rees-Mogg meets energy companies

KEY Liz Truss ally, Jacob Rees-Mogg, has met with the energy companies to discuss a major push into a newly discovered energy source, coal.

"This new-fangled coal will transform Britain's fortunes, as we enter the age of steam and forge an empire on which the sun never sets," Rees-Mogg told the very rich energy executives.

"By harnessing the power of coal, Britain will become the envy of nations across the world, from Rhodesia to Mesopotamia."

PRINCESS DIANA'S CAR SELLS FOR £650,000 AT AUCTION

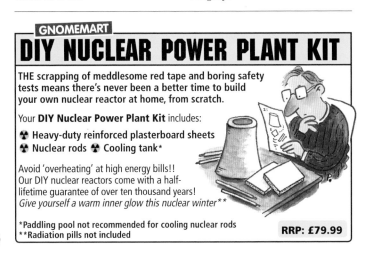

It was an escort from the 1980s

Thought only Andrew was into those

NHS app to cut waiting lists

◼ The NHS has launched a new app, enabling patients to pick where they have their operations and allowing them to search for hospitals with the shortest wait times from their phones.

Said one pensioner, "What's an app?" Said another, "What's a download?" Said a third, "My grandson came around to the care home the other day and started showing me how to get the app, but then all the other residents asked him to help them as well.

"Now he's got such a long waiting list. The NHS need to come up with a new app for grandchildren, so people can pick the one with the shortest wait times."

An NHS spokesman said, "Pensioners may well experience problems with the app but hopefully, they will then join the increasing numbers of disgruntled patients going private, thus shortening the waiting times for other patients awaiting surgery."

GNOMEMART

DIY NUCLEAR POWER PLANT KIT

THE scrapping of meddlesome red tape and boring safety tests means there's never been a better time to build your own nuclear reactor at home, from scratch.

Your **DIY Nuclear Power Plant Kit** includes:

- ☢ Heavy-duty reinforced plasterboard sheets
- ☢ Nuclear rods ☢ Cooling tank*

Avoid 'overheating' at high energy bills!! Our DIY nuclear reactors come with a half-lifetime guarantee of over ten thousand years! *Give yourself a warm inner glow this nuclear winter***

*Paddling pool not recommended for cooling nuclear rods
**Radiation pills not included

RRP: £79.99

Letters

THAT SHITSTORM IN FULL

Flushed away…

…Today's cover is utterly disgusting and reprehensible at every level. Nothing in Boris Johnson's tenure justifies such a vile image. You have gone completely over the top this time and I am seriously reviewing my subscription.

KEVIN MARTIN, Alveston.

…Remove this deeply offensi*** ***
You're not speaking for the **
certainly are not speaking fo**
kicking a man when he's dow**
disreputable.

JULIE & PAUL KE***

…You conflate satire with s***
are too far up your own arse. ***

DENISE JOY KNIG***
Scone, Perth.

…Today's cover (Eye 1577) ***
nor clever. I suppose the same ***
Boris Johnson, but subtle it ain***
me off my breakfast. Not worthy***
esteemed organ.

HEATHER PAGET-BR***
Plaxtol.

…The cover of Eye 1577 was g***
offensive, and not amusing. I used***
to remove it.

DONALD KING.

…I have been a subscriber for ***
years. No more. I have cancelled m***
subscription […] If you are not ash***
you really need to look at some for***
therapy. No, I am not an avid swivel***
Brexiteer banner waver. Just fed up***
ivory tower expressions of self-grat***
smugness… Carry on if you must, bu***
my money.

T. MEDLEY, Lytham St An***

…If the cover of issue 1576 was o***
best, the cover of issue 1577 must be ***
of the worst.

STEVE HEWITT, Norfolk.

…I have never been as disgusted as***
my eye was drawn to the revolting imag***
the front cover. This is not a funny, witt***
satirical or cutting front cover – it is pu***
I have cancelled my annual direct debit***
in protest.

PETER ECKERT.

…I am neither po-faced nor prudish but the front cover of Eye 1577 was utterly revolting, lacking any smidgin of subtlety and so far beyond the "pail" that I am considering cancelling my subscription.

FIONA WILD, Cheltenham.

…Your front cover hits a new low. It is thoroughly despicable, tasteless, utterly puerile in its "humour" and frankly disgusting. This sort of scatological stuff has no place beyond the confines of the gutter press. I have promptly detached it from my subscription copy and binned it, as it is unworthy of a second look and, more pertinently, unfit to be left lying around my house. Have you and your colleagues not even a shred of human decency?

MIKE NEILD, Blackburn.

…Your deplorable anal-erotic offering casts more light on you than it does on Boris Johnson.

PHILIP ASHWORTH, Lr Basildon.

…The 15 July cover was the last straw – unpleasant, unfair, unacceptable and ultimately boring. You do a good job exposing wrongdoing and I enjoy the cartoons, but overall I am sick of the constant sneering and jeering at those who endeavour to lead our nation. Please cancel my subscription and don't send any more issues.

SUSAN PARKINSON-PACKER.

…To think, with all your talent you produce a front cover not even worthy of a schoolboy. Truly pathetic. […] Therefore, after many ***
I have cancelled ***

PRIVATE EYE
No. 1577
15 July –
28 July 2022
£2.99

BORIS JOHNSON MEMORIAL ISSUE
THE PRIME MINISTER'S LEGACY IN FULL

*** Gutray. Well done.

LES ANDERSON, London.

…Good issue. Juvenal would have been a subscriber based on that cover.

PAUL O'SULLIVAN.

…Your latest front cover was so appalling that it made me nauseous. What more fitting tribute could there be to the great man and his legacy?

JOHN ELLERKER, Great Torrington.

…Eye 1577 was easily the best cover I've seen in 30 odd years. I howled with laughter… Excellent stuff. Keep it up. My subscription is safe.

CHRIS KNIGHTS, Hitchin.

…The Eye 1577 cover outclasses all-comers in metaphor, artistic serendipity and memorial durability. Trebles all round!

R.M.CAMERON.

…Your front cover reminds me of my time as a Public Health Inspector. The mistake here is that a force cup has been used rather than a plunger to clear the excrement. So not just a load of shit but a useless tool into the bargain.

JOHN LECHMERE,
Chartered Environmental Health Practitioner, Skelmersdale.

…What a glorious cover. I laughed out loud when I saw it and then set about rearranging the shelf in the well-known Dublin store so that the image would be seen by as many as possible. Up there with the best and I've seen a few over 40 years of handling your organ.
Th**k you.

DAVID CARROLL,
**are.

** expect I'm the 94th person to say that, ***ting to look at as it was, your cover was ***comment on Johnson's destruction of a ***emi-decent country, so I approve of it. ***er, going!

CHRIS BLACKMORE.

***ur latest front cover has elevated the ***the level of a new art form. Pure

RICHARD PRESTON.

** reader for more than 40 years I found ***of Eye 1577 the most repulsive ever. ***new my subscription in perpetuity.

CHIZ SZYMAŃSKI, Nottingham.

***ver that surpasses my expectations by ***gin that I am having it framed. Now ***n find a room in which to hang it…

***AVID HILL, Newark on Trent.

***g at your latest front cover, it can ***atter of time before we see new ***overnment…

***HN PETTIFER, Huntly.

***ver yet. It beats the previous cover ***and sums up Boris's tenure to a

***C ALLEN.

***re paints a thousand turds, ***nailed it. More shit surely ***y from both him and his

***PHEN ROSS.

***n perusing your organ for ***e latest cover is without doubt ***ing and vicious I can
*** good to know standards are not falling. I am still chuckling every time I look at it. Do I need help?

ROCH GARRARD.

…As someone who consumes your organ at the breakfast table, I found your latest cover depicting Johnson's legacy difficult to stomach. It was almost as revolting as your previous covers showing Johnson's face. Keep up the good work.

TOM BOOTH, Bristol.

…Best cover ever. Been laughing out loud to myself for an indescribably and embarrassingly long integer of time. Thanks.

DAN.

…I am so happy to live here, in a country where covers like your latest one is perfectly acceptable. If this photo had been directed at an Arab ruler or a dictator, the consequences could be disastrous. I work for people with dementia and I clean their toilets. I love this country.

V. GRAY.